Columbia University

Contributions to Education

Teachers College Series

No. 233

AMS PRESS
NEW YORK

A DECADE OF PROGRESS IN TEACHER TRAINING

SPECIFIC ADMINISTRATIVE MODIFICATIONS IN MISSOURI TEACHERS
COLLEGES WHICH HAVE TAKEN PLACE DURING THE FIRST
DECADE FOLLOWING THE CARNEGIE SURVEY OF TAX
SUPPORTED NORMAL SCHOOLS IN MISSOURI

AND A

COMPARISON OF THE PRESENT SITUATION WITH THE CONCLUSIONS
AND PROPOSALS OF THE SURVEY COMMISSION

WITH

SUGGESTIONS FOR FURTHER IMPROVEMENT

144029

BY

CLYDE MILTON HILL, PH.D.

TEACHERS COLLEGE, COLUMBIA UNIVERSITY
CONTRIBUTIONS TO EDUCATION, No. 233

LB1899
H5
1972

BUREAU OF PUBLICATIONS
Teachers College, Columbia University
NEW YORK CITY
1927

Library of Congress Cataloging in Publication Data

Hill, Clyde Milton, 1886–
   A decade of progress in teacher training.

   Reprint of the 1927 ed., issued in series: Teachers
College, Columbia University. Contributions to
education, no. 233.
   Originally presented as the author's thesis,
Columbia.
   Bibliography: p.
   1. Teachers colleges––Missouri. 2. Teachers,
Training of––Missouri. I. Title. II. Series:
Columbia University. Teachers College. Contributions
to education, no. 233.
LB1899.H5   1972   370'.73'09778   71-176863
ISBN 0-404-55233-1

Reprinted by Special Arrangement with Teachers
College Press, New York, New York

From the edition of 1927, New York
First AMS edition published in 1972
Manufactured in the United States

AMS PRESS, INC.
NEW YORK, N. Y.   10003

ACKNOWLEDGMENTS

The enthusiastic coöperation of the presidents and faculties of the Missouri State Teachers Colleges made possible the collection of the data upon which this study is based. The careful guidance and many helpful criticisms of Dr. E. S. Evenden, Dr. W. C. Bagley, and Dr. Carter Alexander, of the faculty of Teachers College, Columbia University, determined its merit. The constructive suggestions of Dr. Virginia Craig and Miss Mary Woods, of the Southwest Missouri State Teachers College faculty, resulted in greatly improving its form. The tabulations were made under the direction of Dr. F. B. O'Rear, Registrar of Southwest Missouri State Teachers College, and my secretary, Miss Dorothy Radle. To each of these my obligation is gratefully acknowledged.

Clyde M. Hill

Springfield, Missouri
June 29, 1926.

CONTENTS

A DECADE OF PROGRESS IN TEACHER TRAINING

CHAPTER I

THE PURPOSE, SCOPE, AND METHODS OF THE STUDY

The first Missouri state normal schools were established at Kirksville and Warrensburg in 1870. In 1873 a third was established at Cape Girardeau, and in 1906 schools were located in the southwest and northwest sections of the state, at Springfield and Maryville, respectively. The training of public school teachers at state expense had been advocated since 1842,[1] only three years after the establishment of normal schools in Massachusetts, but the campaign was interrupted by the Civil War. It remained for Joseph Baldwin, who established a private normal school in Kirksville in 1867, to renew in an energetic manner the agitation for state normal schools which resulted in their establishment three years later.

The early history of these schools was characterized by problems growing out of the methods used in their location, inadequate plants and maintenance funds, and the low state standards for admission to teaching. Bonuses beyond the ability to pay were exacted of the towns in which the schools were located. Ambitious communities obligated themselves to assist the new schools to be established within their borders to the extent that in at least two instances they afterwards had to repudiate their pledges.[2] This "purchase of the normal schools" legitimatized exploitation in the opinion of local business men, created jealousies and aroused opposition on the part of communities not fortunate enough to secure a school, and resulted in the unfavorable location of the schools.[3] "It was a decade or more after their organization before the schools could be said to be secure in public opinion," and "the struggle for existence" which resulted "kept the schools impoverished

---

[1] The Professional Preparation of Teachers for American Public Schools. Bulletin No. 14, The Carnegie Foundation for the Advancement of Teaching, p. 34.

[2] Ibid., p. 36.

[3] Ibid., p. 36. See also Humphreys' Factors Operating in the Location of Normal Schools in the United States.

1

and uncertain of their future."[4] Teachers were scarce[5] and, consequently, certification requirements were low. The normal schools were forced to admit very young students with little previous training who desired to be certificated for teaching as soon as possible. The scholarship standards determined by these conditions in the normal schools made their reputations questionable in the minds of institutions of recognized collegiate standing. These handicaps have been overcome only recently, as will be pointed out in subsequent chapters.

Many changes had occurred in the normal school situation in Missouri by 1914. Normal schools had become firmly established as an essential part of the educational system of the state. The total enrollment was several thousands. Students were somewhat more advanced. Since 1905 the schools had received a total biennial appropriation exceeding a half million dollars, and in 1914 they had more than two million dollars invested in buildings and equipment.[6] Doubtless the larger biennial demands which were being made on the state treasury by the normal schools prompted Governor Elliott W. Major in July, 1914, to request the Carnegie Foundation "to consider the problem of the 'supply of adequately trained and prepared teachers' in that state, with reference especially to the question, 'What is the best preparation and what is the duty of the state in meeting it, and how can the state secure the greatest benefit at a minimum expense?' "[7]

In response to this request the Carnegie Foundation undertook an exhaustive study of the situation in Missouri with the hope that it would have more than local application, that it "would not only prove most helpful to Missouri, but would be of the greatest service elsewhere as well."[8] Under the capable leadership of Dr. W. S. Learned and Dr. W. C. Bagley, a group of America's most distinguished educators assumed responsibility for different parts of the work and published the results of the study, together with their conclusions and proposals for the improvement of teacher training, as Bulletin Number 14 of the Carnegie Foundation for the Advancement of Teaching.

[4] Carnegie Bul. No. 14, p. 38.
[5] *Missouri House Journal,* 1857, 19th Adj. Sess., Appendix, pp. 116, 117.
[6] Carnegie Bul. No. 14, p. 441.
[7] *Ibid.,* p. 3.
[8] *Ibid.,* p. 4.

It is a very extensive study and "represents the first comprehensive formulation of good practice in the largest field of professional training for public service in our country, and it is believed that the work has been done with such care that the results here set forth are worthy of the thoughtful study of every earnest and intelligent teacher." [9]

The initiation of the study was coincident with the opening of the World War in Europe. The actual field work started in November, 1914, and most of the data were collected during the school year 1914-1915. When America became involved in the war it was decided to delay the publication of the final report, and, while the findings and recommendations of the survey commission were not generally distributed until 1920, they were made available to the executives of the Missouri normal schools at a much earlier date, thus making it possible for the results of the study to be used in the plans for immediate improvement. The influence of the study has been felt in Missouri for a full decade. The time which has elapsed has been sufficient for the schools completely to reorganize their practice, and this fact is largely responsible for the present study, which is an analysis of the present situation in Missouri teachers colleges in comparison with the findings and proposals of the Carnegie Survey Commission.

Another fact of interest in connection with the original study is that the report was never formally presented to the Missouri legislature. By the time the study was completed Governor Major had retired from office and his successor either was not acquainted with the study or was not interested in it. Consequently the schools were free to accept or reject the recommendations made, without the compulsion of legislative coercion.

As early as 1907 one of the Missouri normal schools had conferred a four-year bachelor's degree, and in 1914 three of the schools conferred twenty-nine such degrees.[10] All of the schools advertised curricula leading to the degree at that time, although the legal right to grant degrees was not given until 1919, when the present teachers college law was passed.[11] It will be observed that the normal schools were legally changed to teachers

[9] Carnegie Bul. No. 14, p. xvi.
[10] *Ibid*, p. 437.
[11] See p. 102.

colleges just midway between the time when the original study was made and the present.

The present study, occurring as it does just ten years after the first study was made, is concerned with certain specific administrative modifications which have taken place in Missouri state teachers colleges during the decade following the Carnegie survey of tax-supported normal schools, in comparison with the findings and recommendations of the Survey Commission. It of necessity is much more limited in scope than was the original study. The phases of the subject considered are those which are of first interest to the colleges themselves, namely, Student Personnel, Teacher Personnel, Curricula, and the Relationship of State Collegiate Institutions. The study was made and the data were treated in accordance with the following outline:

I. The Purpose of the Study:

1. To determine the educational equipment of the present instructional staffs of the Missouri state teachers colleges in comparison with the findings and recommendations of the Survey Commission.

2. To determine the extent to which salaries and conditions favorable to attracting and holding well-trained teachers, such as leaves of absence and teaching loads, have been modified in the decade in accordance with present equipment demands and living costs.

3. To determine curricular modifications as compared with the recommendations of the Survey Commission, and in view of the fact that during the period schools have changed from normal schools to teachers colleges.

4. To determine the steps made in the transition from two-year normal schools to four-year teachers colleges.

5. To determine the significant changes in the student personnel in their relation to administrative modifications.

6. To determine present trends, activities, practices, and issues in relation to the report of the Survey Commission.

II. Outline of the Study:
   1. The educational equipment of the instructional staffs
      A. Training: (*a*) As to number and grade; (*b*) As to source
         1. Higher education
         2. Classification of degrees
         3. Higher education combinations
         4. Retardation in college training
            a. Undergraduates
            b. Graduates
      B. Experience
         1. Kind
         2. Amount
         3. Under what conditions
      C. Professional outlook
         1. Age
         2. Opportunities for professional growth
         3. Professional activities
         4. Contributions to scholarly literature
         5. Present professional study
   Comparison with the findings and recommendations of the Survey Commission
   2. The extent to which the reward elements and teaching conditions are consistent with the demands
      A. Salary
      B. Tenure
      C. Leaves of absence
      D. Teaching loads
   Comparison with the recommendations made by the Survey Commission
   3 and 4. Curricular modifications
      A. During the first half of the decade following survey
         1. Standards of admission
         2. Residence requirements
         3. Prescribed and elective courses
         4. Curriculum differentiation
         5. Organization and content of courses
         6. Practice teaching
      B. The law authorizing the extension of the

courses to include four years of work and the
conferring of degrees
1. Causes leading to the passage of the law
2. Limitations imposed by the law
3. Immediate effect on appropriations
C. During the last half of the decade
1. Standards of admission
2. Residence requirements
3. Prescribed and elective courses
4. Curriculum differentiation
5. Organization and content of courses
6. Practice teaching
Comparison with the recommendations made by the
Survey Commission

5. Student personnel
A. Men as students
B. Secondary students
C. Organization of attendance
D. Admission and classification
E. Student programs of study
F. Administration of credit
G. Graduation and certification
Comparison with the recommendations made by the
Survey Commission

6. Interpretation of the present trends, activities, practices,
and issues:
A. To show their relationship to the survey
B. To show their relationship to the transitional
period in the development from normal schools
to teachers colleges
C. To analyze present tendencies in the development of Missouri teachers colleges

III. Procedures in the Study and Sources of Data:
1. The training, experience, and professional outlook
of the staffs were obtained by personal interviews
and the use of a questionnaire.[12] Since comparisons
with the survey findings were required, it was obviously desirable to use the technique that was used by
the Survey Commission.

[12] See Appendix A, p. 187.

2. The salaries were taken from the Missouri Blue Books and the State Auditor's reports. The reward elements were obtained through personal conferences with the presidents of the colleges and from the author's own files.

3. The curricular modifications were tabulated and checked from the catalogue files of the colleges, from the minutes [13] of the Conference of Higher Educational Institutions, and from syllabi of courses.

4. Facts concerning the student personnel were obtained from the records on file in the offices of the registrars supplemented by a questionnaire.[14]

5. Comparable data were taken from Bulletin Number 14 of the Carnegie Foundation for the Advancement of Teaching.

IV. Conclusions, Proposals.

[13] See Appendices E and F, pp. 204, 207.
[14] See Appendix A, pp. 187-194.

CHAPTER II

STUDENT PERSONNEL OF MISSOURI TEACHERS COLLEGES

PART I

STUDENT PERSONNEL OF MISSOURI NORMAL SCHOOLS IN 1915

The development of first-class, "approved" high schools was slow in Missouri. This was particularly true in the sparsely settled parts of the state. As a result, the aspiring youth in these sections had to look in large measure to the small colleges for his secondary as well as his collegiate training.

Many of the colleges and all of the normal schools had flourishing secondary departments and often permitted students to "complete" a full high school course which admitted to their own collegiate departments in two-thirds or less of the time ordinarily required for such work. This procedure was justified in the opinion of these colleges by the following conditions: Most of their students were over-age country boys who had more than exhausted local opportunities by having repeated, often many times, the work of the eighth grade. They were "thorough" in the common school branches, and, being very ambitious, applied themselves so well that they could actually finish in twenty-four weeks the amount of work in plane geometry and physics which required thirty-six weeks on the part of the boy of normal age who had come up through the eight grades and who, because he had had the advantages of somewhat better instruction in a graded school with a somewhat longer school year, reached high school at an earlier age.[1]

Although the reports of many students clearly indicate that high schools offering two-, three-, and four-year courses were within reach of their homes and that they would not be "hopelessly out of place" in these schools because of over-age,[2] the normal schools of Missouri in 1915 had more students of secondary than of collegiate rank.[3] This large secondary enrollment

[1] Carnegie Bul. No. 14, p. 297.
[2] Ibid., pp. 297, 298, 120.   [3] Ibid., p. 428.

8

was easily explained by the facts that no high school work was required for certification and that many students would teach part of the year and attend the normal schools, instead of local high schools, the rest of the year. They were permitted to shorten both their high school and normal school courses by actually shortening the time required for completing a subject, and by combining high school and college work.[4]

When rural students found it necessary to go from home even a short distance for the purpose of attending high school, they were willing to incur the slightly larger expense at the time by attending a normal school because the shorter time required for the completion of the work made it cheaper in the end. It is not surprising, therefore, to find that there were about three hundred children under sixteen years of age in the secondary departments of the Missouri normal schools, although the median age during the regular session was twenty years.

Even if it were true then that the older students could do the high school work in a shorter time than the students of normal age,[5] the actual age of secondary students enrolled in high school departments of the normal schools was too low to justify the practice of permitting students to complete four years of work in three. A more truthful explanation of the lowering of standards was the desire to attract a large number of students of whatever level of advancement in order to impress the members of the legislature, who, in the matter of appropriations, were more easily appealed to by large numbers than by genuine evidence of a splendid service to the state in the production of capable, trained teachers.

The Carnegie report called attention to this wide range of interest in type of work offered (four years of high school work and two or more years of collegiate work) and to the age of students (twelve to fifty years).[6] These conditions were not only the source of many problems at the time, but have been important factors in the development of the schools during the past decade. In the five normal schools in 1915 about seven thousand five hundred students were enrolled, twenty-eight per cent of whom were men. The median age of all students dur-

[4] Carnegie Bul. No. 14, p. 299.
[5] *Ibid.*, p. 291, note 1, and p. 117.
[6] *Ibid.*, p. 117.

ing the regular session was twenty years; in the summer it was twenty-two years. Most of the students were of American ancestry and natives of the state. "The collegiate students are nearly three-fifths town bred, while but half as many of the secondary students are from town." [7]

Sixty-five per cent of all students, seventy-seven per cent of the secondary students, sixty-two per cent of the collegiate men, and forty-eight per cent of the collegiate women were the children of farmers. Half of the students reporting state that the annual family income was $1000 or less, thirty-three per cent report an annual family income of over $1500. Forty-five per cent of the women and twenty-eight per cent of the men belonged to the latter group. This modest family income would suggest that many of the students were self-supporting. The study shows that half of all of the men and nearly a third of the women were wholly self-supporting. "Of the collegiate group about two-thirds of the men were self-supporting." [8] The median number of children in the families represented was six with "sixteen per cent [of the students from families] of nine or more children." [9]

The three factors which exerted the most influence in the students' choice of teaching as a profession were: other teachers in the family; financial attraction; and the nearness of the normal school to the homes represented. Three-fifths of the students were from families in which there were other teachers. Sixty-five per cent had relatives who had attended normal school and in most cases they had attended the same school in which the students reporting were then enrolled. [10] "Seven-eighths of the women thought teaching their most promising opportunity, while fewer than half of the men were of that opinion." [11] A fourth of the students came from the county in which the school was located, another fourth came from six or seven adjoining counties, about a third came from the more remote counties of the district, and the rest were from scattered localities within and without the state. [12]

[7] Carnegie Bul. No. 14, p. 117.
[8] *Ibid.*, pp. 117, 118.
[9] *Ibid.*, p. 118.
[10] *Ibid.*, p. 118.
[11] *Ibid.*, p. 118.
[12] *Ibid.*, p. 118.

The median attendance of all students in the elementary school was sixty-one months. Two-fifths had their elementary training in rural schools and three-tenths in equal numbers in rural ungraded schools or in graded schools.[13] Four-fifths of the collegiate women and three-fifths of the collegiate men were high school graduates.[14] The others had met such requirements as were demanded for registration as college students, in the secondary departments of the normal schools, by private study or through examination for certificates, the certificate grades being accepted in some instances in lieu of high school credit. The subsequent collegiate work of these students who had not taken full high school training indicated that high school graduates did not fare "conspicuously better or worse than those who take secondary work in the normal school."[15]

Of the total annual enrollment in the normal schools, half of the men and three-fifths of the women had already taught. Of the collegiate group, two-thirds were teachers, while of the secondary students, two-fifths of the men and over half of the women had had teaching experience. It is encouraging, however, to note that during the regular session the conditions are better. Leaving out the summer session, only two-fifths of the students have had teaching experience, and the proportion is greatest, naturally, in the collegiate group, where it is nearly one-half; among the secondary students the proportion dwindles to less than one-third. For three of the schools it was possible to discover the nature of this experience. Rural school teaching predominates, as one would expect; about one-seventh of those in the collegiate group who have taught lacked rural experience, and practically all teachers among the secondary group have been rural teachers, though a quarter of them have had some grade work also. One-fourth of the college students have done both rural and grade work, and about one-tenth have done some high school work. The collegiate women had been teachers only; but about two per cent of the collegiate men had been superintendents and three per cent had been principals. In length of experience, the summer session group shows a median of twenty-one months as compared with sixteen months among regular session students who have taught.[16]

Half of the women reported that they did not intend to teach permanently. This was to be expected because the tenure of women teachers is traditionally terminated by marriage; but it is a significant fact that eighty per cent of the men students

[13] Carnegie Bul. No. 14, p. 119.
[14] *Ibid.*, p. 119. Data from Maryville, Kirksville, and Warrensburg.
[15] *Ibid.*, pp. 123-124.
[16] *Ibid.*, p. 123.

who were being educated at state expense for the profession of teaching stated that they expected to make teaching but a stepping-stone to their permanent occupation.[17] Seventy-five per cent of the men and ninety per cent of the women expected to teach for a while, there being little variation among the schools in this respect.[18] Two-fifths of all the collegiate students expressed their intention of continuing their study in some college or university.

The typical student in a Missouri normal school in 1915 was twenty years old, was of American ancestry, was born in Missouri, had not completed a high school course, was the child of a farmer whose annual income was about $1000, was one of six children, and was partially or wholly self-supporting. He was a member of a family of teachers, some of whom had attended the normal school. He lived near the normal school, which fact, together with the opinion that teaching offered him the most promising immediate employment, accounted for his being there. He had attended the rural elementary school sixty-one months, intended to teach but a few years, and had some ambition to continue his college education.

PART II

PROPOSALS OF THE SURVEY COMMISSION CONCERNING STUDENT PERSONNEL IN 1915

It was the purpose of the study made in 1915 "to reach as nearly as possible the root of existing weaknesses, and to suggest changes likely to correct them not only in Missouri but wherever they may be found."[19] The proposals which are here listed were made in the belief that the more careful selection of students, the devotion of the normal schools to their specific task of teacher training, higher standards of scholarship, and careful placing of the product were fundamental elements in the improvement of the normal schools. The extent to which they have been put into operation and the modifications which seem desirable in the light of the more recent study after a lapse of ten years are presented in the remaining sections of this chapter.

---

[17] Carnegie Bul. No. 14, p. 123.
[18] *Ibid.*, p. 124.
[19] *Ibid.*, p. 387.

The Proposals of 1915

a. The conscious effort to attract or to retain men students in normal schools at a sacrifice of a clear aim and of an intensive organization of work is not in the best interests of the service (pages 292-295).[20]

b. The secondary instruction offered in the normal schools should be abandoned; young pupils should be returned to the high schools for preparation, and state-supported high schools, with organization wholly separate from that of the normal schools, should be provided for older, belated students (page 295).

c. Concessions to irregular attendants have seriously hampered the proper work of the schools and should not continue. Coöperation among the schools in the adoption of prescribed curricula requiring continuous attendance would prove greatly to the advantage both of the student and of the service (page 305).

d. Admission to the normal schools should depend on either a credential issued by the state authority for the inspection and approval of secondary schools or an adequate examination (page 312).

e. The tendency to excessive student programs would be most effectually remedied by resorting to fixed curricula based, not on the number of hours or points, but on the successful completion of a certain series of courses taken in a definite combination and sequence (pages 317-320).

f. Fully to serve its purpose, the normal school should seek to become a selective institution. In determining the degrees of student attainment the relaxation or abandonment of thorough examination without the development of other more accurate and effective methods of measurement is a mistake. "Sizing up" on the part of the instructor can scarcely be considered satisfactory (page 326).

g. The maintenance of accurate, significant records of student work is essential for the moral health of the institution. The administration of credit should be in the hands of disinterested officers acting in accordance with regulations and policies established either by faculty action or preferably by the joint action of all responsible authorities of teacher-training institutions (page 342).

h. (1) Graduation should mark the natural terminus in a symmetrically organized course of training, rather than the achievement of a given number of unrelated credits (page 344).

(2) Certification should be a matter not of statute but of carefully planned administration on the part of the state commissioner of education in coöperation with the training institutions. It should depend not only on initial study and examination, but also on competent scrutiny of ability and growth in service (pages 346-348).

[20] Pages refer to Carnegie Bul. No. 14.

(3) Appointments to positions should involve a clearer and more specific knowledge and record, both of the candidate and of the proposed position, than are of present attempted. To accomplish this the normal school should undertake to establish more intimate and responsibile relations with its dependent schools than now exist. The institution's obligations are not fully discharged until a properly prepared teacher is successfully at work.

i. The administrative practices of an institution, like the patterns of instruction set by its staff, are as vital elements in curricula as are any formal courses; they should be models of good judgment and skillful planning because of their inevitable and powerful influence upon the ideals of prospective teachers (pages 353, 354).[21]

PART III

STUDENT PERSONNEL IN 1926

Fully accredited high schools are now fairly generally distributed throughout Missouri. There is not a county in the state which does not have one or more high schools offering a four-year course with sixteen units of work approved by the accrediting agencies of the state department of education and the state university. While there is yet much to be desired both in the actual quality of the work done in these schools and in their number and distribution over the state, they do exist at the present time in sufficient numbers and are well enough located that the teacher-training institutions no longer are under the necessity of providing secondary training for a large number of students, as was the case in their early history.

Not only has the more general provision for secondary training throughout the state relieved the situation, but the passage of a certification law which requires all candidates for county certificates to have completed a full four-year high school course has prevented the continuance of a large group of over-age men and women as teachers in the state. No longer do mature men and women look to the state schools to provide secondary courses for them in a social group of their own age. With one exception the teachers colleges in Missouri no longer maintain high school departments except in their training schools, and in this college the teaching staffs are quite distinct for the collegiate and

[21] Carnegie Bul. No. 14, pp. 396-397.

secondary classes and under no conditions are secondary students admitted to classes of collegiate rank.

This change in student personnel has made it possible for the teachers colleges to devote their attention to collegiate instruction or has paved the way for improved standards of work, and has simplified administration. Since teachers are no longer expected to teach both college and high school classes it is easier for them to put all of their work on a strictly collegiate level.[22] The better classification of students [23] has provoked and made possible a refinement of aims in the individual courses and has stimulated a general "up-grading" of the work.

With an annual enrollment of between twelve and thirteen thousand individual students of collegiate rank in the five teachers colleges, concessions no longer have to be made which result in the lowering of standards of admission in order to attract a student group of sufficient size to impress the legislature. This does not mean that Missouri teachers colleges are any less willing to serve the needs of their students than they have been in the past, but it does mean that they fully recognize their function in such a fundamental way that they unhesitatingly put the needs of the service in a position of absolute primacy.

TABLE I

SHOWING AGE DISTRIBUTION OF STUDENTS IN MISSOURI TEACHERS COLLEGES
IN 1926

	16 yr. %	17 yr. %	18 yr. %	19 yr. %	20 yr. %	21 yr. %	22 yr. %	23 yr. %	24 yr. %	25 yr. %	26 yr. %	27 yr. %	More than 27 yr. %
Men	4	5	19	27	27	10	3	3	1	1	>1	>1	>1
Women ..	3	7	21	30	24	6	2	2	2	1	1	>1	1
Both	4	6	21	29	25	7	2	3	1	1	>1	>1	>1

Median age = 18.6 years

22 See p. 75.
23 See p. 75.

TABLE II

SHOWING DISTRIBUTION OF STUDENTS IN MISSOURI TEACHERS COLLEGES
IN 1926 ACCORDING TO PLACE OF BIRTH

	Men %	Women %	Both %
Missouri	91	91	91
Mid-West	5	4	4
North	1	1	1
South	2	3	2
East-West	< 1	< 1	< 1
Foreign...........................	< 1	< 1	< 1

TABLE III

SHOWING DISTRIBUTION OF STUDENTS IN MISSOURI TEACHERS COLLEGES
IN 1926 ACCORDING TO TYPE OF HOME COMMUNITY

Type of Home Community	All Students All Colleges %
Farms or villages of less than 1000	49
Villages of 1000 to 2500	16
Towns of 2500 to 5000	11
Cities of 5000 to 25,000	14
Cities of more than 25,000	10
Total	100

Because the teachers colleges have been freed from the many
problems incidental to the offering of work ranging from first
year high school to senior year college and because they now
have a homogeneous group of students, they are able to attack
their work with much less distraction than ever before in their
history.

A survey of student personnel[24] in the Missouri teachers
colleges in January, 1926, by means of a questionnaire,[25] regis-

[24] All data relate to collegiate students only.
[25] See Appendix A.

trars' records, and personal conferences, provided the data for the conclusions recorded here concerning the type of student who is now attending these institutions. The median age of all students is 18.6 years.[26] Ninety-one per cent were born in Missouri, and four per cent in states bordering on Missouri.[27] The ancestry of fifty-four per cent of the students is American; twenty-nine per cent report that their parents are of mixed nationality. Forty-nine per cent of the students live on farms or in villages of less than 1000 inhabitants, sixteen per cent live in cities of 1000 to 2500 inhabitants, eleven per cent in cities of 2500 to 5000 inhabitants, fourteen per cent in cities of 5000 to 25,000, and ten per cent in cities of more than 25,000 inhabitants. The number who live in rural communities is equal to the number who live in urban communities.[28]

TABLE IV

SHOWING DISTRIBUTION OF STUDENTS IN MISSOURI TEACHERS COLLEGES IN 1926 ACCORDING TO PARENTAL OCCUPATION

Parental Occupation		Kirks-ville %	War-rens-burg %	Cape Girar-deau %	Spring-field %	Mary-ville %	Total %	Missouri Occupational Distribution U. S. Census	
								%	Year
Agr.	1926	60	59	36	42	60	50	31.0	1920
	*1915	71	62	56	73	75	65	35.5	1910
Mfg.	1926	< 1	< 1	1	< 1	1	< 1	25.1	1920
	*1915	4	7	8	5	2	6	23.6	1910
Tr.	1026	12	12	25	13	25	17	12.1	1920
	*1915	12	14	14	11	16	13	11.1	1910
Pro.	1926	19	18	31	29	7	22	5.3	1920
	*1915	7	8	14	8	2	9	4.7	1910
Others	1926	9	11	7	16	7	11	26.5	1920
	*1915	6	9	8	3	5	7	25.1	1910

* See Carnegie Bul. No. 14, p. 430. Data for both collegiate and secondary students.

Agr.=Agriculture.   Mfg.=Manufacturing.   Tr.=Trade.   Pro.=Professional Service. Others=All Others.

[26] See Table I.   [27] See Table II.   [28] See Table III.

The fact that the parental occupation of fifty per cent of the students now enrolled in the Missouri teachers colleges is farming [29] is not so significant to the institutions as the fact that fifty per cent of their students have been reared in rural communities, and have had only the limited educational opportunities these smaller communities afford. The kind of responsibility imposed by this situation is well stated in the report of the survey commission of the state teachers colleges of Louisiana, 1924.

That the children of business men and professional men have, on the whole, the best chances to achieve a notable "success in life" is a reasonable inference from the facts recently compiled by Professor S. S. Vischer of Indiana University on the basis of a special inquiry as to parental occupation sent out in collecting data for the current issue (1924-25) of *Who's Who in America*. In summarizing the results of his study, Professor Vischer says (p. 31 of the volume just mentioned):

" . . . a large share of the notables of today have come from certain relatively minor elements, as to numbers, of the population. More than one-third have come from the professional classes which comprised only one-forty-fifth of the population—in 1870. The 5 per cent of the men of America classed as business men contributed 35 per cent of the men and women sketched in 1922-23 edition of *Who's Who in America*. Thus 70 per cent of the notables were fathered by less than 7.5 per cent of the nation's men. In contrast, unskilled laborers fathered almost none of the notables . . . , and, although farmers fathered 23.4 per cent, that per cent is about one-fourth less than their share in proportion to the population.

"While there is a reasonable doubt as to the relative influence of heredity on the one hand and home training, culture, and educational advantages on the other hand in determining these vast differences, it would be futile to deny some influence (and perhaps a preponderant influence) to the latter factor. In any case it is clear that the professional education of recruits for the public-school service (which draws disproportionately from the less favored occupational groups) should make every effort to compensate as far as possible for the cultural handicaps which the student-body is likely to reflect." [30]

The teaching profession in Missouri is not only still drawing a disproportionate share of its recruits from the farms but with the single exception of manufacturing the representation in the teachers college enrollment is in excess of the occupational distribution given for the state in the U. S. Census report for 1920. Although only thirty-one per cent of the people of the state are

[29] See Table IV.
[30] *Report of Louisiana Survey Commission*, 1924, p. 47, note.

engaged in farming, fifty per cent of the students come from farm homes. The parental occupation of seventeen per cent of the students is trade, whereas only twelve per cent of the state's population is so employed. The greatest discrepancy between occupational distribution in the state and teachers college enrollment is in the professional group. Only five per cent of the population of the state belongs to the professional group, while twenty-two per cent of the students are from this group. During the past ten years this enrollment has increased from nine per cent to twenty-two per cent, there being a notable

TABLE V

SHOWING ANNUAL INCOME OF FATHERS OF COLLEGIATE STUDENTS IN 1926

	Less than $501	Less than $801	Less than $1001	$1001–1500	More than $1500	More than $2000	More than $3000	No. of Students Reporting
	%	%	%	%	%	%	%	
Men	2	5	14	15	71	40	26	655
Women ...	2	5	13	13	74	53	27	1025
Both	2	5	14	14	72	51	26	1680
				100%				

TABLE VI

SHOWING ANNUAL INCOME OF FATHERS OF STUDENTS IN 1915
(From Carnegie Bul. No. 14, Table 29, p. 431)

	Less than $501	Less than $801	Less than $1001	$1001–1500	More than $1500	More than $2000	More than $3000	No. of Students Reporting
	%	%	%	%	%	%	%	
Men	16	35	52	20	28	16	7	187
Women ...	6	14	34	21	45	30	15	279
Both	13	28	50	20	30	19	10	1146*
				100%				

* Includes collegiate and secondary students.

increase in each college.[31] It would be of interest to the colleges to ascertain whether there is a tendency for the children of professional men to prepare for teaching or whether they are taking advantage of conveniently located teachers colleges to get a collegiate education without professional aim.

The economic status of the families from which prospective teachers are drawn is a matter of importance to the teachers colleges, since it is likely to reflect the cultural opportunities the students have had. Seventy-two per cent of the students reporting are members of families whose income exceeds $1500, fifty-one per cent of the incomes exceed $2000, and twenty-six per cent exceed $3000. Twenty-eight per cent of the students report annual family incomes of less than $1500, half of which are less than $1000.[32] With a large percentage of the students coming from farm homes it is doubtful if the estimate represents the entire income. It probably represents more nearly only the cash income, but since the median income of the entire group is only $2000, and in view of the depreciated dollar, it is evident that the prospective teachers do not come from the homes which are most favored financially.

TABLE VII

SHOWING SELF-DEPENDENT, PARTLY SELF-DEPENDENT, NOT SELF-DEPENDENT
STUDENTS IN MISSOURI TEACHERS COLLEGES IN 1926

	Men		Women		Both	
	No.	%	No.	%	No.	%
Self-dependent	373	41	452	24	861	30
Partly self-dependent	383	42	464	26	887	31
Not self-dependent	162	17	913	50	1128	39
Total	918	100	1829	100	2876	100

Further evidence for the conclusion that students in the Missouri teachers colleges are under economic pressure is found in the fact that only half of the students are not self-dependent, wholly or in part. Forty-one per cent of the men, twenty-four

[31] See Table IV.
[32] See Tables V and VI.

per cent of the women, and thirty per cent of all the students are entirely self-supporting. An additional forty-two per cent of the men, twenty-six per cent of the women, and thirty-one per cent of all the students are partly self-dependent.[33] This situation suggests, on the one hand, that students who are self-supporting are likely to take their work seriously and make the most of their opportunities; on the other hand, the necessity of giving time and energy to activities not directly associated with their studies dissipates their efforts to the disadvantage of their

TABLE VIII

SHOWING NUMBER OF CHILDREN IN FAMILIES OF STUDENTS IN MISSOURI
TEACHERS COLLEGES IN 1926

No. of Children in Family	% of Families
One	9
Two to four	42
Five to eight	39
Nine to eleven	9
Twelve or more	1

Median No. of Children = 4

TABLE IX

SHOWING NUMBER OF OTHER TEACHERS IN FAMILIES OF STUDENTS IN
MISSOURI TEACHERS COLLEGES IN 1926

No. of Other Teachers in Family	Kirks-ville %	War-rens-burg %	Girar-deau %	Spring-field %	Mary-ville %	Total % Reporting M.	W.	Both	Total No, Reporting M.	W.	Both
None	61	63	65	64	65	63	64	63	625	1269	1894
1 or 2	34	32	31	31	32	32	32	33	322	621	943
3 or more .	4	5	4	5	3	5	4	4	51	79	130
Total .	100	100	100	100	100	100	100	100	998	1969	2967

[33] See Table VII.

studies and class work. Of doubtful validity is the oft-stated claim that through unusual devotion to their studies the students in teachers colleges make better scholastic records than collegiate students generally do.

Not only is the family income small but it has to provide for the needs of large families. Eighty-two per cent of the students are members of families which have from two to eight

TABLE X

SHOWING LOCATION OF HOMES OF STUDENTS IN MISSOURI TEACHERS COLLEGES IN 1926 WITH REFERENCE TO THE COLLEGES

Place of Residence	% of Students
In county in which college is located	30
In district in which college is located	91
In other parts of Missouri	6
In other states	3

TABLE XI

SHOWING RECORD OF HIGH SCHOOL ATTENDANCE OF STUDENTS IN MISSOURI TEACHERS COLLEGES IN 1926

Student in Some High School	Kirks-ville		Warrens-burg		Cape Girardeau		Spring-field		Mary-ville		Total	
	No.	%	No.	%	No.	%	No.	%	No.	%	No.	%
Men	134	100	166	100	135	100	314	100	200	100	949	100
Women	303	100	475	100	262	100	485	100	351	100	1873	100
Both	437	100	641	100	397	100	799	100	551	100	2822	100
Graduate First-class Four-year High School												
Men	131	98	137	82	133	98	267	85	198	99	866	91
Women	301	99	395	83	262	100	437	90	348	99	1740	92
Both	432	98	532	82	395	99	704	88	546	99	2606	92

children. Forty-two per cent of them have from two to four
children, forty-eight per cent have from five to eleven children,
and one per cent twelve or more children. The median number
of children is four.[34]

Sixty-three per cent of the students are the only members of
their immediate families who are teachers, thirty-three per cent
have one or two brothers or sisters who have taught.[35]

Although there are no legal restrictions regarding attendance,
the Missouri teachers colleges draw their students from their
local districts. Thirty per cent of the students come from the
counties in which the colleges are located, ninety-one per cent
from the district, and three per cent from other states.[36]

All of the collegiate students have attended high school.
Ninety-one per cent of the men and ninety-two per cent of the
women are graduates of first-class four-year high schools.[37]
This number includes the graduates of the high school departments of the training schools, all of which meet the requirements
and are approved by the state accrediting agencies. The remaining eight per cent of the collegiate students had not com-

TABLE XII

SHOWING DISTRIBUTION OF TEACHING EXPERIENCE OF ALL STUDENTS WHO
HAVE TAUGHT

	Total No. Report-ing	Students Having Experience		6 mo.	9 mo.	More than 18 mo.	More than 27 mo.	More than 36 mo.	More than 45 mo.	More than 54 mo.	More than 90 mo.
		No.	%	%	%	%	%	%	%	%	%
Men	917	124	13	8	55	37	20	13	6	4	2
Women ..	1829	334	18	4	51	45	19	15	8	5	2
Both	2746	458	16	5	52	43	19	14	7	5	2

100%
Median = 7.9 month

[34] See Table VIII.
[35] See Table IX.
[36] See Table X.
[37] See Table XI.

pleted sixteen units of high school work before entrance. Some of them who had not graduated from high school were admitted to collegiate standing upon the presentation of fifteen high school units, a few established their standing in some subjects by examination, and the rest were admitted to conditional standing in accordance with the conference regulations [38] with the privilege of removing the conditions by the substitution of college credit.

Of the regular resident collegiate enrollment in all the Missouri teachers colleges in January, 1926, only sixteen per cent had held teaching positions between high school graduation and entrance to teachers college. Almost three times as many of the women as men had taught.[39] The median teaching experience of all collegiate students before college entrance was 7.9 months.[40]

TABLE XIII

SHOWING ANTICIPATED TEACHING TENURE OF STUDENTS IN MISSOURI
TEACHERS COLLEGES IN 1926

No. of Yrs.	Kirks-ville %		Warrens-burg %		Cape Girardeau %		Spring-field %		Mary-ville %		Total %		Total %
	M	W	M	W	M	W	M	W	M	W	M	W	Both
1	<1	<1	4	2	4	4	2	3	3	3	3	2	2
2	11	14	14	10	17	20	14	11	14	15	13	13	14
3	14	14	11	11	9	13	9	13	1	12	9	12	12
4	12	10	17	18	13	16	8	13	18	11	13	13	14
5	14	26	12	23	10	20	20	24	13	24	14	25	21
6	<1	5	3	5	1	2	2	4		5	2	5	4
7	0	0	1	2	1	1	1	2	1	<1	1	1	1
8	<1	3	3	3	1	2	0	2	4	3	2	3	2
9	<1	0	0	0	1	0	0	1			<1	<1	<1
10 or more	42	26	34	26	43	22	42	25	46	26	41	26	29
Total ..	100	100	100	100	100	100	100	100	100	100	100	100	100

[38] See p. 156.
[39] See Table XII.
[40] See Table XII.

Of the total number reporting, sixty-six per cent of all students—seventy-three per cent of the women, and fifty-two per cent of the men—expect to teach. Twenty-nine per cent of all students expect to teach ten or more years. Sixty-three per cent expect to teach five years or less; forty-two per cent expect to teach four years or less; fifty-eight per cent expect to teach five years or more. Forty-one per cent of the men who expect to teach at all expect to teach ten or more years. Only twenty-six per cent of the women expect to teach so long. Fifty-two per cent of the men expect to teach five years or less; thirty-eight per cent of them expect to teach less than five years. Of the women, sixty-five per cent expect to teach five years or less, and seventy-four per cent do not expect to teach permanently.[41]

TABLE XIV

SHOWING TYPE OF SERVICE FOR WHICH STUDENTS IN MISSOURI TEACHERS
COLLEGES IN 1926 ARE PREPARING

Type of Service	Kirksville %		Warrens- burg %		Girardeau %		Spring- field %		Maryville %		Total %
	W	M	W	M	W	M	W	M	W	M	Both
Kindergarten .	6		2		13		5		2		3
1st & 2nd gr. .	13		15	<1	12	2	9		9		8
3rd & 4th gr. .	12	<1	15	<1	15	2	9		13	<1	9
5th & 6th gr. .	6		13	2	7	11	11	1	8	5	8
Jr. H. S.	5	4	7	4	4	26	6	6	9	12	7
Sr. H. S.	50	89	43	93	50	48	57	92	45	78	59
Sp. Sch. Subjs.	8	6	4	2	9	11	3	<1	14	3	6
Total	100	100	100	100	100	100	100	100	100	100	100

Fifty-nine per cent of the students who expect to teach are making preparation to teach in the secondary schools. This fact doubtless accounts for the very great preponderance of attention apparently given to the training of high school teachers

[41] See Table XIII.

by all of the colleges.[42]   Thirty-five per cent of all students and
forty-four per cent of the women students are preparing for the
elementary grades and junior high school.   Forty-nine per cent
of the women students are taking courses preparing for high
school teaching and seven per cent are preparing to teach
special subjects, in either high school or the grades.   Of the men
students, eighty-five per cent are preparing for high school
teaching, three per cent for teaching special subjects, eight per
cent for junior high school teaching, and four per cent for intermediate and upper grade teaching.[43]

The typical student in a Missouri teachers college in 1926 is
eighteen years old, is of American ancestry, was born in Missouri, is a graduate from a first-class high school, is the child
of a farmer whose annual income is about $2000, was reared in
a community of less than 2500 inhabitants, is one of a family
of four children, is partially self-supporting while in school,
is attending the college nearest his own home, has no brothers or
sisters who have taught, probably has not held a teaching position or has taught only 7.9 months, expects to teach in a secondary school for about five years, after which he will leave the
profession because of matrimony or to enter some other line of
work.

PART IV

Student Personnel in Missouri Teachers Colleges in 1926 in Comparison With Student Personnel in 1915

Some of the recent surveys of teachers colleges refer to the
training school, the library situation, and the quality of teaching as "phases of the curriculum." It would be equally appropriate to consider the student personnel as a phase of the
curriculum since it is so vital a factor in curriculum planning.
It is one thing to set up an ideal program for teacher training,
and quite another to fit that program, on the one hand, to the
needs of the type of student who seeks to enter the profession,
and, on the other hand, to the needs of the service.

[42] See p. 118.
[43] See Table XIV.

If a student has had thorough training in a cultured community before entering the teachers college, the kind and amount of work necessary and desirable to bring him to the point where he will be acceptable to the profession of teaching and capable of assuming its responsibilities with promise of success, are radically different from what must be given to the student with less favorable early training. Such preparation cannot yet be required of prospective entrants.

Teacher-training institutions justly feel that they have a right to expect their students to have, when they enter college, a desirable background upon which to project their specialized work, but conditions have not yet made it possible for many of the teachers colleges, in recruiting their students, to exercise a great deal of selection beyond the minmum requirements for entrance. If a large number of students are deficient in fundamental elementary and secondary subject matter, the college is compelled to recognize these shortcomings in its plan, in one way or another, because the deficiency must be supplied before the student can be certificated.

In another chapter of this study the extent to which the student personnel can actually determine the curriculum is pointed out. Indeed, in catering to the needs of students the Missouri teachers colleges in their early history all but defeated the very purposes for which they existed.[44] With the improvement of teachers colleges, more and better secondary schools, higher standards for certification of teachers, and somewhat better salaries for teachers, the colleges are exercising more and more care in the selection of students.[45] The better classified, more homogeneous student groups make possible many refinements in requirements and practices in the teachers colleges that in another situation would be extremely difficult if not impossible to obtain. Preliminary to the study of modifications in the curricula in Missouri teachers colleges since 1915, a comparison is made in this section of the student personnel of these institutions in 1915 with that in 1926.

Although there is not a great deal of difference in the median

[44] See p. 9.
[45] See Herzog, *State Maintenance of Teachers in Training.*

ages of the students in 1915 and of those in 1926, the age
deviation in 1915 was much greater than that in 1926. In 1915
the range in ages among the students was from twelve to fifty
years. In 1926 it is from sixteen to forty years, there being
only five per cent of the collegiate students more than twenty-
three, and thirty per cent less than eighteen years of age; whereas
in 1915 thirty-one per cent of the collegiate students were
more than twenty-three and eleven per cent were less than eighteen years of age.[46] Assuming homogeneity in every other respect, many problems of administration, management, and methods of instruction would arise in the first instance which would
not exist in the second.

The problems growing out of mere age disparity were not
nearly so difficult and far-reaching as were the problems incident to the wide range of work needed for these distinct
groups of students. In 1915 more than half of the students
were of high school rank and classes were maintained for four
years of secondary work and four years of college work. In
1926 the Missouri teachers colleges do not offer high school
courses conducted by their regular faculties. All secondary
work is handled by student assistants and in the training schools.
It is to be expected that the general atmosphere of the school
would be determined by its largest group and, in fact, the
normal schools of 1915 were large high schools with some college
classes.[47] In 1926, with no secondary work, the general bearing
of the teachers colleges is collegiate. The students have come
up through first-class high schools, compare very favorably
as regards preliminary training with college students elsewhere,
and make possible an organization and a use of instructional
methods suited to collegiate students. This opportunity for
concentration upon the collegiate phases of the teacher-training
problem has been one of the most important factors in bringing
about the changes that have occurred in Missouri teachers colleges during the last decade.

So far as parental occupation of the students is concerned
there has been no marked change during the ten years that
have elapsed since the survey was made. In 1915 sixty-five

---

[46] Carnegie Bul. No. 14, p. 429, and Table I, p. 15 of this study.
[47] See p. 8.

per cent of the students were the children of farmers; in 1926 fifty per cent of them were from farm homes. The number of students from the professional occupation groups has grown from nine per cent in 1915 to twenty-two per cent in 1926, while the U. S. Census Report shows an increase from 4.7 per cent to 5.3 per cent from 1910 to 1920.[48] It would seem that there is a tendency for the children of farmers to leave the teaching profession and for the children of professional men to take an increasing interest in it. There is just as much reason, however, for assuming that since the teachers colleges are offering four years of college work the children of professional men are taking advantage of the opportunities for collegiate study near home. Perhaps as large a percentage as formerly of the students who enter teaching now are from farm homes. At any rate the largest single group in the teachers colleges now have had only the training afforded by the rural communities, and in so far as that creates a problem, the teachers colleges must face it and plan their work accordingly.

Another respect in which the student personnel has not changed appreciably is the economic status of the homes from which they come. In 1915 the annual family income of half of the students was less than $1000; in 1926 slightly more than half of the students report an annual family income of more than $2000. When allowance is made for the depreciated dollar since 1915, only a slightly larger income is actually represented. The families represented are not so large as they were in 1915. At that time the median size of the family was six; now it is four. Sixteen per cent of the students were from families of nine or more children; now only nine per cent come from such large families. The somewhat larger income and the smaller families may account for the fact that there are not so many students in 1926 who are wholly self-dependent as there were in 1915, the percentages for the men being forty-one and fifty, respectively, and for the women, twenty-four and thirty-three, respectively.

Our interest in these factors, parental occupation, family size and income, is determined by the extent to which they reflect the probable advantages, educational, social, cultural, which

[48] See Table IV.

the students have had when they come to the teachers colleges,[49] and which in turn affect teachers college curricula. In 1915 the normal school planned its work for an over-age, secondary student of rural up-bringing. In 1926 the teachers college must plan its work for a high school graduate who has had secondary schooling because it could be had near his farm home and not because he has left the farm. It is doubtful whether the development of the farm home has kept pace with the growth of educational opportunities.

With better roads, telephones, automobiles, free mail delivery, extension courses and circulating libraries, together with the demands that the better schools would create for these things, it would not be unreasonable to assume some improvement in farm homes during the period covered by this study. The student who enters the freshman college class of a teachers college now, has a better equipment for doing the work than did a student who entered the same class ten years ago. He has received systematic instruction in English, history, mathematics, science, and usually a foreign language. He has no "complimentary" entrance credit nor credit of such doubtful value as that assigned for certificate grades.

Another change which has a direct bearing upon curricula and especially upon the use of the training school, is the change regarding the amount of experience which the students have had when they enter upon their training. In 1915 fifty per cent of the collegiate students had taught; in 1926 only sixteen per cent had taught before entering college. When the students are predominantly an experienced group, the approach to the work must be modified so as to force an analysis of the student's experience in the light of educational principles; otherwise his undirected experience and the body of habits that he has formed will become the most important factor in his training.

The practice teaching of an experienced teacher involves problems which are not present with other students. He must not only develop a technique of teaching, but he must also definitely overcome habits that have been rather firmly fixed. The fact that the relatively inexperienced group now in training

[49] See p. 18.

reflects a feeling on the part of the people that one must not teach until he has made specific preparation for it, is evidence of real progress.

The teaching profession is perhaps different from all other professions in that even its trained members do not expect to make it a permanent vocation. In 1915 only twenty per cent of the men expected to teach permanently; in 1926 forty one per cent of those who expect to teach at all expect to teach for ten or more years. Only twenty-six per cent of the women reporting in 1926 expect to make teaching a permanent occupation; whereas fifty per cent of the women reporting in 1915 were so disposed. Perhaps the difference in maturity of the two groups accounts in part for this difference in expectation of tenure. The expectation of marriage in the younger group would undoubtedly be greater than in the older one.

In comparing training for teaching with training for other professional occupations, as we are constantly prone to do, it is important to take into account that even the women who enter the other professions expect to make the practice of their profession a life vocation. No other profession, perhaps, has to anticipate so short a tenure on the part of its trained members as does teaching.

TABLE XV

SHOWING PERCENTAGES OF MEN STUDENTS ENROLLED AT INTERVALS SINCE
1871 IN MISSOURI TEACHERS COLLEGES

1871	1881	1891	1901	1911	1914	1926
55%	59%	47%	43%	33%	28%	34%

The present percentage of enrollment of men students exceeds that of 1915. Not only is there a larger percentage of men students enrolled, but a slightly larger percentage of them expect to teach permanently. The questionnaires show that many men are taking advantage of the opportunities afforded by the teachers colleges to meet the collegiate, pre-professional requirements of professions other than teaching. The reports also show that many of them expect to teach for a while in

TABLE XVI

SHOWING SIMILARITIES AND DIFFERENCES IN STUDENT PERSONNEL IN
MISSOURI NORMAL SCHOOLS IN 1915 AND IN 1926

Student Characteristics in 1915	Student Characteristics in 1926
1. American ancestry—Born in Mo.	1. American ancestry—Born in Mo.
2. Total annual enrollment of about 7,500 students of secondary and collegiate rank	2. Total annual enrollment of about 13,000 students of collegiate rank
3. 28% of students were men	3. 34% of students are men
4. Median age of all students 20 years	4. Median age of all students 18.6 years
5. 65% of all students were children of farmers	5. 50% of all college students are the children of farmers
6. Average annual family income of majority of students less than $1500	6. Average annual family income of majority of students more than $1500
7. 54% of college men self-supporting	7. 41% of men self-supporting
8. 31% of college women self-supporting	8. 24% of women self-supporting
9. 36% of all students self-supporting	9. 30% of all students self-supporting
10. 62% of all students were of families having teachers as other members	10. 33% of students have brothers or sisters who have taught
11. 50% of students came from the counties nearest the normal school	11. About 50% of students have come from counties nearest the teachers college
12. 80% of collegiate women were high school graduates	12. 92% of collegiate women are high school graduates
13. 60% of collegiate men were high school graduates	13. 91% of men are high school graduates
14. 50% of collegiate women had held teaching positions before entering normal school	14. 18% of women have held teaching positions between elementary school and entrance to college

TABLE XVI—(*Continued*)

Student Characteristics in 1915	Student Characteristics in 1926
15. 50% of collegiate men had held teaching postions before entering normal school	15. 13% of men had taught between elementary school graduation and college entrance
16. 50% of women did not expect to teach permanently	16. 74% of women do not expect to teach permanently
17. 80% of men did not expect to teach permanently	17. 78% of men do not expect to teach permanently
18. 75% of men expected to teach temporarily	18. 52% of men expect to teach temporarily
19. 90% of women expected to teach temporarily	19. 73% of women expect to teach temporarily
20. 82% of men were preparing to teach in high school	20. 85% of men are preparing to teach in high school
21. 45% of women were preparing to teach in high school	21. 49% of women are preparing to teach in high school

order to earn enough money to defray the expenses of their professional training. It would be of interest to know to what extent the presence of these men in the teachers colleges diverts the colleges from a really professional attitude toward their work. These men are often leaders in student activities and undoubtedly exert a large influence in framing student opinion and in creating "atmosphere."

Should the teachers colleges refuse admission to all students who are not definitely preparing for teaching? No college in Missouri now requires students to pledge themselves to teach. At no time when such a pledge was taken was there any effort to follow up students to see whether they taught as they had agreed to do when they accepted training in the normal schools in Missouri. There has never been legal provision for collecting tuition from graduates of Missouri normal schools who failed to teach after having taken their preparation at the expense of the state. Will the up-grading of the normal schools of the country, together with the distinct tendency on the part of the state universities to devote their energies to senior college and graduate study, make junior arts colleges of the normal schools? Would such an arrangement of the state's program of higher education seriously interfere with teacher training? These and

TABLE XVII

Comparing the Typical Normal School Student in 1915 With the Typical Teachers College Student in 1926

Typical Student in 1915	Typical Student in 1926
1. Twenty years of age	1. Eighteen years of age
2. American ancestry	2. American ancestry
3. Born in Missouri	3. Born in Missouri
4. Of high school rank	4. Of collegiate rank
5. Child of a farmer	5. Child of a farmer
6. Annual family income $1000	6. Annual family income $2000 or $1240 when corrected for reduced value of the dollar
7. One of six children	7. One of four children
8. Partially self-supporting	8. Partially self-supporting
9. Attended college nearest his home	9. Attends college nearest his home
10. Other members of family had taught	10. None of his brothers or sisters have taught
11. Had taught twenty-one months	11. Did not teach before entering college
12. Would teach temporarily	12. Will teach about five years
13. Expected to teach in high school	13. Expects to teach in high school

similar problems must receive serious attention in the very near future.

Another problem which is suggested by the Missouri study grows out of the fact that many men are still using the teaching profession as a stepping-stone to professions which pay bigger returns in money and social standing. It would be desirable to know, before condemning the practice utterly, the total influence of these men on the teaching profession. It is not a question of whether it would be better to have these men in the profession permanently or for only a short time. To that question there is only one answer. Does the teaching profession gain or does it lose by having these men for even a short time? Would the teaching profession be better off if these men did not teach at all? What quality of teaching is done by these men while they are teaching? How do these men compare with men who remain permanently in the teaching profession in general intelligence, outlook upon life, and general culture? These are the questions which have not been answered, and upon their answers depends the determination of the policy of the teachers colleges regarding the admission of these men as students.

By way of summary and in order to portray at a glance the change in student personnel in Missouri teachers colleges within the decade, the facts of this section are presented in tabular form in Tables XVI and XVII (pages 32, 33, and 34).

PART V

STUDENT PERSONNEL IN 1926 IN COMPARISON WITH THE PROPOSALS OF THE SURVEY COMMISSION OF 1915, AND ADDITIONAL PROPOSALS

In order to determine the extent to which the Missouri teachers colleges have made progress in the improvement of student personnel in accordance with the proposals of the survey commission it is necessary to analyze the present situation in the light of the proposals made in 1915.

Proposal (a): [50]
The conscious effort to attract or to retain men students in normal

[50] Carnegie Bul. No. 14, p. 396.

schools at a sacrifice of a clear aim and of an intensive organization of work is not in the best interests of the service.

During the decade the percentage of men who signified their intention of teaching temporarily has fallen from seventy-five per cent in 1915 to forty-two per cent in 1926. Twenty-two per cent of the men enrolled in 1926 expect to teach permanently, as against twenty per cent in 1915.

On the whole the situation in 1926 is worse than it was in 1915 so far as *Proposal (a)* is concerned. In Chapter IV [51] it is pointed out that teachers colleges in Missouri with one exception offer the courses leading to A.B. degree, which is a distinct bid for students who do not expect to teach. On the other hand, it is shown in the same chapter that definite curricula for teacher training are prescribed and enforced and that prerequisites are absolute requirements for class entrance. There is apparently little evidence that the men students who do not intend to teach have exerted a great influence unfavorable to definite training programs. They doubtless exert a subtle influence in giving a nonprofessional aim to individual courses in which they predominate. Although positive proof is lacking, it is entirely credible that the presence of these men withdraws the energy of the faculties from the primary function of the colleges.

It is very natural for students who do not expect to teach, but who do intend to enter another profession to desire to meet their pre-professional requirements in a state school, near home, and at state expense. The state has as much obligation, perhaps, to provide this pre-professional training for this group of its citizens as it has to maintain the arts colleges at the university. But that this training should be given at the teachers colleges is another matter. If the state finds that such a policy will make a larger use of the plants and will provide the training at less expense, it should make adequate, additional appropriation to maintain this work and should have a plan of organization and administration which will guarantee that its program of teacher training will not suffer.[52]

[51] See p. 88 (Chapter on Curricula).
[52] California Junior College Plan.

Proposal (b): [53]

The secondary instruction offered in the normal schools should be abandoned: young pupils should be returned to the high schools for preparation, and state-supported high schools, with organization wholly separate from that of the normal schools, should be provided for older, belated students.

Secondary instruction is no longer offered as an integral part of the teachers college program. In four of the colleges no secondary work is done except in training school, and in the fifth a small and rapidly decreasing number of secondary students is taught by student teachers.

Proposal (c): [54]

Concessions to irregular attendants have seriously hampered the proper work of the schools and should not continue. Coöperation among the schools in the adoption of prescribed curricula requiring continuous attendance would prove greatly to the advantage both of the student and of the service.

Concessions are no longer made to irregular students. The students follow prescribed curricula requiring sequential courses. The student bodies change little in personnel during the regular session. Practically all students enter in the fall and remain throughout the college year. With a longer term in the elementary schools of the state there is now no convenient time for students to enter except at the beginning of the fall term, and at the beginning of the summer term. In order to accommodate a few teachers who desire to enter about the middle of the spring term so as to earn fifteen semester hours credit by the end of the summer term, a special term is organized; but these students do not enter classes already in progress and are taught quite independently of the classes of the regular session. If students do not enter classes within one week after class organization, they cannot receive credit for the course. [55]

Proposal (d): [56]

Admission to the normal schools should depend on either a credential issued by the state authority for the inspection and approval of secondary schools, or an adequate examination.

[53] Carnegie Bul. No. 14, p. 396.
[54] *Ibid.*
[55] Conference Agreement, Art. III, Sec. E, p. 158.
[56] Carnegie Bul. No. 14, p. 396.

Students are now admitted only upon the basis of credentials from inspected and approved secondary schools or by entrance examination. The regulations governing the examinations are prescribed by the Conference of State Educational Institutions and all papers are filed for the inspection of the visiting committee.[57] At a meeting of the Conference in March, 1926, it was voted not to admit any student to conditional standing upon the submission of thirteen high school units. In the future no one will be admitted who does not submit at least fifteen units of secondary credit.

Proposal (e): [58]

The tendency to excessive student programs would be most effectually remedied by resorting to fixed curricula based, not on the number of hours or points, but on the successful completion of a certain series of courses taken in a definite combination and sequence.

No student is permitted to carry an excessive program. In the case of students of exceptional ability excess credit may be earned by methods definitely prescribed by the Conference. Prescribed curricula must be pursued.

Proposal (f): [59]

Fully to serve its purpose, the normal school should seek to become a selective institution. In determining the degrees of student attainment the relaxation or abandonment of thorough examination without the development of other more accurate and effective methods of measurement is a mistake. "Sizing up" on the part of the instructor can scarcely be considered satisfactory.

Missouri teachers colleges are not yet selective institutions, although some progress has been made since 1915. The "proving up" [60] and "sizing up" [61] plans are no longer used. Students must meet definite entrance requirements and with few exceptions all courses conclude with thorough, scheduled examinations frequently of the "new type."

[57] Conference Agreement, Art. VI, Sec. A, p. 161.
[58] Carnegie Bul. No. 14, p. 396.
[59] *Ibid.*, p. 396.
[60] *Ibid.*, p. 310.
[61] *Ibid.*, p. 326.

Proposal (g): [62]

The maintenance of accurate, significant records of student work is essential for the moral health of the institution. The administration of credit should be in the hands of disinterested officers acting in accordance with regulation and policies established either by faculty action, or preferably by the joint action of all responsible authorities of teacher-training institutions.

Regulations and policies concerning records and the administration of credit are made by the Conference of State Educational Institutions.[63] Systems are complete, and competent, full-time registrars with clerical help are employed. Blanks and forms are, in the main, uniform in the institutions.

Proposal (h-1): [64]

Graduation should mark the natural terminus in a symmetrically organized course of training, rather than the achievement of a given number of unrelated credits.

Graduation is based upon the completion of prescribed curricula with courses in proper sequence. Minimum requirements are specified by the Conference.[65]

Proposal (h-2): [66]

Certification should be a matter not of statute but of carefully planned administration on the part of the state commissioner of education in co-operation with the training institutions. It should depend not only on initial study and examination, but also on competent scrutiny of ability and growth in service.

Missouri's certification law has not changed since 1915 except that no student who has not completed a four-year high school course is now eligible to make application for a county examination. The state superintendent of schools issues certificates on the evidence of credit earned, rather than on examination, as was the case in 1915. The boards of regents of the teachers colleges have unlimited certification power.[67] Life certificates are still issued upon the completion of two-year and four-year courses. Permanent initial certification is not a stimu-

[62] Carnegie Bul. No. 14, p. 396.
[63] Conference Agreement, Art. IV, Sec. A, p. 158.
[64] Carnegie Bul. No. 14, p. 396.
[65] Conference Agreement, Art. VII and VIII, p. 161.
[66] Carnegie Bul. No. 14, p. 396.
[67] See Revised Statutes of Missouri, 1919, Art. 17, Sec. 11503.

lus to growth in service. Temporary certification until a teacher
has proved her ability over a period of years, and to competent
judges, would be a distinct improvement.

Proposal (h-3): [68]

Appointments to positions should involve a clearer and more specific
knowledge and record both of the candidate and of the proposed position
than are at present attempted. To accomplish this the normal school
should undertake to establish more intimate and responsible relations with
its dependent schools than now exist. The institution's obligations are not
fully discharged until a properly prepared teacher is successfully at work.

In each teachers college well-organized placement bureaus
are to be found, usually in charge of a competent person who de-
votes all or most of his time to a study of the needs of the
schools to be served and to the students' qualifications for
definite lines of teaching. Coöperation among the bureaus of
the different schools exists. An oversupply of teachers in any
field is reported at regular intervals from school to school.
Vacancies which one college is unable to fill are reported to other
colleges.

Proposal (i): [69]

The administrative practices of an institution, like the patterns of
instruction set by its staff, are as vital elements in curricula as are any
formal courses; they should be models of good judgment and skilful
planning because of their inevitable and powerful influences upon the
ideals of prospective teachers.

Stimulated largely by the Conference of State Educational
Institutions, the administrative practices of all the colleges
have improved immeasurably since 1915. The best proof for
this statement is the fact that all of the colleges live up to the
letter of the conference agreements, as is shown by the reports
to the Visiting Committee.[70] In this study no effort was made to
study the actual class instruction but there is much evidence
in the chapter on curricula that the teaching is on a much higher
plane than it was in 1915.

[68] Carnegie Bul. No. 14, p. 396.
[69] *Ibid.*, p. 396.
[70] See Appendix C.

TABLE XVIII

SHOWING EXTENT TO WHICH PROPOSALS OF THE SURVEY COMMISSION IN 1915
REGARDING STUDENT PERSONNEL HAVE BEEN MET IN 1926

Pro-posal	Subject	Page	Extent to Which It Has Been Met
a	Men Students	36	Not met
b	Secondary Work	37	Fully met
c	Concessions	37	Fully met
d	Admissions	37	Fully met
e	Excessive Programs	38	Fully met
f	Student Selection	38	Partially met
g	Student Records	39	Fully met
h (1)	Curricula	39	Fully met
h (2)	Certification	39	Only partially met
h (3)	Appointments	40	Fully met
i	Admin. Practices	40	Largely met

The present study suggests the following additional proposals regarding student personnel for the immediate future:

1. No courses designed to attract students who do not intend to teach should be offered by teachers colleges unless it becomes the stated policy of the state to offer junior college work to students without professional aim and for students who desire to prepare for professions other than teaching. In this event appropriations should be made for the additional work and it should be provided for in such a way as not to interfere with the work or the spirit of teacher training.

2. With the present demand for trained teachers the teachers colleges should select their students by the use of three plans:
   a. Each college should have a well-trained director or department of vocational guidance to study students and assist them in the choice of the field of the service they should enter and to so advise them if it is undesirable for them to make preparation to teach.
   b. Students of less than average ability as shown by intelligence tests, teachers' marks, and the opinion of the department of vocational guidance, together with any other pertinent information, should be dropped.
   c. A system of honor points in addition to class grades should be required for graduation. These should be so arranged as to prevent the graduation of students who are indifferent and who show a total lack of social ability.

3. Upon the completion of curricula temporary certificates should be issued until the teacher has proved, in a manner which will be conclusive and at the same time fair to the candidate, that she can teach.

4. The teachers colleges should through coöperation with the state superintendent of schools or upon their own initiative bring about reforms in certification which will be in harmony with the best practice as found in other states and designed to stimulate the greatest possible pre-service training and in-service growth on the part of the teacher.

5. Through their research divisions careful studies should be made by the teachers colleges of the influence of the teacher who is teaching a few years while making preparation for some other profession. This study should include an analysis of the effect of his presence in the college and the contribution he makes in his short-term teaching. The results of this study will give the data necessary for the determination of policies regarding student pledges for teaching and other restrictions of the services of the colleges to the non-teaching groups.

CHAPTER III

TEACHER PERSONNEL OF MISSOURI TEACHERS COLLEGES

PART I

TEACHER PERSONNEL IN MISSOURI NORMAL SCHOOLS IN 1915

The survey of Missouri normal schools made in 1915 revealed a situation which could well be viewed with alarm. It was all the more serious because it pictured the rather general equipment for and attitude toward teacher training, the most important part of a state's work, as they existed throughout the country. Many states in the United States doubtless were training their teachers in a more effective way than was Missouri; but it is probably true that an equal, if not a larger, number of states had not reached the standards attained by Missouri and a still greater number conducted their teacher training on about the same low plane. In the introduction to the report of the survey, the statement is made that "there are few situations here presented as occurring in Missouri that have not appeared in quite as acute form in many other, perhaps most, American states . . ."[1] One who is interested in the progress in teacher training during the decade from 1915 to 1926 will, therefore, find in this summary of the teacher personnel of the Missouri normal schools in 1915 a situation which was more or less typical of the situation throughout the country.

The study of the personnel of the teaching staffs of the normal schools showed that "in its five normal schools the state maintains two hundred instructors. Nearly one-half are women. Two-thirds are under forty years of age, the median age of the women—thirty-three—being five years less than that of the men. About two-thirds also are of American parentage, and nearly one-half were born in Missouri. Of the men two-thirds came from agricultural, one-sixth from professional, and one-

[1] *The Professional Preparation of Teachers for American Public Schools,* Bulletin No. 14, The Carnegie Foundation for the Advancement of Teaching, p. 5.

tenth from commercial families. Of the parents of the women one-third were engaged in trade, slightly less than one-third in agriculture, and one-fifth in professions." [2] Four-fifths of the men and seven-tenths of the women who were teaching in Missouri normal schools in 1915 were members of families in which there were other teachers, a condition calling attention to the fact that "families that already include teachers are likely to provide others; teachers in general represent families to which school affairs are more or less familiar." [3]

A large majority, about two-thirds, of the normal school teachers received their secondary training in the private academies or in the high school departments which were rather generally maintained in the small colleges and normal schools at that time.[4] Twenty-nine per cent of the teachers had no degrees; one-fourth of this number reported no work above secondary rank, and the others reported from one to three years of collegiate study.[5] Thirty-two of the fifty-eight who had no degrees were teachers of art, music, physical education, or commercial subjects; seven taught academic subjects, eleven were supervisors of practice teaching, and eight taught courses in education. "This reflects a characteristic weakness (in 1915) of the normal schools. One would expect these schools to require, even for their teachers of arithmetic and grammar, at least as well-trained teachers as are demanded by good high schools. This indeed has been the tendency. But while the academic departments have been steadily strengthened by better formal preparation, the professional and supervisory departments have been conducted more largely on the basis of experience unsupported by theoretical training. Nor is it a question of elderly teachers inherited from an old régime; the median age of these deficient teachers is thirty-three. It is certainly unfortunate that eleven out of fifteen teachers in all the schools who were responsible for the critical task of directing the candidate's first practical efforts in teaching, and that eight of the thirty-three teachers giving professional courses possessed an academic training inferior to that of some of their students." [6]

[2] Carnegie Bul. No. 14, p. 99.
[3] *Ibid.*, p. 99.
[4] *Ibid.*, p. 99.
[5] *Ibid.*, p. 100.
[6] *Ibid.*, p. 100.

Seventy-one per cent of the Missouri normal school teachers in 1915 held four-year bachelor's degrees. Thirty-nine per cent of these degrees were from first-class institutions according to the classification of institutions formulated by Dr. K. C. Babcock for the United States Bureau of Education in 1911. The variation among the schools with respect to the training of the teachers was great, but the fact remains that "there can be but one conclusion respecting the normal schools in this regard: they are weak." [7]

Fifty-five per cent of the bachelor's degrees and forty per cent of the advanced degrees held by teachers in Missouri normal schools in 1915 were from Missouri colleges and normal schools. The state university conferred more than a fourth of the number in each group. One-third of the women teachers had been trained in both normal schools and colleges. Thirty per cent of the men were trained in colleges and graduate schools.[8] Twenty-three per cent of the normal school teachers had the sequence of training most common to college and university teachers; namely, high school, college, and graduate work. "Forty per cent of the normal school teachers had both their secondary and higher work in Missouri, while thirty-two per cent were native born and had not left the state previous to receiving their first degree. . . . [9]

"Only about one-fourth of the teachers in Missouri normal schools (in 1915) had ever done recognized study beyond a college course, altho nearly all of them were giving collegiate instruction. Of fifty-two master's degrees, forty-two came from first-class institutions; twenty-two were taken in Missouri, sixteen of them at the university. Of the degrees usually considered as necessary to qualify as teacher to give collegiate instruction, there are seven among the one hundred ninety-nine teachers and officers, six of them taken from first-class institutions, all outside of the state." [10]

The median number of years of experience in teaching of the normal school teachers was twelve. Nine-tenths of it was in elementary and secondary schools. Two-fifths of the entire group had had less than five years of teaching experience in

[7] Carnegie Bul. No. 14, p. 102.
[8] *Ibid.*, p. 102.
[9] *Ibid.*, p. 103.
[10] *Ibid.*, p. 103.

higher institutions. Three-fourths of them had taught in the elementary school, one-fourth had been superintendents in small cities, sixty-three per cent had taught in high schools, and twenty-one per cent had had some experience in college or university teaching.[11]   The study showed that much of this experience "instead of furnishing an all-important background for the present purpose of instruction, is largely unrelated; teachers have in very many cases received their present appointments as promotion out of educational jobs of different sorts and not because of distinguished excellence in the kind of teaching for which they are now asked to prepare students."[12]

Although inadequately prepared for college teaching in a single field "an examination of the teaching programs of 1915-16 shows that eighteen per cent of all the teachers in Missouri normal schools teach (1915-16) more than one subject."[13]   "Nine teachers in the regular session have a combination of three subjects."[14]   Such a combination of work now seems incredible. The situation, however, in this respect in 1915 was much better, with eighty-two per cent of the teachers working in a single field, than it had been previously.   In addition to teaching in more than one field, many of the teachers had very heavy teaching programs.   The weekly teaching load varied from twelve to thirty-five hours.   The median group taught between twenty and twenty-four hours a week.[15]

With the heavy teaching load, the meagre preparation for the work, and the dissipation of energy over so many kinds of work, it is not to be expected that the productive scholarship of the teaching staffs of the normal schools would be large.   As a matter of fact, the two hundred teachers had produced only fifteen bound volumes in a period of twenty years immediately preceding 1916.   "Two-thirds of these were modest textbooks of various kinds, the remainder were doctor's theses or dealt with local history."[16]   Except for two or three, it did not appear from the reports submitted that any teachers could be termed systematically productive in a professional sense aside from their teaching.[17]

[11] Carnegie Bul. No. 14, p. 106.
[12] *Ibid.*, p. 107.
[13] *Ibid.*, p. 107.
[14] *Ibid.*, p. 107.
[15] *Ibid.*, p. 108.
[16] *Ibid.*, p. 111.
[17] *Ibid.*, p. 111.

Practically all of the male instructors in the normal schools were married and their median representative had two children. It is interesting to note that the median parental representative of this group had six children. "The change in family life is noticeable even between the older and the younger teachers. The median parent-family among all those teachers over forty has six children and one-fourth of the families have more than eight; as compared with a median of five with but nine per cent having over eight in the younger group." [18] Only one-eighth of the men have no dependents, while of the women more than half of them have only themselves to care for. Nearly half of the men have more than two dependents, while slightly over one-tenth of the women have as many. One-fourth of the men have more dependents than any of the women except two." [19]

Sixty per cent of the teachers in the Missouri normal schools in 1915 had been in the institution from one to five years. Twenty per cent had served nine years or longer.[20] The median annual salary for men in the Missouri normal schools in 1915-16 was $1800, for women it was $1400, and for both it was $1650.[21] All of those receiving over $2000 are thirty years of age or older. "No one over thirty receives less than $1080. Those receiving $1600 and above number eight per cent of the teachers in their twenties, forty seven per cent of the teachers in their thirties, fifty-six per cent of those in their forties, and all of the remainder. The teachers of the group receiving more than $2000 number twenty-four, all men . . . Only five are over fifty years of age. As a group they have had nineteen years of total experience, and have held their present positions for eight years." [22] "Two-thirds of the number (receiving more than $2000) have their present work clearly correlated with their training and experience, eleven having graduate degrees, in most cases from first-class institutions; four show excellent training without specific experience, and three have had appropriate experience but lack training. . . .[23]

"The sixteen highest paid women receive between $1500 and

[18] Carnegie Bul. No. 14, p. 113.
[19] *Ibid.*, p. 113.
[20] *Ibid.*, p. 113.
[21] *Ibid.*, p. 423.
[22] *Ibid.*, p. 115.
[20] *Ibid.*, p. 115.

$2000. Two are under thirty years of age; three are fifty or over. Five have no four-year degrees; of the remainder, eight hold the degrees of good institutions; four have done graduate work, one holding a Ph.D. from the University of Pennsylvania. As a group they have a median total experience of twelve years, seven of which were in the present position." [24] "Nine of the sixteen teachers show a definite correlation of training and experience with their present work; five lack suitable experience in the elementary schools, and two lack specific training." [25]

In the absence of any retiring system the normal school teachers had to make provision for their future through private savings and some form of insurance. Practically all of the men and about half of the women carried insurance. The amount carried by the women ranged from $1000 to $4300 with three-fourths of them carrying less than $2000. "One-third of the men, on the other hand, have from $2500 to $5000 in insurance, only six per cent holding less than $1500, and the highest group—thirteen per cent—carrying from $8250 to $11,000." [26]

The summary of the teaching personnel of the Missouri normal schools in 1915 up to this point has not considered the relations of the teachers to the working organization of the institutions. There are only a few important points in this connection that have any bearing upon the present study. Although the individual instructors were allowed large freedom of initiative in the conduct of their work, the development of the elective system with its consequent unintentional rating of a teacher upon his ability to attract and hold large numbers in his classes inspired all teachers to seek for their departments as many required courses as possible without regard for the needs of the students.

The plan, furthermore, caused teachers utterly to ignore prerequisites and sequences in courses and to build up the registration in their classes by not being too discriminating in the treatment of their students.[27] The fact that teachers were elected annually (never less frequently than biennially under the provisions of the law), augmented the necessity of large enrollments as evidence of competency and justifying re-election. Under such a system "growth becomes a matter of short, feverish,

[24] Carnegie Bul. No. 14, p. 115.
[25] *Ibid.*, p. 115.
[26] *Ibid.*, p. 114.
[27] *Ibid.*, p. 279.

and often conflicting efforts for recognition instead of a wholesome, harmonious development of the school." [28]

The typical woman teacher in a Missouri normal school in 1915 was thirty-three years of age, was of American parentage, was the daughter of a tradesman or farmer, was one of several teachers in the family. She attended a public high school, normal school, and college, and had a four-year bachelor's degree from a Missouri institution. She had twelve years of experience, most of it in elementary and secondary schools, had taught less than five years in normal school, was re-elected annually, and had had no experience to fit her directly for the work she was doing. She taught from twenty to twenty-four hours a week in one field and had made no contributions to scholarly literature. She received an annual salary of $1400, carried an insurance policy of $1000 and had no dependents. She put her courses on the "bargain counter" and competed with her colleagues for large class enrollments.

The typical male teacher in a Missouri normal school in 1915 was thirty-eight years of age, was of American parentage, was the son of a farmer, was one of five children, was one of several teachers in the family, had attended a public high school, had a four-year bachelor's degree, had not attended school outside of the state, had taught for twelve years, had been superintendent of a small city school, teaching twenty to twenty-four hours a week, had made no contribution to scholarly literature, was married, had two children, had been a member of the staff from one to five years, was re-elected annually, received an annual salary of $1800, carried an insurance policy of more than $1500, and was ambitious to increase his departmental enrollment in order to prove himself an essential part of the organization.

PART II

PROPOSALS OF THE SURVEY COMMISSION CONCERNING TEACHER PERSONNEL IN 1915

The exhaustive study of the personnel of the teaching staffs of the Missouri normal schools in 1915, which revealed the

[28] Carnegie Bul. No. 14, p. 280.

situation described in this chapter, resulted in four major proposals:

(1) Normal school instructors should be transformed into a true "faculty" by classifying them according to merit and service, and by allowing them the exercise of influence characteristic of faculties in good higher institutions in determining the educational policy of the school. They should be absolutely relieved of clerical and administrative duties (page 276).[29]

(2) Their training should conform to collegiate standards, and as these are approximated, their formal hours of class work should be correspondingly diminished and concentrated, their salaries should be much increased, and their tenure of position should be made permanent (pages 105, 110, 114, 280).

(3) Excellence of general education and of professional training and experience should be particularly required of instructors in education, of supervisors of practice teaching, and of critic teachers; these should be the dominant personal elements in any normal school faculty (page 283).

(4) For the sake of teachers in service the summer session should be well staffed with competent and experienced instructors. They should be as well paid as teachers in the regular session. Student assistants are not desirable as instructors in professional institutions for the preparation of teachers (pages 286-292).[30]

In order to compare the recommendations made in 1915 with the situation as it exists in 1926 it is desirable to break up these general proposals into specific recommendations.

1. The instructional staffs of Missouri normal schools should be organized on a professorial basis according to merit and service. This plan of organization is ordinarily found in college and university faculties. (276) [29]

2. Well-organized faculties should exercise predominant influence in the determination of the educational policy of the schools. (277)

3. The administrative staffs should be enlarged to provide for all clerical and administrative duties, thus relieving the teaching staffs who should devote their entire time to teaching. (277)

4. Normal school teachers who teach college classes should receive their formal training early and meet the requirements "usually considered as necessary to qualify a teacher to give collegiate instruction," namely, the Ph.D. degree. (102)

5. Teaching programs for college teachers should not exceed three periods of instruction per day and should be concentrated in a single field or portion thereof. (109)

[29] Numbers in parenthesis refer to pages in Carnegie Bul. No. 14.
[30] Carnegie Bul. No. 14, p. 395.

6. Normal school teachers should receive salaries equal to those paid by the best colleges and the state university for the same training and teaching skill. (115) [a]

7. The tenure of position of normal school teachers should be made permanent. (113)

8. The general education, quality and amount of professional training and teaching experience of the teachers of education courses should equal if not exceed that of the "academic" teachers. (283, 106)

9. Supervisors of practice teaching and critic teachers should meet the same requirements, receive as good or better salaries and enjoy the same professional status as the other members of the instructional staffs. (283, 213)

10. With the relatively larger demand for collegiate courses, the greater maturity of the students, and a plan which permits a student to do all of his normal school work in the summer terms, if he so desires, the teachers in the summer session should meet in every way the requirements of the members of the staffs of the regular sessions. (286-292)

11. Teachers in the summer session should be as well paid as the regular members of the staffs. (290-291)

12. Student-teachers, who obviously are unprepared, should not be allowed to teach college classes. (287)

PART III

TEACHER PERSONNEL IN MISSOURI TEACHERS COLLEGES IN 1926

According to the catalogues of 1925-1926 the Missouri teachers colleges maintain three hundred one teachers on their

TABLE XIX

SHOWING AGE DISTRIBUTION OF TEACHERS IN MISSOURI TEACHERS COLLEGES IN 1926

Ages	21-25	26-30	31-35	30-40	41-45	46 50	51-55	56-60	61-65
	%	%	%	%	%	%	%	%	%
Men	3	15	15	25	18	10	9	4	1
Women ..	2	15	24	24	12	10	11	1	1
Both	3	15	20	24	14	10	10	3	1

Median   Men = 38.3   Women = 37.6   Both = 37.7

[a] Numbers in parenthesis refer to pages in Carnegie Bul. No. 14.

instructional staffs. Of this number one hundred fifty-four are women and one hundred forty-seven are men.

It will be noted that fifty-eight per cent of the men, sixty-five per cent of the women, and sixty-two per cent of both men and women are under forty years of age. The median age of the women—thirty-seven and six-tenths years—is seven-tenths of a year less than that of the men and one-tenth of a year less than the median for the whole group.

TABLE XX

SHOWING MEDIAN AGE OF TEACHERS IN TEACHERS COLLEGES IN MISSOURI, LOUISIANA, MASSACHUSETTS, AND MICHIGAN

	Mo.	La.[1]	Mass.[2]	Mich.[3]
Men	38.3	40.3	46.8	
Women	37.6	33.8	39.9	
Both	37.7	37.8		41.5

[1] *Louisiana Survey*, p. 60.
[2] *Report of a Fact-Finding Survey of Technical and Higher Education in Massachusetts.* Mass. Legislature, House Document, No. 1700.
[3] Moehlman, A.B., *A Survey of Michigan State Normal Schools*, 1922.

Sixty-three per cent of the men, thirty-one per cent of the women, and forty-seven per cent of both came from farm homes. Of the men, nine per cent came from families engaged in trades, eleven per cent from professional families, and seventeen per cent from families in other occupations. Eleven per cent of the women came from commercial families, twenty per cent from professional families, and thirty-eight per cent from families engaged in other vocations. In agricultural and professional pursuits alone do the percentile representations exceed the occupational distribution for the state.

Slightly more than half of the teachers were born in Missouri. About one-third of the parents are natives of the state. Eighty-four per cent of the teachers were born in the middle-west. These data indicate that a large majority of the teachers in Missouri teachers colleges are local in their upbringing and perhaps in their training and interest.

TABLE XXI

SHOWING DISTRIBUTION OF TEACHERS IN MISSOURI TEACHERS COLLEGES IN
1926 ACCORDING TO PARENTAL OCCUPATION

		Men %	Women %	Both %	Missouri Occupational Distribution U. S. Census %	Year
Agriculture	1926	63	31	47	31	1920
	*1915	67.5	31	50	35.5	1910
Trade	1926	9	11	10	12.1	1920
	*1915	11	33	21	11.1	1910
Professions	1926	11	20	15	5.3	1920
	*1915	17.5	22	20	4.7	1910
All Other Occupations	1926	17	38	28	51.6	1920
	*1915	4	14	9	48.7	1910
Sub-total	1926	98	106	204		
	*1915	92	83	175		
Not Reporting	1926	8	18	26		
	*1915	14	10	24		
Total	1926	104	124	230		
	*1915	106	93	199		

* Carnegie Bul. No. 14, p. 419.

TABLE XXII

SHOWING BIRTHPLACE OF TEACHERS AND NATIVITY OF PARENTS OF TEACHERS
IN MISSOURI TEACHERS COLLEGES IN 1926

Location	Birthplace %	Father's Nativity %	Mother's Nativity %
Missouri	54	30	35
Southern State	5	16	12
Northern State	2	3	2
East-West	7	17	10
Mid-West	30	22	30
Foreign	2	12	11
Total	100	100	100

The median number of children in the families of the teachers in Missouri teachers colleges is 3.5. Twenty-nine per cent of the teachers are the only teachers in their families and fifty-eight

TABLE XXIII

SHOWING NUMBER OF CHILDREN IN FAMILIES TO WHICH TEACHERS IN MISSOURI TEACHERS COLLEGES BELONG

	Number of Children in Family										
	1	2	3	4	5	6	7	8	9	10	11
	%	%	%	%	%	%	%	%	%	%	%
Men	6	16	18	13	14	13	9	6	2	3	
Women	7	14	25	19	16	8	7	2	1		1
Both	7	15	21	16	15	10	8	4	2	1	1

Median　　　Men = 3.8　　　　Women = 3.3　　　　Both = 3.5

The table should be read: Six per cent of the men are members of families in which there is one child, etc.

TABLE XXIV

SHOWING NUMBER OF OTHER TEACHERS IN FAMILIES OF TEACHERS IN MISSOURI TEACHERS COLLEGES IN 1926

	Number of Other Teachers in Family						
	None	1	2	3	4	5	6 or More
	%	%	%	%	%	%	%
Men	30	30	16	12	6	1	6
Women	28	29	19	11	5	6	2
Both	29	29	18	11	6	3	4

Median　　　Men = .7　　　　Women = .8　　　　Both = .73

per cent are members of families in which there are fewer than two other teachers. Seventy-one per cent of them are from families of teachers "to which school affairs are more or less familiar." [32]

TABLE XXV

SHOWING THE COMBINATIONS OF TRAINING OF TEACHERS IN MISSOURI
TEACHERS COLLEGES IN 1926

Combination of Training	Men %	Women %
High School, Normal School, College	14	33
High School, College, Graduate	23	15
High School, Normal School	6	8
High School, College	8	13
High School, Normal School, College, Graduate .	26	18
High School		1
Normal School, College, Graduate	8	2
Normal School	1	1
High School, Normal School, Graduate	3	4
College	1	
College, Graduate	3	
Normal School, Graduate	2	
Special School	2	5
Total	97	100

Twenty-three per cent of the teachers have studied in high school, normal school, and college, this combination of training being the largest single one represented among them. The data on the questionnaires [33] indicated that in some instances the normal school training was four years in length and often the college work was in the graduate department. Twenty-two per cent of the teachers report high school, normal school, college, and graduate study. Sixty-five per cent of the men, forty-two per cent of the women, and fifty-three per cent of both definitely report graduate study. Sixty per cent of the men, sixty-eight per cent of the women, and sixty-four per cent of all teachers have been students in normal schools.

[32] Carnegie Bul. No. 14, p. 99.
[33] See Appendix B.

TABLE XXVI

SHOWING HIGHEST DEGREES HELD BY TEACHERS IN MISSOURI TEACHERS
COLLEGES IN 1926

Degrees	Kirks-ville	Warrens-burg	Cape Girardeau	Spring-field	Mary-ville	All Schools
	%	%	%	%	%	%
None	8	0	0	0	7	3
Bachelor's	42	21	40	17	21	28
Master's	42	67	57	70	72	62
Doctor's	8	12	3	13	0	7

Does not include training school staff or teachers of special subjects such as music.

TABLE XXVII

SHOWING HIGHEST DEGREES HELD BY TRAINING SCHOOL STAFFS IN
MISSOURI TEACHERS COLLEGES IN 1926

Degrees	Kirks-ville	Warrens-burg	Cape Girardeau	Spring-field	Mary-ville	All Schools
	%	%	%	%	%	%
None	40	0	0	21	0	8
Bachelor's	56	10	55	58	12	38
Master's	0	90	45	41	88	53
Doctor's	4	0	0	0	0	1

When the training school staffs and the teachers of special subjects are excluded, twenty-eight per cent of the teachers in the teachers colleges have only the bachelor's degree, sixty-two per cent have the master's degree, and seven per cent have the doctorate. The training school teachers are on the whole a little less well trained than the other members of the staff. Eight per cent of them have no degrees, thirty-eight per cent have bachelor's degrees, and fifty-three per cent of them have master's degrees.

When all of the members of the teaching staffs are considered, the percentage of those having no degrees is increased and the

TABLE XXVIII

SHOWING HIGHEST DEGREES HELD BY ALL TEACHERS IN MISSOURI
TEACHERS COLLEGES IN 1926

* Degrees	Kirks-ville %	Warrens-burg %	Cape Girardeau %	Spring-field %	Mary-ville %	All Schools %
None	21	0	4	19	13	11
Bachelor's	48	20	47	20	29	33
Master's	25	70	47	53	58	51
Doctor's	6	10	2	8	0	5

* This table includes teachers of piano, violin, voice, and other special subjects.

TABLE XXIX

SHOWING HOW TEACHERS IN MISSOURI TEACHERS COLLEGES COMPARE
WITH TEACHERS IN SIMILAR INSTITUTIONS IN OTHER STATES
AS REGARDS DEGREES HELD

Highest Degree Held	Mo. %	La.[1] %	Mass.[2] %	Random Selection of 26 Teachers Colleges[3] %
No degree	11	27	51	18
Bachelor's degree	33	50	30	45
Master's degree	51	20	18	31
Doctor's degree	5	3	1	6
Total	100	100	100	100

other percentages consequently lowered. This is due in large measure to the fact that there are a number of teachers of music on the staffs who have had many years of work in their special study but have not attended degree-granting institutions. Two of

[1] *Louisiana Survey*, p. 76.
[2] *Massachusetts Survey*, p. 208.
[3] Data from an unpublished study by Dr. E. S. Evenden, Teachers College, Columbia University.

the colleges have large conservatories of music in which the work is not devoted to teacher training.

TABLE XXX

SHOWING THE SOURCES OF DEGREES OF TEACHERS IN MISSOURI TEACHERS COLLEGES

Colleges Conferring Degrees	Bachelor %	Master %	Doctor %
University of Missouri	28	21	
Missouri Teachers Colleges	37		
University of Chicago	5	20	44
Drury College	4		
Columbia University	5	30	11
University of Kansas	3	3	
University of Michigan	1	2	
Indiana University	1	1	5
University of Wisconsin	1	4	9
Harvard		1	6
Vanderbilt University		1	
University of Pennsylvania			6
Peabody College for Teachers		5	
Other Missouri Colleges	5	3	6
Other Southern Colleges	2	3	5
Other Eastern Colleges	4	2	6
Western and Foreign	4	4	2
Total	100	100	100

The table should be read: Of the total number of bachelor's degrees held by the teachers, 28% were received from Missouri University.

According to the classification of institutions formulated by Dr. K. C. Babcock for the United States Bureau of Education in 1911, a large majority of all the degrees held by teachers in Missouri teachers colleges are from first-class institutions. The list in 1911 did not include Missouri teachers colleges, but they have had a first-class rating since 1918, after which time most of the degrees were conferred.

The question involved is not so much the standing of the degrees of Missouri teachers colleges as the wisdom of the evident policy of recruiting so many teachers from the product of the colleges to be served. It will be observed that not more than twenty-four per cent of the teachers had their under-graduate and graduate training in Missouri institutions. University of Chicago and Columbia University conferred fifty per cent of the master's degrees and fifty-five per cent of the doctor's degrees.

TABLE XXXI

SHOWING THE AMOUNT OF TEACHING EXPERIENCE OF TEACHERS IN MISSOURI TEACHERS COLLEGES IN 1926

	Number of Years of Teaching Experience								
	1–2	3–5	6–8	6–12	13–16	17–20	21–25	26–30	31 or More
Men	3%	14%	16%	23%	14%	11%	7%	3%	10%
Women ..	3	5	15	16	22	10	19	6	4
Both	3	10	15	19	18	11	13	4	7

Medians	Men = 10.4	Women = 13.4	Both = 12.5

Seventeen per cent of the men, eight per cent of the women, and thirteen per cent of all teachers have taught less than six years. Forty-five per cent of the men, sixty-one per cent of the women, and fifty-three per cent of all teachers have taught more than twelve years. The median teaching experience is 12.5 years.

Half of the teachers began teaching before they were twenty-one years of age. Only five per cent were twenty-five years of age when they began teaching. The median age is 19.2 years.

Table XXXIII shows that the teachers had little teaching experience before beginning their college work. The median is .87 years.

Table XXXIV shows in what fields most of the early teaching was done. High school, rural school, and elementary school have provided most of the teachers' practical experience. A little more than ten per cent of the teachers were experienced in college teaching. A proportionate number have taught in normal schools. Just as many teachers have come into the normal school teaching corps without any previous experience as have teachers who have had experience in handling work of collegiate grade.

TABLE XXXII

SHOWING THE AGE AT WHICH TEACHERS IN MISSOURI TEACHERS COLLEGES IN 1926 BEGAN TEACHING

	Age at Which Teaching Began									
	Less than 18	19	20	21	22	23	24	25	More than 25	Median Age
Per cent of Teachers	36	11	14	14	9	5	1	5	5	19.2

TABLE XXXIII

SHOWING AMOUNT OF TEACHING EXPERIENCE BETWEEN HIGH SCHOOL GRADUATION AND COLLEGE ENTRANCE OF TEACHERS IN MISSOURI TEACHERS COLLEGES IN 1926

	Number of Years of Experience												Total with Experience		No Report		Total No.
	None %	1 %	2 %	3 %	4 %	5 %	6 %	7 %	8 %	9 %	10 %	More %	No.	%	No.	%	
Men ...	39	13	9	13	5	7	2	1	1				95	90	11	10	106
Women	42	7	10	12	4	2	2	0	2	2	1	4	110	88	14	12	124
Both ...	40	10	9	11	5	5	2	1	2	1	1	2	205	89	25	11	230

Medians　　　Men = .1　　　Women = 1.2　　　Both = .87

Table XXXIV shows a tendency for the teachers colleges to select their teachers from the staffs of secondary schools and small city superintendents. It is apparent from the data

TABLE XXXIV

SHOWING DIFFERENT KINDS OF EXPERIENCE OF TEACHERS IN MISSOURI
TEACHERS COLLEGES IN 1926

(Groups overlap)

Types of Experience	Men No.	Women No.	Both No.
Secondary School	48	71	119
Grade School	18	62	80
Rural School	48	42	90
Principal of High School	35	14	49
City Superintendent	24	3	27
Principal of Elementary School	12	10	22
College	24	31	55
University	13	10	23
Normal School only	26	27	53
County Superintendent	6	1	7
State Superintendent	1		1
Total Number....................	255	271	526

TABLE XXXV

SHOWING COMBINATIONS OF TEACHING EXPERIENCE OF TEACHERS IN
MISSOURI TEACHERS COLLEGES IN 1926

(Groups mutually exclusive)

Combinations of Experience	Men %	Women %
Administrative, including Varying Teaching Experience	46	24
Elementary and Secondary Schools	7	15
Elementary School only	4	12
Secondary School only................	8	10
Elementary and Secondary Schools and College	6	16
Normal School only	8	10
Secondary School and College	9	3
College only	7	7
Elementary School and College	5	3
Total Per Cent	100	100

of this table that the teachers have had some first-hand acquaintance with the levels of teaching for which they are training others.

Perhaps the most interesting revelation of Table XXXV is that the groups including the greatest number of types of teaching include the largest groups of teachers. If a varied experience is an asset to a teachers college teacher the Missouri colleges are fortunate in this respect. This table emphasizes the fact that teachers colleges do not draw very heavily upon other college faculties for their teachers.

In answer to the question, "Would you choose teaching as a vocation?" sixty-nine per cent reported "yes," nineteen per cent reported "no," and twelve per cent made no report. The reasons assigned by each of the groups are given in the tables which follow.

TABLE XXXVI

SHOWING REASONS ASSIGNED BY TEACHERS IN MISSOURI TEACHERS COLLEGES IN 1926 WHO WOULD NOW CHOOSE TEACHING AS A VOCATION

Reasons	Men %	Women %
Like it	27	39
Renders best service to society	32	23
Enjoy study	2	2
Can help make life livable for coming generation	5	1
Content with fair living wage	2	1
Enjoy working with children		2
Desirable associations	13	13
Cannot derive so much happiness from other work	2	
Flexible working hours		2
Incentive for securing college education	2	
Prepared for the work by native endowments	7	11
Ideal home life possible	2	
Better salary than other work for women		1
Teachers are doing big things in the world today	2	
Cultural opportunities and social prestige	3	5
Others	1	
Total	100	100

TABLE XXXVII

SHOWING REASONS ASSIGNED BY TEACHERS IN MISSOURI TEACHERS COLLEGES
IN 1926 WHO WOULD NOT NOW CHOOSE TEACHING AS A VOCATION

Reasons	Men %	Women %
Insufficient financial returns	28	16
Expense of travel, study and research too great	8	11
Prefer administrative work to teaching		6
Prefer some of the other work now open to women		30
Teaching breaks health early		5
Not enough time to do other interesting things	4	11
Object to constant moving	4	
Uncertain tenure of service		11
Object to continually shifting education practices	4	
Tendency to lose initiative and become satisfied with mediocre attainments	4	
Restriction of freedom of action and speech		5
No future in teaching profession	16	
Politics involved make it unpleasant	8	
Men teachers not regarded as men of affairs	4	
No ethics in the profession	4	
Prefer other professions	16	5
Total	100	100

The Missouri teachers colleges in 1926 are all members of the North Central Association of Colleges and Secondary Schools. The regulations of the association limit the amount of teaching

TABLE XXXVIII

SHOWING THE LENGTH OF TEACHING SCHEDULES IN MISSOURI TEACHERS
COLLEGES IN 1926

	Number of Teaching Hours per Week					
	Less than 18	18–20	20–24	25–29	30–34	35 or More
Per Cent of Teachers	85	8	4	1	1	1

to 18 hours a week. The faithfulness with which the colleges are now meeting this requirement is shown by Table XXXVIII and is in interesting contrast to the situation in 1915.

The median teaching schedule is less than eighteen hours a week. Ninety-three per cent of all teachers are scheduled for less than twenty hours a week. Not only are the teaching schedules reasonable but the classes in most instances are not overlarge, as Table XXXIX shows. The median weekly teaching schedule in Louisiana teachers colleges is twenty hours.[34]

Twenty per cent of all the classes enroll less than ten students, forty-nine per cent enroll between ten and thirty students, thirty-one per cent enroll more than thirty students, six-

TABLE XXXIX

SHOWING THE PROPORTION OF LARGE AND SMALL CLASSES IN VARIOUS SUBJECTS IN MISSOURI TEACHERS COLLEGES IN 1926

Classes	Less than 10 Students %	10 to 30 Students %	More than 30 Students %
English	9	12	18
Latin	10	1	1
French	3	2	1
German	5	1	1
Mathematics	2	8	3
Spanish	2	2	
Agriculture	7	2	3
Household Arts	2	5	3
Sociology and Economics	4	3	13
Geography	2	2	
Commerce	7	10	3
Physical Education	2	9	7
History	2	8	8
Expression	2	1	1
Education	15	14	28
Science	12	11	8
Art and Music	14	9	2
Total	100	100	100

The table should be read: Of all classes having enrollments of less than 10 students 9 per cent are English classes.

[34] *Louisiana Survey*, p. 94.

teen per cent enroll more than forty students, and six per cent enroll more than fifty students.

During the last few years the teachers in Missouri teachers colleges have contributed one hundred books and articles which may be classed as contributions to scholarly literature. Of this number several are dissertations, a few are textbooks for elementary and secondary schools, and the majority are articles for publications of a more or less local nature. Since the contributions represent the work of fifty-one teachers, perhaps none of the writers can be thought of as a regular contributor to educational literature. With the more reasonable teaching loads it is to be hoped that the teachers in teachers colleges will take advantage of their opportunity to undertake investigations of a research nature in their fields and make distinct contributions to the scientific study of the professional training of teachers.

In 1915 the median salary for all teachers in Missouri normal schools was $1650.[35] According to the Official Manuals of Missouri for the respective years the median salary for all teachers

TABLE XL

Showing Number of Dependents of Teachers in Missouri Teachers Colleges in 1926

	Number of Dependents										
	0 %	1 %	2 %	3 %	4 %	5 %	6 %	7 %	8 %	9 %	10 %
With Dependents Wholly Dependent											
Men..............	9	22	34	23	7	3	1			1	
Women	84	10	5	1							
Both	47	17	18	13	4	2	1			1	
With Dependents Partially Dependent											
Men	67	11	15	3	2	2					
Women	57	18	17	7	1						
Both	62	15	16	5	1	1					

Note: The table should be read: 9 per cent of the men have no one who is wholly dependent upon them, etc.

[35] See p. 47.

in 1920 was $2040; in 1925 for women it was $2088, for men it was $2979, and for both it was $2340. The purchasing power of the dollar in 1924 was sixty-two cents [36] in comparison with one hundred cents in 1915. Taking this into account, the teachers were actually getting $1451 in 1925 in comparison with $1650

TABLE XLI

SHOWING SAVINGS OF THE TEACHERS IN MISSOURI TEACHERS COLLEGES
IN 1925

Insurance Premiums	Men %	Women %
Up to $25	5	3
$ 26 to 50	5	9
51 to 100	12	14
101 to 150	13	10
151 to 200	10	7
201 to 250	8	4
251 to 300	6	5
301 and more	32	16
Total	91	68
Median	$154	$191
*Median in Louisiana Teachers Colleges.	$150	

Other Savings	Men %	Women %
Up to $100	7	6
$101 to 200	5	5
201 to 300	7	7
301 to 400	6	7
401 to 500	11	12
501 to 600	5	9
601 and more	27	26
Total	68	72
Median	$382	$392
*Median in Louisiana Teachers Colleges.	$455	

* *Louisiana Survey*, p. 67.

[36] *World's Almanac*, 1925, p. 362.

in 1915. While the salaries of teachers in Missouri teachers colleges have increased forty-one per cent in the ten years, they have increased fifty per cent at the state university. During the decade salaries of teachers in the best elementary schools have increased one hundred twenty-nine per cent, in junior high schools one hundred fifty-one per cent, and in senior high schools eighty-eight per cent.[37]

It will be noted that the median number of dependents in both groups is two. Almost half of the faculty members have no dependents, which fact is accounted for by the large percentage of unmarried women teachers. This explains why the men carry much more insurance than the women do. Although their salaries are somewhat lower, the women on the whole save as much by other investments as the men do.

The median age of the men and the median annual expenditure for life insurance indicate that the typical policy is the equivalent of a $5000 non-participating, straight life policy. If we use the same method for making the estimate, the face of the typical policy carried by the women is $2500.

It is difficult to present in tabular form the data from the questionnaires which portray the relations of the teachers to the working organizations of the colleges. The statements are grouped under rather large headings with the hope that an adequate impression of the situation will be depicted. The teachers are practically unanimous in the opinion that they participate to a desirable extent in the determination of the educational policies of their colleges.

Fifty-two per cent report that they are absolutely free in their teaching, forty-four per cent report conditions as satisfactory, and four per cent report that they are hampered. As a rule there is no supervision of classroom teaching and the teachers are not enthusiastic about such supervision as they have. Most of the collective investigations in which members of the staffs have engaged during the past year have had to do with curricula and the preparation of syllabi of courses. There are only two members of the teachers college staffs who feel that the institutions they serve do not stimulate and expect professional growth on their part.

[37] *N. E. A. Research Bulletin*, Vol. I, No. 3, May 1923, p. 25.

It is generally reported that faculty meetings are of such a nature as to improve the staffs professionally. Attendance upon and participation in the work of educational organizations is encouraged to the extent of defraying at least a part of the expense of attending such meetings. Liberal leaves of absence with part pay are granted by all the colleges.[38] Extra-classroom activities and teaching loads are not so excessive as to prevent the possibility of growth through study and general reading. In one college alone twenty-nine faculty members, by taking advantage of their leaves of absence, have earned higher degrees during the past eight years.

The systematic administration of carefully prescribed curricula [39] and the evaluation of a teacher's work by other criteria than the number of students in his classes have made possible a concerted, impersonal effort for the "wholesome, harmonious development" of the colleges. Each teacher has opportunity to present to properly constituted committees of the faculty the claims for recognition of his courses as a part of required curricula. He is no longer dependent upon the undesirable methods of inducing students to enter his classes through the offer of "cheap" credit or because of personal obligations which he may have created.

The typical woman teacher in a Missouri teachers college in 1926 is thirty-seven and six-tenths years of age, is the daughter of a farmer or professional man, is of American parentage, was born in Missouri, is one of a family of four children, of whom one other is a teacher. She attended a high school, normal school, and college, has a master's degree from a first-class university, began teaching before she entered college, has taught thirteen years in the elementary school, high school, and college. She would select teaching as a vocation now because she likes it and because she feels that it offers opportunity for service to humanity. She is teaching less than eighteen hours a week, receives an annual salary of $2088, carries an insurance policy of $2500, and has no dependents. She is happy in her work and feels that she exerts due influence in the determination of the educational policies of her college. Her college expects and stimulates professional growth on her part and

[38] See Appendix H.
[39] See p. 134.

she responds by earning advanced degrees by taking advantage of the leaves of absence her college grants her.

The typical male teacher in a Missouri teachers college in 1926 is thirty-eight and three-tenths years of age, is of American parentage, was born in Missouri, is the son of a farmer, is one of four children, is one of two teachers in the family, attended high school, normal school, and college, has a master's degree from a first-class university, has made no contribution to scholarly literature, has taught ten years, taught between high school graduation and college entrance, has served as superintendent of a small school, would choose teaching now as a vocation, teaches sixteen hours a week, receives an annual salary of $2979, carries an insurance policy of $5000, has two dependents, augments his annual salary by $200, saves about $400 a year, and is happy in his work.

PART IV

TEACHER PERSONNEL IN 1915 IN COMPARISON WITH TEACHER PERSONNEL IN 1926

The history of the normal school movement in this country affords an explanation of the presence of some of the factors in the problems that have been involved in the development of the teaching staffs of these institutions. Usually normal schools were established in new states in response to a demand for an immediate supply of teachers. The scarcity of trained teachers forced low certification requirements. Students who entered the early normal schools had little previous training above the elementary schools and wished to review the common school branches in order to pass examinations for certificates to teach. A large percentage of the work, therefore, of these normal schools was composed of review courses in elementary subjects supplemented by "method and device" courses in the same fields. College-trained teachers were not to be had for the meagre salaries paid and, indeed, were not deemed necessary in view of the elementary nature of the work offered. Successful local "practitioners" were usually employed as normal school teachers and they were selected upon the basis of their teaching records and without regard to specific training for the work to be done.

At a later period in their history normal schools might be characterized as "method-haggling and device-hunting institutions." "Methods" were conceived to be the only necessary equipment of the prospective teacher. It made little difference what a teacher taught so long as she taught it well. Here again, the person best prepared to teach in the normal school was the public school teacher who had succeeded in acquiring through her own practice the "tricks and devices of the trade." Fundamental and extensive knowledge was not regarded as a positive handicap, but it certainly was not looked upon as essential in the equipment of the normal school teacher.

In their study of problems involved in standardizing state normal schools, Professors Judd and Parker call attention to factors influencing the development of normal school standards in these words:

Normal schools have grown up in isolation. While the colleges have been in the closest touch with each other through the organization of entrance examination boards and accrediting institutions, and while high schools have been brought together by standard definitions of units, normal schools have stood apart. The typical normal school derives its financial support from legislative appropriations, receives its students without competition from a territory over which it exercises exclusive control, and has no difficulty in placing its graduates in positions which they regard as satisfactory. Furthermore, so urgent has been the demand in the country for teachers that school boards and superintendents have not been able to make rigid selections, with the result that standards of training have not been forced upon the normal schools from without.[40]

When normal schools first began seriously to consider the improvement of scholarship in their faculties, they were immediately brought face to face with two major problems. Successful local school men had formed the "habit" of being appointed to normal school positions, and since the schools were state institutions they were not always free from the necessity of making political appointments. On the other hand none of the universities of the country were giving attention to the training of teachers for normal school positions, and in the absence

[40] U. S. Bureau of Education, Bulletin, 1916, No. 12, p. 7.

of a definite source of supply it was extremely difficult to secure university trained men and women who were informed about, and in sympathy with, the professional training of teachers.

The period under consideration, 1915 to 1926, is coincident with the teachers college movement in America. A majority of the normal schools have definitely entered the senior collegiate field and are offering courses leading to baccalaureate degrees. In so doing they impose upon themselves the necessity of meeting generally accepted standards for collegiate instruction and chief among these is the training of the faculties. As is pointed out elsewhere,[41] Missouri normal schools were legally converted into teachers colleges in 1919 although they conferred four-year degrees as early as 1907. Perhaps the best single criterion for judging the progress of colleges during a given period is the progress made in the measurable qualities of their teachers. It is the purpose of this section to show just what changes have taken place in the teaching personnel of Missouri teachers colleges during this important period in their history.

During the decade the median age of the women instructors has increased from thirty-three years to thirty-seven and six-tenths years. The median age of the men has remained the same; namely, thirty-eight years. In 1915 two-thirds of the teachers were under forty; in 1926 about an equal proportion, sixty-two per cent, are under forty. The age of the teaching staffs in 1926 is about the same as it was in 1915. Since many of the present teachers were teaching in the colleges at the time of the Carnegie Survey the additions to the faculties have evidently been young men and young women. Table XXI shows that the teachers in the Missouri teachers colleges in 1926 are from about the same occupational groups as in 1915. There is a slightly smaller number from the trades and the professions, although, according to the U. S. Census for 1920 both groups have increased in the state during the decade. There seems to be nothing of special significance in these facts except that at neither time has there been enough over-ageness to interfere with vigorous work nor enough under-ageness to indicate insufficient preparation or inadequate experience. Since

[41] See p. 102.

they come in about equal numbers from the types of homes in which the students have been reared and since they have attended schools in the communities in which the students will teach, the teachers in the Missouri teachers colleges have an understanding and a sympathy which is of great benefit to them in their work.

More than eighty-seven per cent of the teachers in Missouri teachers colleges in 1926 and about sixty-six per cent of the normal school teachers in 1915 received their secondary education in public high schools. Of the teachers in 1926 only about five per cent had received their secondary work in the high school departments of the colleges; whereas in 1915 more than thirty per cent were products of these departments. This probably indicates a longer period of secondary training in the present group [42] and certainly signifies a better acquaintance with high school problems in which most of the students in 1926 are primarily interested.[43] In 1915 seven per cent of the teachers reported no training above the high school and twenty-nine per cent had no degrees. In the present faculties (1926) there are no teachers without collegiate training, and only eleven per cent are without bachelor's degrees. This number for both periods includes teachers of special subjects who have perhaps spent as much time in study as teachers who have attended degree-granting institutions. When this group is not considered, there were sixteen per cent without degrees in 1915 and three per cent in 1926. Thirty-seven per cent of the bachelor's degrees held by faculty members of Missouri teachers colleges in 1926 were conferred by the colleges themselves and fifty-six per cent were from other, first-class institutions. This is in sharp contrast to the situation in 1915, when only thirty-nine per cent of the degrees were from institutions of unquestionable standards. Seventy-four per cent of the bachelor's degrees and thirty per cent of the higher degrees held by the teachers in 1926 were from Missouri institutions as compared with fifty-five per cent and forty per cent, respectively, in 1915.

The state university conferred sixteen per cent of the bachelor's degrees and ten per cent of the master's degrees in 1915, but in 1926 it conferred twenty-eight per cent of the bachelor's

[42] See p. 55.
[43] See p. 118.

degrees and twenty-one per cent of the master's degrees. In
1915 twenty-three per cent of the teachers had the type of training represented by study in high schools, colleges, and universities. In 1926 this number had dropped to eighteen per cent.
If we add to this group the group who had studied in high
schools, normal schools, colleges, and universities, forty per
cent of the present teaching staffs have had a desirable sequence
of training for teaching in college faculties. A large percentage
of the teachers in Missouri teachers colleges are "Missouri
trained" so far as their undergraduate work is concerned, but
when an attempt is made to evaluate this training in comparison
with that found in 1915, it is necessary to recognize the improvement in Missouri teachers colleges which have afforded
much of it, to consider the larger number of degrees from the
state university, and to recall that this undergraduate work has
been supplemented in most cases by graduate work of which
at least ninety per cent was done in universities of the highest rank to be found in the country.

In 1915 twenty-five per cent of the normal school teachers
in Missouri had done recognized graduate study; in 1926 more
than fifty-six per cent had done graduate work in America's
best universities. In 1915 of fifty-two master's degrees, forty-
two came from first-class institutions. In 1926 all of the

TABLE XLII

SHOWING TRAINING OF TEACHERS IN MISSOURI TEACHERS COLLEGES
IN 1915 AND IN 1926

Type of Training	1915	1926
	%	%
No training above high school	7	0
No bachelor's degrees	29	11
Teachers of non-technical subjects bachelor's degrees	16	3
Bachelor's degrees from first-class institutions	39	93
Master's degrees	26	51
Master's degrees from first-class universities	21	51
Doctor's degrees	4	5

master's degrees are from first-class institutions. There were in 1915 less than four per cent of the teachers who held doctor's degrees; in 1926 five per cent have such degrees.

While the training of the teachers in Missouri teachers colleges leaves much to be desired, the summary in Table XLII is most encouraging.

The median number of years of teaching experience (12) is the same for both groups, and this experience is in both instances in the elementary and high schools of the state. In 1915 twenty-one per cent of the teachers had had, before coming to the normal school, experience in college teaching. In 1926 this number had been increased by only six per cent. Although ten years have elapsed since the original study was made and there are many of the teachers on the staffs now who were teaching in 1915, the median age of the group has increased only four years. It has evidently been the practice to recruit the teaching staffs by the addition of young teachers of good training, who, however, have had limited experience in teaching. The teachers colleges have been unable to attract good teachers who have already established themselves as college teachers. Aside from the fact that the ability to purchase this experience would also indicate ability to purchase additional training, one would hardly be justified, in the light of present knowledge, in saying that the teachers colleges have suffered any great disadvantage in this respect.

A factor second only in importance to the training of the teachers, which might be used as an index of the improvement of an institution in a given period of time, is the teaching load assigned the staff members; if a teacher is to do an artistic piece of teaching he must have not only ability but also favorable working conditions. Without time for study, and planning, and recreation, one cannot be expected to teach long with an optimum of enthusiasm and skill. Three aspects of the teaching load must be considered: the number of class periods a week, the size of the classes, and the range and variety of the work.

In 1915 the median teaching load in Missouri normal schools was between twenty and twenty-four hours a week; in 1926 it is less than eighteen. In 1915 twenty-one per cent of the classes had an enrollment of less than ten students; in 1926 this number had decreased by one per cent. Twelve per cent of the classes in 1915, as compared with thirty per cent in 1926, enrolled more than thirty students. In 1915 nine per cent of the classes contained more than fifty students, but in 1926 this number had been reduced to six per cent. On the whole the amount of deviation in the size of classes in 1926 is less than in 1915, the mode being less than thirty students in both cases. This more compact grouping of classes is doubtless due to modifications in curriculum requirements, especially regarding free electives.[44] It indicates, among other things, that there is a much more economical use of the teaching staffs than formerly. In practically no case does a teacher teach courses of both collegiate and secondary rank. To do so is a violation of the regulations of the North Central Association of Colleges and Secondary Schools under whose rulings the Missouri teachers colleges operate. The necessity of combining collegiate and secondary teaching is obviated because there are practically no classes of secondary rank in the colleges. Only four per cent of the teachers report teaching in more than one department and these are all closely related, e. g., history and political science. In some cases teaching in two fields is the result of substitution for other teachers who are on leave of absence and therefore is only temporary. In 1915 eighteen per cent of the teachers taught regularly in more than one department. With about two-thirds of the teaching schedule, with all classes on the collegiate level, with all of the courses in a single field, with reasonable class enrollments, it is to be expected that the teaching in Missouri teachers colleges in 1926 is on a much higher plane than the less favorable conditions in 1915 would permit.

The extent to which the teachers in Missouri teachers colleges are better paid for the better teaching they are able to do is made clear by a comparison with the rewards they receive now and those received in 1915. The median salary for men has increased from $1800 to $2979. For women it has increased from $1400 to $2088, and for both it has increased from $1650 to $2340, or forty-two per cent. During this time the full pro-

[44] See p. 130.

fessorial salaries at the University of Missouri have increased from a median of $2416.66 to a median of $3971.51. The median salary of associate and assistant professors has increased from $1728.60 to $3045. The increase in the median salary of all teachers above the rank of instructor at the university is from $2200 in 1915 to $3370.60 in 1926, or fifty per cent. It is evident that in comparison with the university faculty the teachers college teachers are underpaid; the discrepancy is even greater when it is taken into account that the university professors receive additional compensation for summer school teaching, whereas the faculties of the teachers colleges are paid on an annual basis which includes the summer school. On the whole the university teachers are better trained than are the teachers college teachers. In comparison with many universities of equal standing throughout the country the university teachers in Missouri do not receive adequate salaries.[45] Missouri does not yet recognize the importance of improving the instruction in her institutions for the training of her public school teachers and has not adequately acknowledged the progress that has been made. Even the hope one feels, when he contemplates the figures just referred to, vanishes quickly when he realizes that with the reduced value of the dollar these men and women are actually receiving less [46] for the improved service in 1926 than they did for the inferior service in 1915.

Although salaries have not increased in proportion to living costs, other reward elements are much improved. In 1915 only one normal school in Missouri granted its teachers leaves of absence for further study with part pay. In 1926 each school gives its teachers such leaves, and while there is much variation in the generosity of the regulations governing leaves, all make it possible for ambitious teachers to continue their training if they wish to do so.[47] Under the new law of 1919 [48] the tenure of teachers is much more certain than formerly. Boards of regents may now determine the length of term for which a teacher is employed. In practice, teachers are now employed during satisfactory service and, on the whole, need have no

[45] U. S. Bureau of Education, *Statistics of State Universities and Colleges*, Dec. 21, 1925.
[46] See p. 78.
[47] See Appendix H.
[48] See Revised Statutes of Mo. (1919) Art. 12, Sec. 11502.

TABLE XLIII

SHOWING SIMILARITIES AND DIFFERENCES IN TEACHER PERSONNEL IN
MISSOURI TEACHERS COLLEGES IN 1915 AND IN 1926

Characteristics of Teaching Staffs in 1915	Characteristics of Teaching Staffs in 1926
1. Median age, thirty-eight	1. Median age, thirty-eight
2. Sixty-six per cent under forty	2. Sixty-two per cent under forty
3. Two-thirds of American parentage	3. Eighty-eight per cent of American parentage
4. Fifty per cent born in Missouri	4. Fifty-four per cent born in Missouri
5. One of five children	5. One of four children
6. Fifty per cent from farm homes	6. Forty-seven per cent from farm homes
7. Twenty-one per cent from trades	7. Ten per cent from trades
8. Twenty per cent from professions	8. Fifteen per cent from professions
9. One of several teachers in the family	9. One of few teachers in the family
10. Sixty-six per cent had attended high school	10. Eighty-seven per cent have attended high school
11. Seven per cent had no training of collegiate rank	11. One hundred per cent have training above high school
12. Sixty per cent had attended normal schools	12. Sixty-four per cent have attended normal schools
13. Seventy-one per cent had bachelor's degrees	13. Eighty-nine per cent have bachelor's degrees
14. Thirty-nine per cent of the bachelor's degrees were from first-class institutions	14. Ninety-three per cent of the bachelor's degrees are from first-class institutions
15. Fifty-five per cent of the bachelor's degrees were from Missouri institutions	15. Seventy-four per cent of the bachelor's degrees are from Missouri institutions
16. Missouri university conferred sixteen per cent of the bachelor's degrees	16. Missouri university conferred twenty-eight per cent of the bachelor's degrees
17. Twenty-six per cent had done recognized graduate study	17. More than fifty-six per cent have done recognized graduate study

TABLE XLIII—(*Continued*)

Characteristics of Teaching Staffs in 1915	Characteristics of Teaching Staffs in 1926
18. Twenty-six per cent had master's degrees	18. Fifty-six per cent have master's degrees
19. Eighty-one per cent of the master's degrees were from first-class institutions	19. Ninety-six per cent of the master's degrees were from first-class institutions
20. Four per cent had doctor's degrees	20. Five per cent have doctor's degrees
21. The median teaching load was more than twenty hours a week	21. The median teaching load is less than eighteen hours a week
22. Twenty-one per cent of the classes had less than ten students	22. Twenty per cent of the classes have less than ten students
23. Twelve per cent of the classes enrolled more than thirty students	23. Thirty per cent of the classes have more than thirty members
24. Nine per cent of the classes had a membership exceeding fifty	24. Six per cent of the classes have more than fifty members
25. Teachers taught courses of collegiate rank and courses of secondary rank	25. Teachers teach courses of collegiate rank only
26. Eighteen per cent of the teachers taught in more than one department	26. Less than four per cent of the teachers teach in more than one department and then only temporarily
27. The median salary was $1650	27. The median salary is $2340—corrected value $1451
28. Leaves of absence were allowed by one school	28. Leaves of absence are allowed by all schools
29. Elected for one year only	29. Elected during satisfactory service
30. Limited participation in determination of institutional policy	30. Satisfactory participation in determination of school policy
31. Supervisors subordinate and poorly trained, poorly paid	31. Supervisors coördinate with other teachers, equally trained and paid
32. Uncomfortable pressure for large class enrollment	32. Comfortable teaching conditions

TABLE XLIV

COMPARING THE TYPICAL TEACHER IN MISSOURI TEACHERS COLLEGES IN
1915 AND THE TYPICAL TEACHER IN 1926

Typical Teacher in 1915	Typical Teacher in 1926
MEN	
1. Thirty-eight years of age	1. Thirty-eight years of age
2. American parentage	2. American parentage
3. Born in Missouri	3. Born in Missouri
4. Son of a farmer	4. Son of a farmer
5. One of six children	5. One of four children
6. Had attended public high school	6. Has attended public high school
7. Had a bachelor's degree	7. Has a master's degree
8. Had not attended school outside state	8. Has attended school outside the state
9. Had taught twelve years	9. Has taught twelve years
10. Taught twenty or more hours a week	10. Teaches eighteen or less hours a week
11. Received an annual salary of $1800	11. Receives an annual salary of $2979, which represents only $1877 when corrected for reduced value of the dollar
12. Carried $1500 life insurance	12. Carries $5000 life insurance
WOMEN	
1. Thirty-three years of age	1. Thirty-seven years of age
2. American parentage	2. American parentage
3. Daughter of a farmer	3. Daughter of a farmer
4. Born in Missouri	4. Born in Missouri
5. One of several teachers in family	5. One of few teachers in family
6. Had bachelor's degree from Missouri college	6. Has master's degree from first-class university
7. Had taught twelve years	7. Has taught thirteen years
8. Taught twenty or more hours a week	8. Teaches eighteen or less hours a week
9. Received an annual salary of $1400	9. Receives an annual salary of $2088, which represents only $1294 when corrected for the reduced value of the dollar
10. Carried a life insurance policy of $1000	10. Carries a life insurance policy of $2500

concern about tenure. Boards cannot dismiss teachers without cause. The reasons justifying dismissal and the procedure are specified in the statutes.

In personal matters, such as savings, insurance, number of dependents, and extent to which salaries are augmented by outside work, there is little variation from 1915 to 1926. On the whole, more insurance is carried and savings are somewhat greater in the latter year.

The relation of the teachers to the working organization of the institutions is much more wholesome in 1926 than it was in 1915. The truth of this statement is vouched for in the testimony of the teachers themselves. Teachers participate in the determination of school policy. Training school supervisors are given in every way equal standing with other members of the teaching staffs, and are expected to meet the same academic and professional requirements. In 1915 the survey commission was made to feel that there was a "feverish" struggle going on in all the normal schools for departmental and personal recognition. Stimulated by rating systems based almost entirely upon class enrollment, teachers resorted to the most unprofessional practices in order to attract and hold large numbers of students. In 1926 there is abundant evidence both in the statements of the teachers and from observation that this type of thing has practically, if not entirely, disappeared. At least there is nothing in the present administration which gives encouragement to such practices.

The changes which have occurred in the teaching personnels of the Missouri teachers colleges in the last decade are depicted more clearly in the tabulation of the salient facts in Tables XLIII and XLIV.

PART V

TEACHER PERSONNEL IN 1926 IN COMPARISON WITH THE PROPOSALS OF THE SURVEY COMMISSION OF 1915, AND ADDITIONAL PROPOSALS

The survey commission made very definite proposals concerning the improvement of the teaching staffs of the Missouri normal schools. This section is devoted to an examination of these recommendations in comparison with the accomplishments of the colleges during the decade.

Proposal 1.
The instructional staffs of Missouri normal schools should be organized on a professorial basis according to merit and service as is ordinarily found in college and university faculties.

That all of the colleges have made progress in the direction of faculty organization on the professorial plan is evident from statements in the respective catalogues and from the Missouri Manual, which shows the salary schedules of the different schools. Much remains to be done. The history of the faculty organizations in the several schools has prevented earlier and more rapid progress in this matter.

Proposal 2.
These well-organized faculties should exercise predominant influence in the determination of the educational policy of the schools.

Practically all of the faculty members stated in their reports in the questionnaires [49] that they do exercise such influence.

Proposal 3.
The administrative staffs should be enlarged to provide for all clerical and administrative duties, thus relieving the teaching staffs who should devote their entire time to teaching.

All of the colleges have full-time registrars and adequate clerical staffs to take care of all of the administrative duties. In some of the schools the committee system is still used, but the committees of the faculties are not administrative or executive. They are largely concerned with the study of problems for the faculty. They provide the data necessary in the determination of the educational policies of the colleges.[50]

Proposal 4.
Normal school teachers who teach college classes should receive their formal training early and meet the requirements "usually considered as necessary to qualify a teacher to give college instruction"; namely, the Ph.D. degree.

A majority of the teachers now have the master's degree. Only five per cent have the doctor's degree, although many report

[49] See Appendix B.
[50] See p. 86, paragraph 8.

graduate study beyond the master's degree. Missouri teachers colleges must demand more training on the part of the teaching staffs. By the end of another decade it is reasonable to expect as large a percentage of the teachers with the doctor's degree in the teachers colleges as is to be found in the best arts colleges.[51]

Proposal 5.
Teaching programs for college teachers should not exceed three periods of instruction per day and should be concentrated in a single field or portion thereof.

This proposal has been fully met. The median number of class periods per week is less than eighteen. In no case is it the permanent policy of the college to assign work in more than one department. There are a few instances in which teachers are now substituting temporarily outside of their field of special training.[52]

Proposal 6.
Normal school teachers should receive salaries equal to those paid by the best colleges and the state university for the same training and teaching skill.

If training is measured in terms of degrees held, the teachers in the teachers colleges are now receiving almost as much salary as is received by the group with equal training on the staff of the university. The difference in teaching skill of these two groups is difficult to estimate. On the whole, the teachers in the teachers colleges are underpaid. Salaries will have to be increased before more training can be required.[53]

Proposal 7.
The tenure of position of normal school teachers should be made permanent.

In practice this proposal has been fully met. The law does not make the tenure permanent, but it gives the boards of regents the power to determine the tenure and guarantees the teacher against dismissal without cause.[54]

Proposal 8.
The general education, quality and amount of professional training and

[51] See p. 73.
[52] See p. 74.
[53] See pp. 75-76.
[54] See p. 76.

teaching experience of the teachers of education courses should be equal to that of the "academic" teachers.

In 1926 the teachers in the departments of education must meet exactly the same requirements as are met by the teachers in other departments.[55]

Proposal 9.
Supervisors of practice teaching and critic teachers should meet the same requirements, receive as good or better salaries, and enjoy the same professional status, as the other members of the instructional staffs.

According to the reports of both groups of teachers and the salary statements in the Official Manual of Missouri, no distinction is made between them in any respect.[56]

Proposal 10.
With the relatively larger demand for collegiate courses, the greater maturity of the students, and a plan which permits a student to do all of his normal school work in the summer terms, the teachers in the summer sessions should meet in every way the requirements of the members of the staffs of the regular sessions.

This proposal has been fully met. No college can maintain its standing in the State Conference or in the North Central Association of Colleges and Secondary Schools if the teachers of all college classes, regardless of the time of year in which they teach, do not meet the minimum requirements. Some of the colleges provide no opportunities for practice teaching in the summer terms. Since such courses are demanded of all candidates for the degrees and the life certificates, it is no longer possible to complete the work in these colleges by attending in the summer only.[57]

Proposal 11.
Teachers in the summer session should be as well paid as are the regular members of the staffs.

The supply of well-trained teachers available for summer school teaching is such that they can be obtained for less salary than is paid during the regular session. So long as this condition prevails it is not necessary or desirable to increase their stipend.

[55] See p. 158.
[56] See p. 75.
[57] See p. 158.

Proposal 12.

Student-teachers, who obviously are unprepared, should not be allowed to teach college classes.

Student-teachers are not now permitted to teach college classes.[58]

TABLE XLV

SHOWING EXTENT TO WHICH THE PROPOSALS OF THE SURVEY COMMISSION IN 1915 REGARDING TEACHER PERSONNEL HAVE BEEN MET IN 1926

Pro-posal	Subject	Page	Extent to Which It Has Been Met
1	Faculty Organization	81	Largely met
2	Faculty participation in adminis-tration	81	
3	Clerical Staffs	81	Fully met
4	Faculty Training	81	Partially met
5	Teaching Loads	82	Fully met
6	Salaries	82	Only partially met
7	Tenure	82	Fully met
8	Teachers Education	82	Fully met
9	Training School Staffs	83	Fully met
10	Summer Faculty	83	Fully met
11	Summer Salaries	83	Not met and not desirable
12	Student Teachers	81	Fully met

The study in 1926 indicates that the following conditions should be met as the next step in the development of the faculties of the teachers colleges in Missouri:

1. The teaching staffs should be organized on the basis of definite professional rank so that a young teacher will be able to see his way from the bottom to the top. Such a plan will do away entirely with the feeling that personal favoritism or political prestige is necessary in order to obtain recognition, and will make the teachers colleges more attractive to young teachers of the type that should be employed by them.

2. Definite salary schedules based upon professional rank and service to the college should be adopted by all colleges.

3. The master's degree should not be considered as adequate preparation for teachers in Missouri teachers colleges. Additional training of at least two years of graduate study usually rewarded with the doctorate degree should be considered the ultimate minimum.

[58] See p. 158.

4. The amount of training is of no greater importance than the kind of training. Teachers of prospective teachers must have obtained as a part of their own training a sympathy with, and a knowledge of, the work to be done by their students. If we assume adequate higher training, desirable personal qualities, and teaching skill, the following conditions should be met by all new teachers as a guarantee of the right background for their work:

a. They should be the products of good school systems in order to have come in contact with good teaching while students in the grades and high school.

b. They should have had enough experience in teaching children to be acquainted with the problems involved, especially those having to do with the selection of subject matter suitable for the different teaching levels.

c. Their teaching experience should be in schools which are well supervised and in which in-service training opportunities have been good. Other things being equal, some supervisory experience is desirable.

d. Normal school training, especially practice teaching, is desirable.

e. Graduate courses in education should have been directly concerned with the professional training of teachers.

f. All graduate work should have been in institutions which are in sympathy with the scientific study of education.

5. With the present sources of trained teachers for positions in teachers colleges it will be necessary for these colleges to anticipate their needs and encourage young people of ability by promise of employment to follow prescribed courses of study. Suppose an enlargement of the training school is anticipated and a third grade supervisor will be needed in three years: the following plan is recommended as a desirable way to provide such a teacher:

a. Select a young woman possessing the desired personal qualities, who has a bachelor's degree and who has shown marked ability in her practice teaching.

b. Employ her at a modest salary as an assistant to the best supervisor in the training school staff. Advise the supervisor to give the young teacher every opportunity to become acquainted with the problems involved in supervision as well as in demonstration teaching.

c. During the next year and two summer sessions have her go at her own expense to a graduate school in which she will be able to get courses bearing directly upon the work of the intermediate school, supervision and the professional training of teachers. During this time she will receive her master's degree and a half year of additional graduate credit.

d. During the third year assign her to field duty in three capacities. She should spend three months working with the best county superintendents in the section, assisting them with their work in actual supervision. The second three months she should have definite teaching and supervisory work in two or three of the best consolidated schools available. The last three months should be spent with the best city superintendents and grade supervisors in the capacity of an assistant. During this year she should receive a small salary and traveling expenses.

e. The following summer should be devoted to the preparation of teaching material and the curriculum of the intermediate school. After this time she will be assigned to the supervision of the third grade with full responsibility.

A plan of this kind will not need to cost the college more than $2500, for which it will receive a year's service of an assistant supervisor and a year's work in field service which will benefit the schools of the state. This is a small amount in comparison to the present cost of preparing supervisors who are drawing full salary and who are malpracticing on the children and student-teachers. The cost to the candidate need not exceed $1500, for which she will have a year and a half of graduate study and two years of directed experience.

6. Not only are well-trained faculties necessary but it is equally essential to be able to retain the services of these teachers against competition from other colleges. This desirable permanency can be had if salaries are adequate, and not otherwise. For equal training and an equal term of service annually, teachers college teachers should receive no less than the salaries paid in the state university.

7. Upon the assumption that teachers will be employed as young as is consistent with adequate training and experience, the teachers colleges should provide the most desirable opportunities for in-service training for their teachers.

8. Members of the faculties who prefer administrative work to teaching should be so assigned or they should seek positions elsewhere. It is extremely difficult for a teacher to divide his time between teaching and administration. He is quite likely to "hold to one and despise the other."

9. Conferences of the faculties of all of the colleges, jointly or by departments, should be held annually and at state expense.

10. Provision for frequent contact with the public schools of the district should be made for all teachers in order that they may develop and retain a coöperative interest in the work of the public schools they are employed to serve. Similarly, the administration of the training school should be such as to bring each teacher into vital contact with it in the way in which his particular talents will make the contact of the greatest mutual benefit.

11. With rapidly increasing enrollments and more required courses, classes in teachers colleges are becoming much larger. Salaries necessary

to attract and retain good teachers of thorough training must be much larger than at present. It is not likely that the appropriations will increase in a ratio adequate to provide the greatly enlarged faculties which will be necessary to teach students in classes now considered of maximum size. The staffs of teachers colleges, therefore, should address themselves to the serious study of a technique for teaching much larger groups with the same satisfaction to themselves and the students as now obtain.

CHAPTER IV

CURRICULA OF MISSOURI TEACHERS COLLEGES

PART I

CURRICULA OF MISSOURI NORMAL SCHOOLS IN 1915

An attempt to present within the present bounds a comprehensive view of the Missouri normal school curricula in 1915 involves a number of problems. Since there existed no coordinating agency, there was much variation among the five schools in this, as well as in other matters. It is not easy to state facts regarding curricular practices without judging their worth either by implication or by direction. Our purpose is to acquaint the reader with the situation as it actually existed and to portray both its good and its bad features. From the very nature of the case those aspects which were capable of improvement received the major emphasis. The resultant rather dismal picture does not mean that there was little good in these schools or that the conditions described were peculiar to Missouri normal schools. By selecting carefully among the normal schools of any state at this time one could describe conditions that would create any impression he might desire to make. A selection here is necessary, but it is made with the idea of representing the common practices in Missouri normal schools with regard to curricula. In some instances an individual school may have been an exception to the specific point under discussion, but the facts disclosed by the survey justify the presentation of certain important features as the salient characteristics of curricular policies of Missouri normal schools in 1915.

Not the least important index of a school's own interpretation of its function is its standards of admission. Missouri normal schools announced in their catalogues in 1915 that students would be admitted to college curricula who had completed fifteen units of high school work or who were classified as special students over twenty-one years of age. Before students could complete courses in the normal schools leading to teaching certificates they were expected to meet the entrance requirements and pursue certain prescribed courses of study in the normal department; but since the check of a student's work was made about the time he was to receive the certificate there was little opportunity to force him to take his work in the proper sequence. Students of high school rank and students of collegiate rank were admitted to the same classes. As a result practically all of the work was neither secondary nor collegiate. Indeed, it had such a jumble of aims that it had little educational value.[1] The extent to which this mixing of students of different grades of advancement was carried, is indicated by the conditions found to exist in thirty-seven classes which were carefully analyzed. Six of these had students registered in them "having to their credit sufficient work to be rated in each of the eight years of the secondary school and college curricula; one class only was confined to students in as few as two grades, and the median as well as the modal range of distributions covered five years."[2] "More than two-thirds of the classes contained both secondary and collegiate students; thirteen were attended chiefly by secondary students and the same number contained a majority of college students."[3]

"Similarly with the elements of age and teaching experience: students less than twenty years of age, usually with no teaching experience, are classified indifferently with students twenty-five or thirty years of age, or even older, who have taught for many years. Among the thirty-seven classes above examined, twelve had more than ten per cent of their students in each of these extreme age groups; three had twenty per cent in each extreme group. In point of teaching experience of their members, these thirty-seven classes ranged from three, in which ten per cent or fewer had experience, through every percentile decade to two classes in which one hundred per cent had had experience."[4]

It should be said that this practice of mixing students of different grade levels in the same classes came as the result of

[1] Carnegie Bul. No. 14, p. 315.
[2] *Ibid.*, p. 315.
[3] *Ibid.*, p. 315.
[4] *Ibid.*, p. 315.

placing what was conceived to be the personal welfare of the student above the needs of the service, together with the careless administration of the admission requirements, rather than as a result of a lack of appreciation of what constituted good practice. Each normal school catalogue for the period specifically stated that the minimum requirement for entrance to college classes was fifteen units of high school credit.[5] A school is to be commended for catering to the needs of its individual students provided that in so doing it does not defeat the very purpose for which it exists. The attempt to shorten the student's course of training often results in weakening it so that he emerges with credit on the books but totally lacks the qualities his training is supposed to develop. There were many evidences of carelessness in the administration of credit for admission. Transcripts of high school credit were ordinarily not to be found in the offices of the registrars. Credit blanks contained such meagre statements as "Graduate of ......," "Attended .... yrs."[6] It was difficult to tell whether credit made at the normal school was of secondary or collegiate rank, because of inadequate information on the record cards. It was frequently assumed that students submitting evidence of credit in certain courses must have credit in prerequisite courses; consequently, a credit in solid geometry carried with it a credit of one unit in algebra and one unit in plane geometry.[7] "Lump credit" was often recorded on the record cards. It represented the estimate, in terms of high school units, that the president placed upon the previous experience of the student whom he probably knew personally. To say that there were no exceptions to this practice and to have it appear that there was not a large number of students who had submitted first-class high school credits would grossly misrepresent the situation. These cases are cited because of their potent influence upon curricula construction, regulation, and administration. Although the procedure cannot be justified, it is but fair to say that this and similar "habits" were the outgrowth of an honest desire of devoted men to make the normal schools most helpful to the students who attended them.

[5] Catalogue 1915, Kirksville, p. 23.   Catalogue 1915, Warrensburg, p. 45.   Catalogue 1915, Cape Girardeau, p. 34.   Catalogue 1915, Springfield, p. 33.   Catalogue 1915, Maryville, p. 23.

[6] Carnegie Bul. No. 14, p. 330.

[7] *Ibid.*, p. 331.

The admission of students at almost any time of the year to membership in the classes "makes a curriculum organized for a purpose and followed in sequence impossible; or at least it places a very high premium upon an indiscriminate or loosely grouped elective system for the sake of ease in administration." [8] The changes in student body from term to term made necessary the too frequent repetition of courses for small groups and prevented the organization and sequential treatment demanded in a well-constructed and administered curriculum.[9] The state laws which permitted the early admission of students to certification for teaching and which did not require high school attendance as a prerequisite to certification, provided examinations could be passed without it, were responsible for much of the irregularity in admission to college classes. Students after securing teaching positions desired courses in the normal school which would specifically fit them for the work they were to do. Many of the professional courses, especially in specialized fields like primary teaching, were organized for collegiate students; but it did not seem wise to refuse to admit students who were actually employed to teach primary classes and who did not meet the entrance requirements. In many instances these students had no idea of completing the requirements for any of the normal school certificates or diplomas and, therefore, they added to the need, which they could easily demonstrate, the further "argument" that they desired to take the courses as "special students." Whatever the causes for their admission to collegiate classes were, and however important it appeared to permit such registration, the fact remains that with such a plan interest was destroyed, standards were lowered and there was "confusion, waste, duplication of work." [10]

In another chapter attention was called to the undesirable effect of the elective system on the standards maintained by teachers in their classes.[11] The free election of courses had a most decided effect upon curricula. It nullified all curricula in

[8] Carnegie Bul. No. 14, p. 302.
[9] *Ibid.*, p. 302.
[10] *Ibid.*, p. 303.
[11] See p. 75.

the sense of their being prescribed programs of study providing definite training for specific levels or fields of specialization in teaching. No matter upon what grounds attempts may be made to justify the system, it implied "an equivalence of educational values among different courses which on their face are not equivalent in their value as preparation for specific types of teaching"; [12] it put the desires of the student and ease of administration above the needs of the service [13] and, therefore, could not be justified on any scientific, educational basis. The claim that the elective system improves the attitude of the student who is enthusiastic in the pursuit of subjects of study of his own choosing could not be verified. "Interest, enthusiasm, and hard work are elements that, in so far as they depend upon the exercise of the student's choice, are the product of his initial decision as to the goal at which he hopes to arrive." [14]

The Missouri normal schools recognized the fundamental importance of curriculum differentiation. All of the schools published in their catalogues [15] curricula recommended for teachers and did not emphasize other types of training, although curricula without professional aim were announced as available. Specific curricula were recommended for the different levels of grade teaching and for departmental teaching in high schools, the amount of differentiation from the general course being determined by the ability of the individual school to offer a variety of work. The variation as to the kind and amount of work recommended by the different schools as the best preparation for the different branches of the teaching service indicates that there was little agreement as to basic principles of curriculum making.

The most striking feature of the situation is the lack of uniformity, and this in spite of the fact that the normal schools were all preparing teachers for schools of different sections of a single state in which the conditions were practically identical. The curricula for the training of special teachers

[12] Carnegie Bul. No. 14, p. 146.
[13] *Ibid.*, p. 145.
[14] *Ibid.*, p. 147.
[15] Catalogue 1915, Kirksville, p. 24. Catalogue 1915, Warrensburg, p. 45. Catalogue 1915, Cape Girardeau, p. 35. Catalogue 1915, Springfield, p. 32. Catalogue 1915, Maryville, p. 23.

TABLE XLVI

Subject	Kirksville[1]		Warrensburg[2]		Cape Girardeau[3]		Springfield[4]		Maryville[5]	
	Hrs.	%	Hrs.	%	Hrs.	%	Hrs.	%	Hrs.	%
Education ...	25	41.6	25	41.6	25⅓	42.2	17½	45.8	22½	37.5
English	7½	12.5	7½	12.5	6	10.0	5	8.3	7½	12.5
History	7½	12.5	0	0.0	6	10.0	0	0.0	0	0.0
Specials	5	8.3	0	0.0	8	13.3	7½	12.5	0	0.0
Electives	5	8.3	27½	45.8	6⅔	11.1	17½	29.5	25	41.6
Science	7½	12.5	0	0.0	8	13.3	2½	4.1	5	8.3
Lib. Science ..	2½	4.0	0	0.0	0	0.0				
Total ...	60		60		60		40		54	

[1] Catalogue, 1915, Kirksville, p. 24.
[2] Catalogue, 1915, Warrensburg, p. 46.
[3] Catalogue, 1915, Cape Girardeau, p. 35.
[4] Catalogue, 1915, Springfield, p. 35.
[5] Catalogue, 1915, Maryville, p. 26.

show the same characteristics that are found in the general curriculum. (See Table XLVI above.)

In placing the welfare of the individual student above the welfare of the teaching service the normal schools not only prevented a strict, systematic administration of curricula but they actually permitted the policy to be carried so far that it resulted in the schools merely recommending "rather large program patterns from which individual curricula may be constructed"[16] instead of professional curricula in the true sense of the term. The individual curricula of students working under these general recommendations show how they can meet the requirements for certification and at the same time be wholly unprepared for the service for which they are certificated and incidentally recommended. Responsible practice teaching paralleled by two courses supposed to be consecutive and both prerequisite to teaching;[17] the presentation of two units of

[16] Carnegie Bul. No. 14, p. 167.
[17] *Ibid.*, p. 413.

algebra from high school and an additional unit of secondary algebra taken in the normal school as three of fifteen entrance units; [18] a term of history of secondary grade taken between two terms of history of collegiate grade; [19] a course in the teaching of English with only high school English as a background; [20] are illustrations of the working out of the so-called curricula in which much unrestricted election was permitted. "A miscellany of general studies; put together in a haphazard fashion, with a few courses in educational theory and practice introduced where they will most conveniently 'fit in' " [21] does not constitute, even in loose terminology, a professional curriculum.

Another, and perhaps the most important, element in curriculum differentiation in normal schools is the "professionalization" of subject matter in the courses making up the curriculum. The selection and treatment of the subject matter in a course in American history for teachers in the elementary school would differ as much from the ordinary "arts" course in the subject as a course in chemistry for dietitians would differ from the general chemistry course which is studied without professional aim. When the term is used in this sense, it is just as important for us to apply the tests of "professionalization" to the "professional" courses as to the "academic" courses. For example, the introductory course in psychology in Missouri normal schools in 1915 was "apparently conceived . . . as furnishing the student with an introduction to psychological study for its own sake, rather than as a 'practical course' dealing with facts and principles directly applicable to the problems of teaching." [22] More advanced courses dealt with pedagogical applications but practically without exception these courses were elective. A student could complete the prescribed program for elementary teaching with a single course in psychology which neither provided a basis for explaining, interpreting or formulating principles for improving teaching practice, nor furnished "a working theory of the mental life as a basis for understanding the larger problems of education." [23] Most of the professional courses were planned to be immediately helpful to the students, so much so that many of them were "device" courses which paid

[18] Carnegie Bul. No. 14, p. 414.
[19] *Ibid.*, p. 414.
[20] *Ibid.*, p. 414.
[21] *Ibid.*, p. 168.
[22] *Ibid.*, p. 179.
[23] *Ibid.*, p. 181.

little attention to fundamental principles. The extravagant offerings of education courses, an average of 64.7 semester hours for each school,[24] together with the lack of complete syllabi and careful planning, resulted in much duplication of subject matter even in required courses.

The question of the "professionalization" of the subject matter of "academic" courses for teachers is one on which there is wide difference of opinion both as to its desirability and as to the nature and extent of modification necessary for "professionalization." It is not our purpose here to defend or condemn it as a principle of curriculum making. The summary of the kind of work offered in the Missouri normal schools in 1915 from this point of view is given in order that comparisons with present practices may be made and present trends determined.

An examination of courses, including the study of syllabi, class visitation, and conferences with normal school teachers in 1915 seemed to justify the statement that "from whatever point of view they are examined, one cannot fail to be impressed by the very slight difference in apparent aim between the work done in the normal schools and the work done in non-professional schools and colleges of similar grade."[25] The traditional academic courses were not appreciably modified to meet a professional need. An opinion which prevailed among the academic teachers was expressed by a teacher of English in these words:

I can hardly be so foolish as to spend a part of my time giving the training and part showing how to give it to others. I expect that the students who expect to teach composition will make careful note of the methods and practices of this course. I do give the students considerable training in grading each others' themes, but that ought to be done in any theme course, and is done in most university courses in composition.[26]

Most of the "special" subjects, music, art, handwork, showed "a commendable adaptation to the professional needs of the students," in that they emphasized the types of work and materials that could be used in the elementary schools.[27] Commercial courses, home economics, and manual training were made to serve so many interests in addition to that of teacher training that

[24] Carnegie Bul. No. 14, p. 406.
[25] *Ibid.*, p. 228.
[26] *Ibid.*, p. 230.
[27] *Ibid.*, p. 242.

they had a heterogeneous enrollment which made professionalization impossible.

The limitations set for this study preclude any detailed treatment of practice teaching, a subject which merits an intensive and elaborate study in itself. It is, however, an element in curriculum making that cannot be totally ignored in any study which attempts to compare conditions existing at different periods in a teacher-training situation. A statement of the place of practice teaching in the students' program, its relation to the other departments of the normal school and the facilities for meeting the demands upon it, will be sufficient for our purposes.

The amount of practice and participation in the training school required in the two-year elementary curriculum of each of the normal schools in 1915 follows: Kirksville 5 hours; [28] Warrensburg 7½ hours; [29] Cape Girardeau 8 hours; [30] Springfield 5 hours; [31] Maryville 5 hours.[32] In the absence of professionalized subject-matter courses the amount of contact with the training school was extremely limited, never representing more than 12½ per cent of the students' total 60-hour program. The limited requirement in practice teaching may have been due to the limited facilities for providing for it, there being about a third as many students available in the practice schools as minimal standards required.[33]

A second reason for the general inadequacy of the courses in observation and practice teaching may be found in the subordinate position that the training school has often been forced to assume in its relationships with other normal school departments. This subordination is noticeably revealed in the neglect in many cases to provide for the training school quarters and equipment that are at all comparable either with the quarters and equipment provided for the normal school classes, or with what the better school systems provide for their elementary schools.[34]

The relation of the training school and other normal departments is well stated in the following paragraph:

By far the most significant weakness of the courses in observation, participation, and practice teaching is the general lack of a satisfactory correlation of all the work of the normal school with the training school. Not only does the training school as a rule occupy a subordinate position in the normal school organization instead of being the pivotal point and

[28] Catalogue, 1915, Kirksville, p. 34.   [29] Catalogue, 1915, Warrensburg, p. 47.   [30] Catalogue, 1915, Cape Girardeau, p. 35.   [31] Catalogue, 1915, Springfield, p. 35.   [32] Catalogue, 1915, Maryville, p. 27.   [33] Carnegie Bul. No. 14, p. 195.   [34] *Ibid.*, p. 197.

focus of all departments, but the work of the training school seems in many, if not most, cases to be detached, to lack a fundamental relation to what is taught and learned in the classrooms "upstairs." It is no unusual thing for the normal school student to complain that the theory that has been taught to him in the courses in psychology, principles of teaching, and special methods (to say nothing of the purely "academic" courses) has no perceptible connection with the work of the training school. This is sometimes due, no doubt, to the fact that the "theory" is impracticable, and that those responsible for the practice teaching know it, and in consequence will have no commerce with it; but it is oftener due merely to a complete mechanical separation of the training department both from the department of educational theory and from the academic departments,—a separation which results in the total ignorance of each party regarding what the other is teaching or practising, if not, indeed, in actual opposition or open friction.[35]

The prominent characteristics of normal school curricula in Missouri in 1915 were these:

1. The published requirements for admission to collegiate curricula were fifteen units of high school credit, but the loose administration of the requirements permitted students of a wide range of advancement, age, and experience to enroll in the same classes with the inevitable result of low standards of teaching and a general corruption of aims.

2. The admission of students at irregular intervals forced wasteful repetition of courses, disorganized class work, and imposed additional burdens upon overloaded teachers.

3. The general use of a system of unrestricted electives with its false theory of equivalence resulted in making the student's prejudices and immature judgment paramount to the known needs of the teaching service in the formulation of a course of study to be pursued. Consequently, the so-called curricula were nothing more than large program patterns.

4. Variation in curricula among the schools indicated that there were no generally accepted principles for curriculum making for training the state's supply of teachers.

5. Curricula were differentiated for the different levels of the teaching service and for special fields of teaching, but the constant consideration of "the student's immediate welfare" permitted these to become a haphazard arrangement of miscellaneous subjects.

6. Subject matter courses were in no sense professionalized.

[35] Carnegie Bul. No. 14, p. 199.

7. Little of the work of the student brought him in contact with the training school. Practice teaching occupied a very subordinate place in his program.

8. Training school facilities were inadequate as to kind and amount and housing.

9. There was no satisfactory correlation (in one instance open friction existed) between the training schools and the normal schools.

PART II

Proposals of the Survey Commission in 1915 Concerning the Improvement of Curricula

The study of curricula in Missouri teachers colleges led to a series of proposals which are repeated here, and inspired a supplementary volume of "proposed 'curricula' designed for the professional preparation of teachers for American public schools." [36] The volume contains "provisional suggestions . . . for coöperative discussion on the part of training institutions and students of education." Its recommendations will be considered incidentally in a later section of this chapter in which the present (1926) curricula of the Missouri teachers colleges are analyzed.

The conclusions and proposals relating to the collegiate curricula in the survey report were as follows:

(1)[37] The minimum standard of admission to all professional teaching curricula should be the requirement of graduation from an approved four-year secondary school, or its equivalent by examination; this standard should be fixed at once. Service as teacher in a public school without recognized professional training of collegiate character should be made impossible.

(2) A schedule of progressive increase in residence requirements should be established. The expressed goal of this program should be, in effect, an identical residence requirement for all public school teachers from the first to the twelfth grades, urban and rural alike,— a requirement of four school years of organized professional preparation of collegiate character.

(3) In order to make possible a standard admission and residence requirement for professional curricula in the case of women, the profession of teaching should be made attractive to them through-

[36] Published by the Carnegie Foundation in February, 1917.
[37] The numbering has been made consecutive regardless of omissions from the text.

out the state as a permanent life career. Their marriage should not be considered as a bar to such service, but rather as an added qualification. ·

(4) After a brief period of orientation and self-discovery on common ground, all professional curricula should, in the interests of the public service, have in view definitely distinguished positions, to the preparation for which their entire resources may contribute. In so far as formulated disciplines exist that clearly promote skill and power in the given position, the principle of free or group election should give place to prescriptive sequences prepared by experienced observers. In the longer curricula, where reasoned equivalence may be secured, or is a matter of indifference, option may be allowed, but the greatest possible effectiveness of the teacher in the position chosen should be the first consideration throughout.

(5) The differentiation of curricula according to the position in view, a principle already partly recognized for primary and high school teachers, should be completely worked out, and should be applied as well to the middle and upper grades, and to the work of school administration.

(6) Curricula of collegiate grade that have for their purpose the preparation of teachers should be professionalized throughout in the sense that every course should be chosen with specific reference to the contribution that it makes to the teacher's equipment. This would, by definition, include courses of a distinctly "liberal" type (pages 166-172, 228-247).[38]

(7) The focal characteristic of every such curriculum should be participation in the actual work of teaching; consequently the training school should be looked upon and administered as the central feature of the normal school organization (pages 192, 224).

(8) No professional curriculum for teachers should look exclusively toward the development of specific *skill* in teaching. It should aim as well to make the teacher professionally intelligent: competent to coöperate in the construction of large educational plans and policies, or at least to measure the full significance of constructive proposals. This broader aim of ensuring professional intelligence will naturally receive greater emphasis in the longer curricula, but it should find a definite expression even in the briefest preparation (pages 179-182).

(9) The so-called "professional" courses—psychology, the history of education, principles of teaching, school management, practice teaching, and the like—should be judged not only by the extent to which they increase specific skill in classroom procedure, but also by their contribution to the broader professional intelligence and insight of the teacher. In connection with the latter aim, the

[38] The page numbers refer to Carnegie Bulletin No. 14.

claims of biology, sociology, and economics should be considered as well as those of the professional courses now recognized as such (pages 179-182).

(10) The sequence of professional work should represent a progression from the concrete courses that deal primarily with classroom procedure to the more abstract summarizing and systematic courses. The latter consequently will appear at or near the end, and will be elaborated most fully in the longer curricula (pages 183, 186, 189, 191, 224).

(11) A general course in "pure" psychology is of doubtful value as an introduction to professional study. The introductory course should deal rather with the concrete applications of psychology to teaching (educational psychology), leaving the more abstract course in psychology until later. All courses should exemplify and expressly emphasize the psychological principles which they involve (pages 182, 183).

(12) A general course in the history of education is probably out of place in one-year or two-year curricula. Such a course, however, should serve an important purpose in one of the later years of the longer curricula. Most courses would gain both in force and in coherence by briefly tracing the development in their own practice. These partial glimpses should then be gathered firmly into a complete picture by a systematic course in educational development as a whole (pages 184-187).

(13) The courses generally known as principles of teaching (general method) and school management will yield the best results if associated closely with the work in participation and practice teaching (pages 189, 191).

(14) As far as possible, the distinction between courses in "special methods of teaching" and courses in the subject matter itself should be eliminated. Every professional curriculum should embody thorough courses of distinctly collegiate character in all of the subject matter that the student proposes to teach. In these courses the specific organization of materials for elementary or secondary teaching should be fully discussed, and the approved methods of teaching should be both exemplified and justified. All teachers of the so-called academic subjects should hold a direct and responsible relationship to the training school (pages 199-202, 227).

(15) In each specific curriculum, a course that aims to organize and integrate the work of that field for which the curriculum prepares (primary teaching, intermediate grade teaching, junior high school teaching, and so forth) should be offered in the final year (pages 224, 227).

(16) The importance of the training school in the scheme of curriculum construction above outlined suggests—

(a) Much more extensive training-school facilities than most normal schools now provide; intimate and to some extent controlling relations should be developed with the local public school system (pages 192-197).

(b) Control by the normal school of the principal school or schools in which students serve as teachers for practice. This should not preclude a supplementary use of other schools for apprentice-teaching (page 193).

(c) A recognition of the status of the supervisor and critic teacher as equal or superior to that of the "academic" teacher (page 213).

(d) The unification of the headship of the education department with the direction of the training school and of practice teaching in one person.

(e) The safeguarding of the interests of training-school pupils by permitting not more than three-fourths and preferably not more than one-half of the teaching to be done by student-teachers (page 194).

(f) The provision of a separate school for experimental purposes, and the limitation of the training school to practice teaching and teaching for purposes of demonstration (page 221).

(g) The employment of teachers of educational theory and teachers of "academic" subjects as supervisors of teaching under the general control of the director of training (page 202).

(h) A systematic gradation of the work in observation, participation, group-teaching, and responsible room-teaching (pages 224, 225).

(17) In each collegiate curriculum of two years or more, a term or a semester should be left after the period of responsible room-teaching, for the summarizing courses mentioned above (pages 183, 224).

(18) Each prescribed professional curriculum should have in view the symmetrical development of an individual's knowledge and skill as required for an analyzed purpose. It is not a mere series of independent courses juxtaposed by title. It is rather one complex, carefully devised tool operated by different instructors to a common end. Its success depends upon the extent to which these instructors, by constant study, conference, and mutual criticism, learn to re-enforce and supplement each other in the content of their teaching. Differences should be worked out in advance or omitted. Each curriculum should constitute a harmoniously interrelated body of instruction progressively directed toward a definite result that is clearly understood by all.

(19) The present administration of the curricula in the Missouri normal schools is wasteful and ineffective, due to duplication of classes, to an extravagant elective system, and to the complete lack of the intercollegiate differentiation of specialized curricula. Differentiation and concentration of prescribed curricula in accordance with

the previously ascertained needs of the state are suitable remedies for the existing situation (pages 258-265).

PART III

CURRICULA OF MISSOURI TEACHERS COLLEGES IN 1926

During the first half of the decade immediately following the Carnegie survey of Missouri normal schools they operated under the Normal School Law of 1870 which gave the boards of regents full authority to prepare the courses of study.[39]

The Fiftieth General Assembly of the State of Missouri in 1919 passed the "Teachers College Law," which changed the names of the normal schools to teachers colleges, authorized the extension of their curricula, and gave them the degree-granting privilege. The sections of the present law relating to curricula are:

The board of regents of each state teachers college shall have power to prescribe, for its college, courses of instruction which shall include such subjects in the arts and sciences as are usually taught in teachers colleges, normal schools, or schools of education.[40]

Each board shall have power and authority to confer upon students, by diploma under the common seal, such degrees as are usually granted by teachers colleges and normal schools.[41]

Although appropriations were meagre and faculties were poorly prepared and overworked, all of the Missouri normal schools in 1915 advertised courses of study leading to the degree of B.S. in Education. One of them announced courses leading to the degrees of A.B., B.S. in Education, and B.S in Home Economics.[42]

Curricula leading to baccalaureate degrees had been offered in the Missouri normal schools since 1902.[43] In 1909 a bill was presented to the legislature proposing a revision in the normal school statutes, making these schools state teachers colleges; but other legislation got in the way of its passage and it was withdrawn. When the bill was finally passed in 1919, it merely

[39] Revised Statutes of Missouri, 1909, Article 17, Section 11076.
[40] Revised Statutes of Missouri, 1919, Article 17, Section 11502.
[41] *Ibid.*, Article 17, Section 11503.
[42] See Missouri Normal Schools Catalogues for 1915: Kirksville, p. 25, Warrensburg, p. 48, Cape Girardeau, p. 38, Maryville, p. 28, Springfield, p. 36.
[43] A course leading to the A. B. degree appears in the catalogue of the Cape Girardeau Normal School for 1902.

legalized what the schools had been doing for many years, although few students had received four-year degrees from the normal schools at this time.[44] In another section of this study the apparent, immediate effects of the passage of the bill on the curricula and practices of the schools is pointed out but to trace the actual transforming of the normal schools into teachers colleges will cover a period of twenty-four years. In our present study of curricula, therefore, we are considering the last ten years of this period of development and the fact that the four-year courses were actually legalized at the middle of this period was but an incident in the process.

As has been pointed out elsewhere,[45] the administration of curricula in Missouri teachers colleges is no longer a haphazard affair. Students are not admitted to collegiate curricula who have not satisfied the standard requirements for college entrance.[46] Residence requirements are consistent with the best collegiate practice.[47] A distinction is made between work of junior and of senior college rank, and all the colleges demand that at least forty per cent of the work offered for the degree be of senior college rank.[48] A general scholarship record equal to or above the median group must be maintained by all students who receive the college degrees.[49] The University of Missouri and all of the teachers colleges offer courses by correspondence and extension, but since this non-residence work is of doubtful value in the minds of some, the amount that can be offered in meeting the requirements for the degree is limited by the Conference to thirty-three per cent.[50]

With the original data upon which this study is based are filed random samplings of transcripts of credit of students who received degrees from Missouri teachers colleges in 1925. Two of them are reproduced here to show the distribution of courses as applied in the four-year schedule of individual students. They also show the care with which records are kept and the form in which transcripts of credit are made.

[44] See p. 114.
[45] See p. 130.
[46] See p. 156.
[47] See p. 162.
[48] See Catalogue, Springfield, 1926, p. 26.
[49] *Ibid.*, p. 29.
[50] By Conference action, March, 1926. See Chapter V.

CASE I

(See transcript on pages 105 and 106)

It will be noted that the files of the teachers college contain
not only the complete record of **Mr. A** while a student in the
college but his complete high school record as well. An analysis
of the transcript reveals the following facts: Forty-four per
cent of the work is of senior college rank. With the exception
of two courses this work was taken during the junior and senior
years. Less than ten per cent of the work during these years
was of junior college rank. The distribution of courses is:

Course	Semester Hours
Education	30
Political and Social Science	25
History	27.5
English	15
Science	7.5
Latin	2.5
Physical Education and Health	10
Industrial Art	5
Music	2.5

The absence of mathematics both in the high school and in the
college courses and the small amount of science, all of which is
chemistry, are striking. Two-thirds of the work in education
was taken in the last two years of the course and in the following order: Educational Psychology, Principles of Teaching,
Educational Sociology, Teaching of History and History of
Education, High School Problems and Teaching and Observation, Tests and Measurements, School Administration, Educational Sociology, Teaching and Observation and Teaching of
Social Science. It should be noted that Mr. A's schedule lacked
an introductory course in education for general exploratory purposes. The history of education is not well placed and the only
opportunity for integration at the close is a course in teaching
the social sciences which may serve the purpose admirably if
it is properly planned.

The faithfulness with which the printed requirements for
graduation have been met by Mr. A is apparent from the following table.

*Uniform transcript form adopted by the University
and State Teachers College of Missouri*
For explanation of terms see back of sheet

NORTHEAST MISSOURI STATE TEACHERS COLLEGE
OFFICE OF THE REGISTRAR
KIRKSVILLE, MISSOURI

Date....Feb. 15, 1926..........

Official Transcript of the Record of—
..........................Mr. A..........................
Home Address.............Kirksville, Mo. ....
I. Attendance. Admitted. (Date)........September, 1921.............

Degree..........B.S. in Ed. ....{ Attended..14...terms (12) weeks
......summer sessions (10) weeks

II. Status..............Postgraduate..................................
III. Entrance Credits. Sources (a)..Kirksville High School..............
..............................Graduated (year) ..1921......
(b) ....(c)..........................

Below—first column, subjects; second, units; third, source.

English....	4	..	Latin......	2	..	Gen. Biol.			Agr.		..	Sociology....		..
Algebra....	1	..	Greek......		..	Gen. Sci.		..	Voc. Agr. ..		..	Economics...		..
Pl. Geom. .		..	Anc. Hist...	1	..	Botany....		..	H. H. Art ..		..	Com. Law...		..
Sol. Geom.		..	M.&M.Hist.	1	..	Zoology...		..	Voc.Ho'.Ec.		..	Com. Geog.		..
Adv. Arith.		..	Eng. Hist..		..	Hygiene...		..	Drawing ...		..	Com. Arith.		..
Trigonom..		..	Amer. Hist.	½	..	Chemistry.	1	..	Mech.Draw.		..	Bookkeep. ..	1	..
French....	1	..	Amer. Govt.	½	..	Physics ...		..	Man. Train.	1	..	Sten. & Typ.	1	..
German...		..	Com'y Civ.		..	Ph. Geog. .		..	Music......		..	Teach. Train.		..
Spanish....	1	..	....		..	Physiology		..	Ph. Ed.	½	..	....		..

How Admitted........Certificate from first-class high school. ....
....
IV. College Credits

Course	Descriptive Title	Course Number	Term— Date	Semester Hours	Grade	Credit
Practical English		21a	Sept. '21	2½	S	2½
Sociology		9a	" "	2½	S	2½
Chemistry		1a	" "	2½	G	2½
Educational Psychology		1b	" "	2½	S	2½
Practical English		21b	Dec. '21	2½	G	2½
Sociology		9b	" "	2½	G	2½
Chemistry		1b	" "	2½	G	2½
Basketball		3	" "	1¼	G	1¼
Chorus		9	" "	1¼	G	1¼
Sociology		9c	Mar. '22	2½	G	2½
Chemistry of Metals		3	" "	2½	G	2½
Business Law		17	" "	2½	S	2½
Principles of Teaching		3	" "	2½	G	2½
Economics		103a	June "	2½	G	2½
American Government		1a	" "	2½	C	0
Auto Mechanics		6a	" "	2½	S	2½

NOT VALID WITHOUT IMPRESSION SEAL OF THE COLLEGE
Total, or amount forwarded,

Continued on page 106

NORTHEAST MISSOURI STATE TEACHERS COLLEGE
OFFICE OF THE REGISTRAR
KIRKSVILLE, MISSOURI

Sheet No.........2..........   Date......Feb. 15, 1926......
..........................Mr. A..............College Credits (continued)
                                                        Brought forward—

Course Descriptive Title	Course Number	Term— Date	Semester Hours	Grade	Credit
Business English	19	Sept. '22	2½	G	2½
M. & M. History	1a	" "	2½	G	2½
Physiology	7a	" "	2½	G	2½
Auto Mechanics	6b	" "	2½	G	2½
M. & M. History	1b	Dec. "	2½	G	2½
Economics	103b	" "	2½	S	2½
American Government	1b	" "	2½	S	2½
Basketball	3	" "	1¼	G	1¼
Chorus	9	" "	1¼	G	1¼
M. & M. History	1c	Mar. '23	2½	S	2½
Word Study	9	" "	2½	E	2½
Rural Sociology	5	" "	2½	G	2½
Teaching of History	25	" "	2½	G	2½
American Literature	3a	Sept. "	2½	G	2½
American History	7a	" "	2½	G	2½
Ancient History	3a	" "	2½	G	2½
History of Education	107	" "	2½	G	2½
Europe since 1815	108b	Dec. "	2½	S	2½
Soc. and Econ. History of America	113c	" "	2½	G	2½
High School Problems	16	" "	2½	G	2½
Teaching and Observation	217b	" "	2½	S	2½
Europe since 1815	108a	Mar. '24	2½	S	2½
Party Government	107	" "	2½	G	2½
Soc. and Econ. American History	113a	" "	2½	S	2½
Tests and Measurements	133	" "	2½	G	2½
19th Century Literature	101a	Sept. "	2½	G	2½
American Constitutional History	111a	" "	2½	E	2½
Latin American History	109a	" "	2½	E	2½
School Administration	129a	" "	2½	S	2½
Journalism	131b	Dec. "	2½	S	2½
Principles of Coaching	101b	" "	1¼	G	1¼
Basketball	3	" "	1¼	G	1¼
Educational Sociology	102	" "	2½	S	2½
Teaching and Observation	126	" "	2½	S	2½
American Constitutional History	111c	Mar. '25	2½	S	2½
Financial Organization	113	" "	2½	S	2½
Common Diseases	111	" "	2½	G	2½
Teaching of Social Sciences	117	June "	2½	E	2½
Total					125 hours

TABLE XLVII

SHOWING EXTENT TO WHICH MR. A HAS MET THE PRINTED REQUIREMENTS
FOR GRADUATION FROM A MISSOURI TEACHERS COLLEGE

Courses	Semester Hours Required [1]	Semester Hours to Mr. A's Credit
Education	25 to 30	30
English	7.5	15
Major (History)	22.5	27.5
Minor (Political Science)	15	25
Minor (Physical Education)	10	10
Social Science	5	Minor
Science or Mathematics	5	5
Physical Education	5	5
Free Electives	20	7.5 and excess in major and minors

[1] Catalogue, 1926, Kirksville.

CASE II

(See transcript on pages 108 and 109)

In the case of Miss B thirty-three per cent of the credit is of senior college rank, all of which was taken during the last two years of her course. The distribution according to departments is as follows:

Course	Semester Hours
Education	27.5
English	37.5
History	15
Spanish	10
Sociology	10
Geography	7.5
Science	5
Mathematics	2.5
Music	7.75
Physical Education	6.25
Expression	2.5
Art	2.5
Home Economics	2.5

MISS B'S RECORD

THE NORTHWEST MISSOURI
STATE TEACHERS COLLEGE
MARYVILLE

Official Statement of Credits

Office of Registrar.   *Date February 10, 1926*

Miss B has the following credit on the records of the State Teachers College, Maryville:

Quarter and Year	NAME OF COURSE	Cat. No.	Grade	Credit	
16 units entrance credit accepted from Burlington Jct., Mo., High School					
Fall-1920:	Gen. Psychology	11	M+	2.5	sem. hr.
	Eng. Composition	11	S+	2.5	" "
	Current History	13	M	2.5	" "
	Penmanship	11	I	1.25	" "
	Physical Education	12	M	1.25	" "
Winter-1920:	Eng.-Types in Literature	12	M+	2.5	" "
	Physical Education (Health)	14	M	2.5	" "
	Sociology (The Family)	15	M	2.5	" "
	Piano	11a	M	2.5	" "
Spring-1921:	Ed. Psychology	12	S	2.5	" "
	School Economy	51	I	2.5	" "
	Journalism	24	M	2.0	" "
	Biology	11	M	2.5	" "
	Physical Education	61	M	.5	" "
Spring-1922:	Piano	11c	M+	1.25	" "
Fall-1922:	Intro. to Teaching	22	S	2.5	" "
	H. S. Methods	101a	M+	2.5	" "
	Eng. Juvenile Literature	16	M+	2.5	" "
Winter-1922:	Prin. of Teaching	55	I	2.5	" "
	Public Speaking	61	S	2.5	" "
	Historical Survey of Europe	11b	S−	2.5	" "
	Advanced American History	12b	S	2.5	" "
Spring-1923:	History of Education in U. S.	81	M	2.5	" "
	Composition and Grammar	15	S+	2.5	" "
	Fine Arts	11a	M	1.25	" "
	Music	11a	S	1.25	" "
Summer-1923:	Eng.-History of Am. Literature	61a	S	2.5	" "
	College Algebra	61a	M−	2.5	" "
	Economic Geography	51	M	2.5	" "
	Music Appreciation	81	S	2.5	" "
Fall-1923:	Journalism	124a	M	2.5	" "
	Spanish	11a	S	2.5	" "
	Sociology	78	S−	2.5	" "
	Hist. Confederacy & Constitution	124a	M	2.5	" "

Continued on page 109

Quarter and Year	Name of Course	Cat. No.	Grade		Credit	
Winter-1923:	Journalism	124b	M	2.5	sem. hr.	
	Spanish	11b	S	2.5	"	"
	Sociology	151	M+	2.5	"	"
	Biology	13	M+	2.5	"	"
Spring-1924:	Practice Teaching	105	M+	2.5	"	"
	Eng.-Hist. of Eng. Literature ...	62a	M+	2.5	"	"
	Spanish	11c	M	2.5	"	"
	Geographic Influences	81	M−	2.5	"	"
Summer-1924:	Child Study	120	M	2.5	"	"
	Personal Hygiene	75	S	2.5	"	"
	Spanish	11c	M	2.5	"	"
	Human Geography	102	M	2.5	"	"
Fall-1924:	Practice Teaching	105	S+	2.5	"	"
	Technique of Drama	170	M	2.5	"	"
	Eng.-Browning	105	M−	2.5	"	"
	Social Problems	24	S−	2.5	"	"
Winter-1924:	Hist. of Eng. Literature	62b	M−	2.5	"	"
	Hist. of Eng. Language	102	M	2.5	"	"
	Home Ec.-Clothing	13	S−	2.5	"	"
Spring-1925:	Teaching H. S. English	140	M+	2.5	"	"
	Eng.-Tennyson	104	S−	2.5	"	"
	Am. Literature	131	M	2.5	"	"
	Ideals in Am. History	172	M	2.5	"	"
Credit earned by Correspondence:	Adv. Am. History	12a	S	2.5	"	"
At Conservatory:	Piano		M+	1.25	"	"

Miss B received both the B.S. in Education and the B.A. degrees on May 27, 1925.

The major fields of knowledge are represented in the schedule. With the exception of the too early introduction of high school methods and history of education, the sequence of educational courses is not out of harmony with the principle which places an orientation course first, practice teaching relatively late, followed by an integrating course. In this case as in Case I the integrating course is a methods course. Rather more of the education work occurs in the first two years of the course than is considered best practice in a four-year course.[51]

[51] Carnegie Bul. No. 14, p. 182.

Table XLVIII shows the extent to which the printed requirements for graduation have been met by Miss B.

TABLE XLVIII

SHOWING EXTENT TO WHICH MISS B HAS MET THE PRINTED REQUIREMENTS
FOR GRADUATION FROM A MISSOURI TEACHERS COLLEGE

Courses	Semester Hours Required [1]	Semester Hours to Miss B's Credit
Education	27.5	27.5
English	5	Part of Major
Foreign Language	7.5	10
Social Science	7.5	10
Science	7.5	5
Mathematics	5	2.5
Major (English)	15	37.5
Minor (History)	10	15

[1] Catalogue, 1926, Maryville.

These are typical cases and on the whole show a rather careful administration of the regulations governing the curricula requirements.

Criteria formulated by the best expert opinion [52] for judging the curricula of teachers colleges may be classified under three general headings: Differentiation, Content, Organization.

Differentiation

1. Differentiated curricula determined by the character of the work to be done and the subjects to be taught should be provided for the four generally recognized teaching levels, namely, kindergarten-primary, intermediate, upper grade or junior high school, and secondary.

2. Specialized curricula should be provided for cognate subject groups in the levels and fields of teaching in which best practice recognizes the desirability of departmental teaching.

Content

3. All curricula should provide for a cross-section of the better-known fields of human knowledge even though major emphasis of some is demanded by the type of service for which preparation is being made. This principle implies sufficient flexibility in administration to take into account the students' secondary training, especially in two-year curricula.

[52] Provisional Curricula for Professional Training of Teachers, 1917. Louisiana Survey, pp. 120-122.

4. The courses constituting the curriculum, while providing for breadth, depth, and newness of subject materials, must also provide a scholarship relevant to the adaptations in subject matter which the student must make in the instruction of children and pertinent to the functional point of view.

5. The curriculum should provide activities and materials which will strengthen the personal and social equipment of the students and put them in possession of the skills and controls known to be an essential part of the teacher's equipment.

Organization

6. All courses in the curriculum should be arranged with respect to their sequential relationship within and without the subject and should provide for the integration at all points of theory and practice by the parallel treatment of courses in the classroom and the training school.

7. The introductory courses in all curricula should be identical and planned to give the student a view of the entire field that he may make an intelligent choice of the level of the service for which he will prepare. All curricula should provide for very little "free election."

8. The professional treatment of subject matter makes possible the reduction of the number of courses in education, especially those dealing with the special methods of individual subjects. It is important to provide courses for orientation, followed by parallel theory and practice courses. Independent practice teaching should come late in the schedule and be followed by a thorough integration course.

The curricula offered in Missouri teachers colleges in 1926 will be examined by applying these criteria. The data are taken from the catalogues of the five colleges and unless otherwise stated the most general curriculum for the training of elementary teachers is considered.

According to the first criterion the teachers colleges should provide curricula differentiated so as to give training of specific significance for the different teaching levels. The tables which follow show the number and kinds of curricula offered by the five colleges in 1926 and also show what the tendencies have been in curricula differentiation since 1915. Since students who complete prescribed courses representing two years of college work are permanently certificated in Missouri for elementary teaching, all of the colleges offer both two-year and four-year curricula; hence, tables are given for curricula leading to life certification for elementary teaching and for curricula leading to the degree.

TABLE XLIX

SHOWING THE NUMBER AND KINDS OF DIFFERENTIATED CURRICULA LEADING TO CERTIFICATION FOR TEACHING IN ELEMENTARY SCHOOLS OFFERED BY MISSOURI TEACHERS COLLEGES FROM 1916 TO 1926

("x" indicates that the curriculum is offered)

Curricula	1916					1917					1918					1919					1920					1921					1922					1923					1924					1925–26				
	K	W	C	S	M	K	W	C	S	M	K	W	C	S	M	K	W	C	S	M	K	W	C	S	M	K	W	C	S	M	K	W	C	S	M	K	W	C	S	M	K	W	C	S	M	K	W	C	S	M
General	x	x	x	x	x	x	x	x	x	x	x	x	x	x	x	x	x	x	x	x	x	x	x	x	x	x	x	x	x	x	x	x	x	x	x	x	x	x	x	x	x	x	x	x	x	x	x	x	x	x
Rural																																	x																		x
Primary		x		x			x	x				x					x	x				x	x				x	x				x	x				x					x					x			x
Interm.																																	x																		x
Upper																																	x																		
Kgn.-Prim.																																	x																		
Mus. Sup.		x		x			x		x			x	x	x			x	x	x			x	x	x			x	x	x			x	x	x			x	x	x			x	x	x			x	x	x	
Art. Sup.		x		x			x		x			x	x	x			x	x	x			x	x	x				x	x			x	x	x			x	x	x	x		x	x	x			x	x	x	
H. Ec.		x		x			x		x			x	x	x			x	x	x			x	x	x				x	x			x	x	x			x	x	x			x	x	x			x	x	x	
Commerce		x					x					x					x					x											x							x											x
Agri.		x					x					x					x					x											x																		
Man. Art																																																		
Jr. H.S												x					x																																	
Total	1	7	1	5	1	1	7	2	4	1	1	8	4	4	1	1	8	5	4	1	1	7	5	4	1	1	3	5	4	1	1	5	11	4	1	1	5	4	4	3	1	5	4	4	1	1	5	4	4	5

K—Kirksville. W—Warrensburg. C—Cape Girardeau. S—Springfield. M—Maryville.

For several years the teachers colleges in Missouri have offered differentiated curricula representing sixty hours of work and leading to the life certificate. It appears from Table XLIX that Kirksville makes no provision for differentiation at this level but the system of electives in the general course is such that students can, upon advice of members of the faculty, differentiate their courses as much as is possible in the other schools. The plan, with proper restrictions, is as effective as any other, but in the absence of printed requirements there is danger of simply meeting requirements quantitatively and without regard for specific teaching requisites.

In 1923 specialized curricula in the junior college for secondary teaching were abandoned by the colleges. This date is coincident with the requirement of four years of college training for teaching in first-class high schools. Some of the colleges arranged their four-year curricula so that temporary teaching certificates could be issued at the end of the second year. Students could drop out of college to teach in unapproved and third-class high schools on temporary certificates, and then return to college and continue their courses without the loss of time which would be incurred by meeting the requirements for the permanent certificate for elementary teaching at the end of the second year. In 1026 four of the colleges announce differentiated curricula for the training of elementary teachers and the fifth makes such differentiation possible, thus satisfying the first criterion proposed for judging curricula. (See Table LI).

The number of differentiated curricula leading to the degree increased from a total of twenty-five in all schools in 1916 to a total of thirty-six in 1919. This is the maximum number offered in any one year in the history of the teachers colleges. It is probable that the normal schools sought to regain their enrollment at the close of the war by offering a variety of courses sufficient to appeal to a great number of interests. By 1921 the number of curricula dropped to twenty-one. A part of the decline was due to the fact that the teachers colleges were not approved for the training of teachers of vocational agriculture. Specialized courses for supervisors of art and music were dropped and this training was cared for by the choice of majors and minors in the general curricula. The total number of curricula increased again in 1925 to thirty. This increase was due

TABLE L

Showing Differentiated Curricula Leading to Degree of B. S. in Education and Other Degree Curricula in Missouri Teachers Colleges from 1916 to 1926

Curricula	1916					1917					1918					1919					1920					1921					1922					1923					1924					1925-26				
	K	W	C	S	M	K	W	C	S	M	K	W	C	S	M	K	W	C	S	M	K	W	C	S	M	K	W	C	S	M	K	W	C	S	M	K	W	C	S	M	K	W	C	S	M	K	W	C	S	M
General	X	X	X	X	X	X	X	X	X	X	X	X	X	X	X	X	X	X	X	X	X	X	X	X	X	X	X	X	X	X	X	X	X	X	X	X	X	X	X	X	X	X	X	X	X	X	X	X	X	X
Primary			X	X	X			X	X	X			X	X	X			X	X	X			X	X	X			X	X	X			X	X	X			X	X	X			X	X	X			X	X	X
Interm.			X	X				X	X				X	X				X	X				X	X				X	X				X	X				X	X				X	X				X	X	
Upper			X	X				X	X				X	X				X	X				X	X				X	X				X	X				X	X				X	X				X	X	
Rural		X	X	X	X			X	X	X			X	X	X			X	X	X		X	X	X				X	X				X	X				X	X				X	X				X	X	
Jr. H. S.																												X					X					X					X					X		
High Schl.		X	X	X	X		X	X	X	X		X	X	X	X		X	X	X	X		X	X	X	X		X	X	X	X		X	X	X	X		X	X	X	X		X	X	X	X		X	X	X	X
Voc. or General		X	X				X	X				X	X				X	X				X	X				X	X				X	X				X	X				X	X				X	X		
Home Ec.		X	X	X	X		X	X				X	X				X	X				X	X	X			X	X	X			X	X	X			X	X	X			X	X	X			X	X	
Voc. Agri.		X			X		X					X					X					X	X	X			X	X	X			X	X	X			X	X	X			X	X	X			X	X	
Music							X					X					X					X	X	X			X	X				X	X	X			X	X	X			X	X	X			X	X	
Art							X					X					X					X	X				X	X				X	X				X	X				X	X				X	X	
Commerce		X					X					X					X					X	X					X					X					X					X					X		
A. B.																	X																																	
B. S. in H. Ec.		X	X				X					X					X				X	X		X				X																						
Grade Sup.																	X					X		X				X																						
Phys. Ed.		X	X				X	X				X	X				X	X		X								X																						
Manual Arts	X					X					X					X					X																													
Voc. Mech. Trades		X					X					X								X		X		X			X																X							
Art & Music																																																		
Total	2	8	8	2	5	2	9	10	2	2	4	9	10	2	2	5	10	11	8	2	4	10	6	9	2	5	8	8	6	3	4	6	9	6		3	6	8	6	5	3	5	9	7	4	3	4	5	8	10

* These curricula permit various combinations of majors and minors from principal academic fields.
K—Kirksville. W—Warrensburg. C—Cape Girardeau. S—Springfield. M—Maryville.

to the enlargement of the offerings of the college at Maryville. It is to be inferred from Table L that there is a strong tendency to offer a general curriculum with specialization provided for by a restricted choice of majors and minors. If the combinations of subjects are clearly specified and adequate provision made for the elements common to all curricula, this plan of differentiation is probably satisfactory; but it is more liable to maladministration than if it were difficult for students to transfer from one curriculum to another without loss of credit.

The number of curricula specified in the catalogue is less important than the extent to which there is actual differentiation in accordance with the predictable needs of the service. In Tables LI and LII following, an effort is made to show the extent and kind of differentiation in two colleges.

It is apparent from Table LI that only eight courses are common to all curricula and of this number five are fundamental courses in education. Practice teaching is differentiated according to the level of the work for which the student is preparing. Twelve courses appear in only one curriculum, eighteen appear in more than half of them, and sixteen appear in two-thirds or more of them. There are thirty-six different courses which are required in one or more curricula. The table does not include the majors and minors which are required in all curricula.

English is the only course that is common to all curricula represented in Table LII. Thirteen courses are common to half or more of the curricula. In some cases election is permitted within the field. Sixteen of the thirty-six courses appear in only one curriculum. Twelve specific courses are required in the curriculum for high school teaching, twenty-two for the primary curriculum, sixteen for the sixty-hour intermediate curriculum, and fourteen for the sixty-hour rural curriculum. The A.B. and B.S. curricula contain the least amount of prescribed work, but this is to be expected since they are without professional aim.

It is reasonable to conclude from an examination of these tables that there is a real differentiation of courses in the several curricula offered by the Missouri teachers colleges. In the prescribed work in education fundamental courses are common to all curricula and usually occur as the first work offered in

TABLE LI

SHOWING AMOUNT AND KIND OF DIFFERENTIATION IN 120-HOUR CURRICULA
DESIGNED TO PREPARE FOR DIFFERENT LEVELS OF TEACHING SERVICE
BASED ON PRACTICE AT SPRINGFIELD IN 1926

Subject	Kindergarten Primary	Intermediate	Upper Grade	Rural	Junior High School	High School	% of Curricula in Which the Course Appears
Intro. to Education	x	x	x	x	x	x	100
Ed. Psychology	x	x	x	x	x	x	100
Prin. Teaching	x	x	x	x	x	x	100
Observation	x	x	x	x	x	x	100
Primary Methods	x			x			32
Prac. Teaching*	x	x	x	x	x	x	100
Teach. Plays & Games ..	x						16
Kgn. Curriculum	x						16
Inter. Gr. Methods		x					16
Teach. El. Subj.		x	x	x	x		66
Upper Gr. Methods			x				16
Psych. Jr. H. S. Subj. ..					x		16
Junior H. S.					x		16
Hist. Education					x	x	33
Teach. Jr. H. S. Subj. ..					x		16
Teach. H. S. Subj.						x	16
Psych. H. S. Subj.						x	16
Eng. Composition	x	x	x	x	x	x	100
Children's Literature ...	x	x					33
Story Telling	x	x		x			50
Biology	x	x	x	x	x		83
Nature Study	x						16
American History	x	x	x	x	x		83
Sociology	x	x	x	x	x		83
Science (Gen.)	x	x	x	x	x	x	100
Geography		x	x	x	x		66
Gen. Mathematics		x	x	x	x		66
Word Study		x	x	x	x		66
Voice Training		x	x				33
Gen. Science			x		x		33
Home-Making				x			16
Agriculture				x			16
Foreign Language.......	x	x	x	x	x	x	100
Music	x	x	x	x			66
Indus. Art	x	x		x			50
Fine Arts	x	x					33
Elect.-Education........	x	x	x	x	x	x	100
Elect.-Academic	x	x	x	x	x	x	100
Elect.-Specials	x	x	x				50
Total Req. Courses ...	23	25	22	23	22	13	

"x" indicates that course is required.

* Differentiated according to curriculum.

TABLE LII

SHOWING AMOUNT AND KIND OF DIFFERENTIATION IN 120-HOUR CURRICULA LEADING TO DIFFERENT DEGREES AND FOR DIFFERENT TYPES OF SERVICE BASED ON THE PRINTED REQUIREMENTS OF WARRENSBURG IN 1926

Subject	B. S. in Ed. for H. S. Teachers	B. S. in Ed. for Primary Teachers	A. B.	B. S.	60-Hour Intermed. Teachers	60-Hour Rural Teachers	% of Curricula in Which the Course Appears
Ed. Psychology	x				x	x	50
Prin. Teaching	x				x	x	50
Hist. Education	x						16
Ed. Tests & Measurements	x	x					50
Observ. & Teaching	x	x			x	x	66
Elect. in Education	x						16
Primary Methods		x					16
Kindergarten Theory		x					16
Child Psychology		x					16
Mental Tests		x					16
Meth. in Gr. History		x			x	x	50
Teachers Arithmetic		x			x	x	16
Meth. in Phys. Education		x					16
El. Education					x	x	33
Methods in Art					x		16
Inter. Gr. Methods					x		16
Meth. in Music					x		16
Elect.-Tech. Subj.	x	x					33
Elect.-Economics	x	x					33
Foreign Language			x	x			33
Eng Composition	x	x	x	x	x	x	100
Juvenile Literature		x			x	x	50
American History					x	x	32
Elect.-History	x	x	x	x			65
Hygiene		x			x	x	33
Geography					x	x	33
Household Physics					x	x	33
Nature Study		x			x	x	50
Agriculture						x	16
Elect.-Science	x	x	x	x			66
Mathematics					x	x	33
Elect.-Mathematics	x	x	x	x			66
Industrial Arts		x					16
Fine Arts		x					16
Music		x					16
Child Welfare		x					16
Major	x	x	x	x			67
Minors	x	x	x	x			66
Free Electives	x	x	x	x	x	x	100

"x" indicates that the course is required.

the course. The differentiation in education is to be found in the courses in methods in subjects, or in methods for the different grade levels. Practice teaching is limited to the grade of work for which the curriculum is planned. The large number of specialized curricula for high school teaching emphasizes the attention given to the training of secondary teachers by Missouri teachers colleges. The fact that these specialized curricula have persisted in the catalogues for ten years indicates that there is a real demand in the colleges for them, or it reveals propaganda on the part of the colleges in behalf of the training of secondary teachers. It cannot be said, however, that they do not differentiate curricula or fail to offer complete and carefully planned courses for the training of elementary teachers. Until the public demands and is willing to pay for collegiate training beyond the junior college, it is not likely that many elementary teachers will avail themselves of the opportunities for more advanced training now afforded by the teachers colleges. So long as the teachers colleges actually train a majority of the high school teachers of the state, and so long as the schools look to them to provide such teachers in large numbers, it is their duty to make as adequate provision for training as possible and in so doing to see that they do not necessarily neglect the more important work of training elementary teachers. It has been demonstrated that the actual cost of teacher training is inversely proportional to the size of the student group.[53] As a matter of economy, would it not be desirable for the state to encourage many types of work in the teachers colleges with the idea of concentrating large numbers of students in a few centers? Is the training of high school teachers so radically different from the training of elementary teachers that the presence of both groups in the same school is mutually detrimental? Is not a prospective high school teacher more likely to get professionalized subject matter courses in a teachers college the entire energy of which is devoted to teacher training than he is in an arts college in which it is impossible to differentiate courses to suit the numbers of professional aims represented in the student personnel?

[53] Hamilton, *Fiscal Support of Teachers Colleges.*

If there are adequate appropriations for teachers colleges to maintain the necessary quantity of work for the training of high school teachers, there is no more valid argument for the opinion that prevails in some sections that the arts college should train the high school teachers than would apply with equal force for the training of elementary teachers. The Missouri teachers colleges in providing for the training of both elementary and secondary teachers are but serving the state in their legitimate fields of activity.

TABLE LIII

SHOWING THE NUMBER OF SEMESTER HOURS REQUIRED IN THE VARIOUS SUBJECTS FOR THE 60-HOUR CERTIFICATE FOR ELEMENTARY TEACHING AT KIRKSVILLE, FROM 1916 TO 1926

	1916	1917	1918	1919	1920	1921	1922	1923	1924	1925
Education ...	25	22.5	17.5	17.5	17.5	15	12.5[5]	15	12.5	12.5
English	7.5	7.5					5[5]	5[5]	7.5[5]	7.5
History	7.5	[2]7.5					5	5	7.5	5[4]
Science	7.5	[3]7.5					5[5]	5[5]	5	5[4]
Pol. Science .. or Sociology							2.5[5]	2.5[5]		2.5[4]
Public Health							2.5[5]	2.5[5]	2.5[5]	2.5[5]
Mathematics .							2.5[5]	2.5[5]	2.5[5]	5[4]
Latin							2.5[5]	2.5[5]		
Geography ...							2.5[5]	2.5[5]	2.5	2.5[4]
Lib. Econ. ...	2.5	2.5								
[1]Specials	5	5	5	5	5	5	7.5	7.5	5	5
Pref. Major ..			7.5	7.5	7.5	7.5				
Pref. Minor ..			5	5	5	5				
Phys. Educ. ..			2						2.5	
Electives.....	5	7.5	25	25	25	27.5	12.5	12.5	12.5	15

[1] Music and Art. [2] 2.5 hr. may be Political Science. [3] Half may be Mathematics.
[4] Choice of 5 hours. [5] Courses specified.

The third criterion for judging curricula states that the important fields of human knowledge should be represented in the student's training. The extent to which Missouri teachers colleges are meeting this standard is shown by Tables LIII to LVII.

TABLE LIV

Showing the Number of Semester Hours Required in the Various
Subjects for the 60-Hour Certificate for Elementary
Teaching at Warrensburg from 1916 to 1926

	1916	1917	1918	1919	1920	1921	1922	1923	1924	1925
Education ...	22.5	22.5	22.5	22.5	22.5	17.5	17.5	17.5	17.5	15
English	2.5	2.5	2.5	2.5	2.5	5	5	5	5	5
‡Group Elect.						15	15	15	15	15
†Tech. Subjects		5	5	5	5					
*General Electives	35	30	30	30	30	22.5	22.5	22.5	22.5	25

* Not more than 10 hr. from technical subjects.
† Requiring no preparation. Music. Art.
‡ Must include three five-hour courses selected from History, Mathematics, Physical Science, Biological Science, Languages, Economics, Technical Subjects.

TABLE LV

Same Data for Cape Girardeau from 1916 to 1926

	1916	1917	1918	1919	1920	1921	1922	1923	1924	1925
Education ...	18	18	18	19	19	19	16	16	16	16
English	6	6	6	6	6	6	6	6	6	6
History	6	6	6	6	6	6	6	6	6	6
Biology	6	6								
Physics or Chemistry ...	6	6								
Foreign Language									12	12†
Drawing	2	2	1.5							
Music	2	2	1.5	1.5	1.5					
Manual Arts .	2	2	1.5	1.5	1.5					
Science			12	12	12	12	6	6	6	6
Indust. Arts..				1.5	1.5					
Restricted Electives ..	12	12	13.5	13.5	13.5	11		12		
*Phys. Ed. ..	0	0	0	0	0	0				
Elect from Specials ...						6	4.5			
General Electives							21.5	14	8	8
Mathematics .									6	6

* Required without credit.
† Required unless 2 high school units are offered for entrance.

TABLE LVI

Showing the Number of Semester Hours Required in the Various Subjects for the 60-Hour Certificate for Elementary Teaching at Springfield from 1916 to 1926

	1916	1917	1918	1919	1920	1921	1922	1923	1924	1925
Education ...	27.5	25	25	22.5	22.5	22.5	22.5	22.5	22.5	22.5
English	5	5	5	5	5	5	5	5	5	5
Health	2.5	2.5	2.5							
Agri. or Home-Making ...		5	5	5	5	5	5	5	5	5
Geography ...		2.5	2.5	2.5	2.5	2.5	2.5	2.5	2.5	2.5
Sociology		2.5	2.5	2.5	2.5	2.5	2.5	2.5	2.5	2.5
Arithmetic ...		2.5	2.5							
Am. History .		2.5	2.5	2.5	2.5	2.5	2.5	2.5	2.5	2.5
Biology				2.5	2.5	2.5	2.5	2.5	2.5	2.5
Gen. Math. ..				2.5	2.5	2.5	2.5	2.5	2.5	2.5
Story Telling .				2.5	2.5	2.5	2.5	2.5	2.5	2.5
Word Study .				2.5	2.5	2.5	2.5	2.5	2.5	2.5
Specials		10	10	5	5	5	5	5	5	5
Electives	25	2.5	2.5	5	5	5	5	5	5	5

TABLE LVII

Showing the Number of Semester Hours Required in the Various Subjects for the 60-Hour Certificate for Elementary Teaching at Maryville from 1916 to 1926

	1916	1917	1918	1919	1920	1921	1923	1924	1925
Education	25	25	20	20	20.5	20	17.5	17.5	17.5
English	7.5	7.5	7	7	7.5	7.5	7.5	7.5	5
Home Economics ...	2.5	2.5	3	2.5					
Biology	2.5	2.5	3	2.5	2.5	2.5			
Geography	2.5	2.5	3	2.5	2.5	2.5			
Social Science			3		2.5	2.5			
History				2.5	2.5	2.5			
Commerce						2.5			
Phys. Education ...					3.75	2.5			
Health						2.5			
Specials			8	6	3.75	5	5	5	5
Electives	20	20	13	17	14.5	10	30	30	32.5

For the certificate for elementary teaching the colleges at Kirksville and Springfield require courses in English, History, Science, Sociology, Mathematics, Geography, Music and Art, thus bringing the student into contact with each of the larger fields except the foreign languages. It will be noted that Kirksville especially provides for an administration of the curriculum which takes into account the student's high school courses of study.

The teachers colleges at Warrensburg and Maryville permit electives in the elementary course but they must be chosen from groups representing the different fields of knowledge. The Cape Girardeau teachers college requires English, History, Science, and Mathematics in all curricula. Foreign language is required unless two high school units were submitted for entrance credit.

In the specialized curricula in all of the colleges the conditions

TABLE LVIII

Showing the Number of Semester Hours Required in the Various Subjects for the Degree of B.S. in Education at Kirksville from 1916 to 1926

	1916	1917	1918	1919	1920	1921	1922	1923	1924	1925
Education ...	30	30	25	25	25	25	25	25	25	25
English	7.5	7.5							7.5	7.5
History	7.5	†7.5							7.5	5‡
Science	12.5*	12.5*							5	5‡
Pol. Sci. and Sociology ..										2.5‡
Pub. Health .									2.5	2.5
Latin										
Geography ...									2.5	2.5‡
Mathematics .		5							2.5	5‡
Lib. Econ. ...	2.5	2.5								
Phys. Ed.			4						2.5	
Specials	5		5	5	5	5	5	5	5	5
Dept. Major .			22.5	22.5	22.5	22.5	22.5	22.5	22.5	22.5
1st Minor ...			15	15	15	15	15	15	15	15
2nd Minor ...			10	10	10	10	10	10	10	10
Electives	22	22	42.5	42.5	42.5	42.5	42.5	42.5	12.5	12.5

* Half may be Mathematics.
† 2.5 hr. may be Political Science.
‡ Specified substitutions in related fields are permitted.

of the third criterion are met, although the sixty-hour course does not permit of more than a few of the courses in each field and they are most general in nature.

It will be observed in Tables LVIII to LXII that the curricula of all of the colleges leading to the degree require some work in each of the fields of knowledge. Warrensburg accomplishes this end through the selection of courses from specified groups which must be chosen in addition to the majors and minors. On the whole, the Missouri teachers colleges meet the requirements of the third criterion rather satisfactorily.

TABLE LIX

SHOWING THE NUMBER OF SEMESTER HOURS REQUIRED IN THE VARIOUS SUBJECTS FOR THE DEGREE OF B.S. IN EDUCATION AT WARRENSBURG FROM 1916 TO 1926.

	1916	1917	1918	1919	1920	1921	1922	1923	1924	1925
Education ...	27.5	27.5	27.5	27.5	27.5	30	30	30	30	25
English	2.5	5	5	5	5	5	5	5	5	5
Major Subj. .	25	25	25	25	25	25	25	25	25	25
Minor Subj. .	10	10	10	15	15	15	15	15	15	15
*Group Elec-tives								15	15	15
General Elec-tives	55	52.5	52.5	47.5	47.5	45	45	30	30	35

* Must include three five-hour courses selected from History, Mathematics, Physical Science, Biological Science, Economics, Technical Subjects.

Although the teachers practically without exception claim to give a professional slant to their courses, the facts revealed by an examination of syllabi, catalogue descriptions, and class visits would not, by the greatest stretch of the imagination, justify the statement that the work in the actual class instruction is given a professional treatment such as is contemplated in our fourth criterion.[54] In this respect the Missouri teachers colleges, and for that matter teachers colleges throughout the country, are weakest. The situation is largely due to the fact that many ex-cellent teachers in teachers colleges are still of the opinion that no special treatment of subject matter for teachers is neces-

[54] See p. 111.

sary. They expect young teachers to be able to apply the principles they learn in the education courses in the selection of subject matter for their students and therefore leave the most difficult of all the teacher's problems for her to work out unaided. The almost total lack of textbooks written to exemplify this point of view has made it difficult for teachers who have little or no training in the professionalization of courses to make modifications in their syllabi which result in a professional treatment of the subject.

TABLE LX

SHOWING THE NUMBER OF SEMESTER HOURS REQUIRED IN THE VARIOUS SUBJECTS FOR THE DEGREE OF B.S. IN EDUCATION AT CAPE GIRARDEAU FROM 1916 TO 1926

	1916	1917	1918	1919	1920	1921	1922	1923	1924	1925
Education ...	24	24	24	24	24	24	24	24	24	24
English	6	6	6	6	6	6	6	6	6	6
History	6	6	6	6	6	6	6	6	6	6
Science			6	6	6	6	6	6	6	6
Mathematics..			6	6	6	6	6		6	6
*Foreign Language.......	12	12*	12*	12*	12*	12*	12*		12*	12*
Elect. from Courses of Jr. College Rank								14	8	8
†Restricted Electives....								12		
Biology	6	6								
Major Subj. .	24	24	24	24	24	24	24	24	24	24
1st Minor Subjects.....	12	12	12	12	12	12	12	12	12	12
2nd Minor Subjects.....	12	12	12	12	12	12	12	12	12	12
Elect. from Courses of Sr. College Rank									4	4
Free Electives	18	12	12	12	12	12	12	4		
Phys. Science.		6								

* Required unless 2 high school units are offered for entrance.
† According to level of grade teaching.

TABLE LXI

SHOWING THE NUMBER OF SEMESTER HOURS REQUIRED IN THE VARIOUS
SUBJECTS FOR THE DEGREE OF B.S. IN EDUCATION AT
SPRINGFIELD FROM 1916 TO 1926

	1916	1917	1918	1919	1920	1921	1922	1923	1924	1925
Education ...	35	35	35	30	30	30	30	30	30	30
English	5	5	5	5	5	5	5	5	5	5
History				5	5	5	5	5	5	5
Foreign Lang.				5	5	5	5	5	5	5
Mathematics .				5	5	5	5	5	5	5
Science				5	5	5	5	5	5	5
Major Subj. .	20	30	30	25	25	25	25	25	25	25
1st Minor ...	12.5	20	20	15	15	15	15	15	15	15
2nd Minor ...	7.5	20	20	15	15	15	15	15	15	15
*Phys. Ed. ...										
Free Elect. ..	37.5	10	10	10	10	10	10	10	10	10
Health	2.5									

* Required with or without credit.

TABLE LXII

SHOWING THE NUMBER OF SEMESTER HOURS REQUIRED IN THE VARIOUS
SUBJECTS FOR THE DEGREE OF B.S. IN EDUCATION AT
MARYVILLE FROM 1916 TO 1926

	1916	1917	1918	1919	1920	1921	1923	1924	1925
Education	30	30	25	25	25	25	25	25	27.5
English	7.5	7.5	8	7	7	7.5	7.5	7.5	5
*Foreign Language .	5	5	10	10	10	10	10	10	7.5
Social Sci. incl. Hist..					2.5	10	10	10	7.5
Phys. Science	5	5	8	7	7	7.5	7.5	7.5	7.5†
Mathematics			3	5	5	5	5	5	5
Biology	5	5	6	5	5	5	5	5	
Sanitation and Hy-giene	2.5	2.5				2.5	2.5	2.5	
History	5	5	6	7	7				
Specials	5	5	3	2	6.5	5	2.5	2.5	2.5
Major			24	24	24	24		15	15
Minor			12	15	15	15		10	10
Electives	55	55	15	17	6	3.5	45	20	32.5

* Required unless 2 units of entrance credit are offered.
† Physical and Biological.

The following table shows the number of catalogue descriptions of courses in Missouri teachers colleges which include any reference to the needs of the prospective teacher. In compiling this table if a single phrase was found that one would not expect to find in the description of the same course in an arts college, it was listed as having some professional bearing.

TABLE LXIII

SHOWING PERCENTAGE OF COURSES OFFERED AT REGULAR INTERVALS IN
VARIOUS DEPARTMENTS WHOSE CATALOGUE DESCRIPTIONS IN 1925
SHOW EVEN SLIGHT EVIDENCE OF PROFESSIONALIZATION

	Kirks-ville	Warrens-burg	Cape Girardeau	Spring-field	Mary-ville	All Schools
	%	%	%	%	%	%
English & Public Speaking	19	26	22	23	12	20
Mathematics	36	33	15	23	24	26
Science	22	20	18	14	10	19
Soc. & Pol. Science	26	9	4	10	6	11
Foreign Language	10	10	17	8	9	11
Agriculture	10	5	10	10	17	10
Household Arts ...	30	20	20	22	16	21
Phys. Ed. & Health	30	50	61	62	51	51
Art (Fine & Ind.)	20	− 1	18	41	52	24
Music	20	50	26	60	31	37

Although the greatest generosity was used in the selection of evidence of professionalization and the special methods courses were included in the list, it is very clear that there is little consciousness of the great need of a differentiated treatment of subject matter for teachers on the part of the teachers college faculties. The terminology has not even penetrated the backs of the catalogues, and the actual professional treatment of courses in the classroom is a long way off. Physical education and music rank highest in evidences of professionalization. Among the "academic" subjects mathematics ranks highest. Its high rank is due to the relatively small number of courses offered and the listing among them of at least one special methods course and usually a course in general mathematics. The Missouri teachers colleges should make their greatest progress during the next decade in the development of syllabi of courses which will "provide a scholarship relevant to the adaptations of subject matter the student must make in the instruction of children and pertinent to the functional point of view."

The types of training provided in Missouri teachers colleges may be roughly grouped under the headings of basic education and technical knowledge. The curricula imply the desirability of the acquisition of classroom skills, but little is done to assure the college that the prospective teacher is actually in possession of these skills when she is graduated. The amount of work done in the training schools is relatively meagre and is devoted largely to the teaching of a single subject. To be sure, the theory courses are rich in suggestions which form the background for the acquisition of these desirable skills. But skill implies not only knowledge; it implies also expertness in execution and performance. This expertness can be acquired only through practice of sufficient amount and variety.

Subject matter courses are designed for the development of general scholarship and differ little from the courses taught in the arts college. There is provision for limited contact with the training school. Consequently, the theory courses in the teachers colleges are given the impossible task of equipping the prospective teacher with technical knowledge, technical skills, general teaching ability including the reorganization of her college subject matter. At the same time there must be developed in each teacher the professional point of view upon which her success and the advancement of the profession depend. The following table shows the wide range of courses in education offered by the Missouri teachers colleges. A study of this table and a study of the curricula emphasize the importance of having definite analyses made of the teacher's "job" to the end of providing in the training courses for the positive acquisition of the equipment the teacher precisely needs. It is evident that the Missouri teachers colleges recognize the importance of the fifth criterion. They believe the curriculum should provide activities and materials which will strengthen the personal and social equipment of the students and put them in possession of the skills and controls known to be an essential part of the teacher's equipment. It is also evident that there is uncertainty as to these skills and the best way to provide for them.

TABLE LXIV

SHOWING NUMBER OF SEMESTER HOURS OF WORK OFFERED IN THE VARIOUS SUBJECTS IN THE DEPARTMENTS OF EDUCATION IN THE MISSOURI TEACHERS COLLEGES IN 1926

K—Kirksville, W—Warrensburg, C. G.—Cape Girardeau, S—Springfield, M—Maryville

	K.	W.	C. G.	S.	M.
Psychology (Gen.)				2.5	2.5
Educational Psychology	2.5	2.5	6	5	2.5
Adoles. Psychology	2.5	2.5	3		2.5
Child Psychology	2.5	2.5	3	2.5	2.5
Teach. Exceptional Children		2.5			
Psychol. Jr. H. S. Subj.				2.5	
Psychol. H. S. Subj.				2.5	
Psychol. Elem. Sch. Subj.				2.5	
Ed. Tests & Meas.	5	2.5	3	2.5	2.5
Mental Tests		2.5	3	2.5	2.5
Social Psychology			3		
Statistics					2.5
High School Problems	5	2.5		2.5	
Jr. High School	5	2.5	3	2.5	2.5
High Sch. Administration		2.5			2.5
Prin. Sec. Ed.			3		
Advisement of Girls			2		2.5
Social Control in H. S.					2.5
High School Methods					5
Principles Teaching	2.5	5	3	2.5	2.5
Primary Methods		2.5	3	5	2.5
Kindergarten Methods				2.5	
Kindergarten Curriculum				2.5	
Intermediate Grade Methods		2.5		2.5	2.5
Upper Grade Methods				2.5	
Grade Methods				5	
Teaching Jr. H. S. Subjects				7.5	
Elem. Education	5	2.5			
Kindergarten & Prim. Education .	5	2.5			
Kindergarten Theory		7.5			
Kindergarten Development					2.5
Primary Curriculum					2.5
Primary Supervision				2.5	

TABLE LXIV—(*Continued*)

	K.	W.	C. G.	S.	M.
Teaching Practical Supervision . . .			7.5		
Prac. Teach. in Elem. Sch.	7.5	5	7	7.5	2.5
Prac. Teach. in High Sch.	7.5	5		7.5	
Prac. Teach. in Rural Sch.				5	
Intro. to Education				2.5	2.5
Observation		5	6	2.5	2.5
Elem. & Jr. H. S. Curriculum				5	
County Sch. Organization				2.5	
Administration			3	2.5	2.5
Supervision		2.5	3	2.5	2.5
Primary Supervision					
School Surveys		2.5		2.5	
Elem. Course of Study		2.5			
Curriculum Construction		2.5			
School Adm. & Supervision	5				
Ed. Sociology	2.5	2.5	3		2.5
Ethics		2.5			
School Economy		2.5	3		2.5
Modern School Systems		2.5			
Child Welfare		2.5			
Public Education in U. S.			3		
Health Education					2.5
Rural Com. Activities				5	
Rural Observation					2.5
Adm. Rural Schools				2.5	
Supr. Rural Schools				2.5	
Rural Sch Methods				2.5	
Rural Health				2.5	
Rural Surveys				2.5	
Rural School Economy	2.5				
Rural Sociology	2.5				2.5
Rural Education	2.5		3		
Rural Sch. Adm. & Supervision . .	2.5	2.5	3		2.5
Consolidated School			3		2.5
Hist. Elem. Education				2.5	
Hist. Second. Education				2.5	
Hist. Education in U. S.		2.5		2.5	2.5
History Education	2.5		3	2.5	2.5
History Modern Elem. Education .		2.5			2.5

The Missouri teachers colleges arrange the courses in each curriculum with regard to sequence and continuity of thought units. Four of the five colleges specify prerequisites of courses in the catalogues, and students are not admitted to classes unless the prerequisites have been met. There may be exceptions in cases of special merit but on the whole the regulations are rigidly administered. It is obviously difficult in sixty-hour curricula to offer a wide range of work and at the same time provide for continuity of subject matter. The extent to which the colleges have observed this principle is shown in Table LXV based upon typical curricula in operation in Warrensburg and Springfield.

It will be observed that the departments of education and English arrange their work in sequence. While the student is working in the training school he is carrying related theory courses.

The work in the other departments is well arranged, except that the large number of fields to be covered in the short time forces the introduction of short units of work of a very general nature in some of the major departments.

Contact with the training school at more points, both in the courses in educational theory and in the academic courses, would strengthen the work. It would provide for the integration of theory and practice with the desirable effect of professionalizing the one and of placing the other on both a scientific and an artistic basis. The tables on pages 122 ff. show a decided tendency on the part of all of the colleges to prescribe most of the work accepted for the degree. According to the statements in the catalogues this prescribed work has been arranged with the idea of providing an organization of subject matter which is sequential and which preserves continuity of thought units.

The first term's work is identical in all the curricula in the Missouri teachers colleges. With one exception all the schools require a course in the introduction to teaching, which is designed to give the student an initial large view of the field of teaching and to acquaint him with a technical vocabulary. The content of this course is such that the student should be able to make an intelligent choice of curricula after completing the first term's work. The following table shows the amount of required and

TABLE LXV

SHOWING CONTINUITY AND SEQUENTIAL ARRANGEMENT OF REQUIRED COURSES
IN 60-HOUR INTERMEDIATE CURRICULA OF
MISSOURI TEACHERS COLLEGES IN 1926

SUBJECTS	1'ST. TERM	2'ND TERM	3'RD TERM	4'TH TERM	5'TH TERM	6'TH TERM
EDUCATION						
ELEM. EDUCATION	W					
INTRO. TO TEACHING	S	W				
ED. PSYCHOLOGY	S		W		S	
PRIN. TEACHING		S		W		
TEACHING AND OBS.			S	W S	W S	
METHODS			S	S	W	
ENGLISH						
COMPOSITION	W S					
COMPOSITION		W S				
LITERATURE			W S			
SCIENCE						
HYGIENE	W					
PHYSICAL			W			
AGRICULTURE					W	
NATURE						W
BIOLOGY					S	
SOCIAL SCIENCE						
HISTORY		W				W S
GEOGRAPHY			W S			
SOCIOLOGY					W	S
ECONOMICS					W	
MATHEMATICS						
GENERAL				W S		
SPECIALS	S					
ART		S			W	
MUSIC	S			W		
EXPRESSION		S		S		

LEGEND

W = WARRENSBURG   S = SPRINGFIELD
- - - - - - CONNECTS · SUBJECTS·IN·SEQUENTIAL · ORDER
————— CONNECTS · SUBJECTS WHICH · REPRESENT
          CONTINUOUS · THOUGHT · UNITS
▯ = SHOWS · SUBJECTS PARALLELED·BECAUSE·OF· RELATIONSHIPS

elective work in the sixty-hour and the one hundred twenty-hour curricula of the Missouri teachers colleges. It will be seen in the tables on pages 119 ff. that the amount of free election of courses has declined in the last few years. This is particularly true of the curricula which lead to degrees.

TABLE LXVI

SHOWING PERCENTAGE OF REQUIRED AND ELECTIVE COURSES IN 60-HOUR AND 120-HOUR CURRICULA IN MISSOURI TEACHERS COLLEGES IN 1926

	Kirksville		Warrensburg		Cape Gir.		Springfield		Maryville	
	60 hr.	120 hr.	60 hr.	120 hr.	60 hr.	120 hr.	60 hr.	120 hr.	60 hr.	120 hr.
	%	%	%	%	%	%	%	%	%	%
Required ...	75	50	34	27	66	47	92	46	46	53
*Major & Minor		40		33		40		46		20
Free Electives	25	10	41	30	13	3	8	8	54	27
Restricted Electives			25	100	20	10				

* Students are permitted to choose majors and minors and may elect courses within the fields of specialization.

According to the eighth criterion, the reduction in the number of courses in education may be regarded as an index to the amount of professionalization in the subject matter courses. Since the amount of theoretical education has not been decreased in ten years [55] we have further evidence that there is little such professionalization of courses in Missouri teachers colleges. Attention has been called to the fact that in all of the colleges orientation courses in education are followed by parallel courses in theory and practice and that independent practice teaching comes late in the course and is followed by courses which give opportunity for integration. In this respect the Missouri teachers colleges satisfy the requirements of the eighth criterion.

The prominent characteristics of the curricula of Missouri teachers colleges in 1926 may be summarized as follows:

[55] See pp. 122 ff.

1. The Missouri teachers colleges offer differentiated curricula of sufficient number and variety to meet the demands made upon them.

2. Carefully planned and well-administered curricula afford an opportunity for specialization in secondary teaching.

3. All curricula require students to come in contact with the important fields of human knowledge, but the sixty-hour curricula contain short general courses in most of the major subjects.

4. Very few of the courses offer a professional treatment of subject matter. They provide a general scholarship no more suited to the needs of teachers than to the needs of students without professional aim. It is here that the greatest weakness of the Missouri teachers colleges is to be found.

5. Although training school facilities have improved greatly in recent years in Missouri teachers colleges, limited use is made of them. The amount of practice teaching required in no case exceeds seven and one-half semester hours. The subject matter courses are entirely independent of the training school, and students are graduated without having had opportunity to acquire and demonstrate the possession of the skills necessary for effective teaching.

6. As a rule, courses are arranged with respect to sequential relationship.

7. All curricula require broad introductory courses in education and very little unrestricted election is permitted.

8. The teachers colleges require from twenty-five to thirty semester hours in education for the degree. The plan of organization is: (1) general introductory courses; (2) parallel theoretical and practice courses; (3) independent practice teaching, and (4) integration courses.

PART IV

CURRICULA OF 1926 IN COMPARISON WITH CURRICULA OF 1915

The summary in this section shows the modifications that have been made in the curricula of Missouri teachers colleges since 1915. In the preceding sections of this chapter the details of the curricula and their administration were pointed out; hence only the conclusions developed there are restated at this point.

1. In 1915, due to the loose administration of the regulations, students were admitted to college classes in Missouri normal schools without regard to prerequisites in subjects or the amount of credit. The practice resulted in an unfortunate mixing of students with varying interests and degrees of ability to do the work. In 1926 all students must submit at least fifteen units of secondary credit for entrance to any college classes and for individual courses additional prerequisites must be met. Students are carefully classified as to their fitness for the work to be done, classes are homogeneous as to advancement and aims, and, consequently, the work is on a higher plane of excellence than was possible in 1915.

2. Students are not admitted except at the beginning of terms, thus preventing the wasteful repetition of courses and disorganized class work that was common in 1915. At the middle of the spring term some of the colleges organize new classes for students who desire to enter at this time.

3. Differentiated curricula were offered in 1915 as well as in 1926 but in 1915 they were simply large program patterns. Now they are definitely prescribed courses of study, allowing few free electives and admitting few substitutions.

4. The uniformity in the requirements in fundamental subjects among the different colleges indicates a general policy in curriculum making and is in interesting contrast to the situation with all of its variation in 1915.

5. Little progress has been made in the professionalization of subject matter in the ten-year period. It is probable that in 1915, with the students very close to their "jobs" and in need of immediate help, the courses were more nearly presented from a professional point of view than they are now.

6. Since 1915 four of the colleges have built or rebuilt training school buildings and are much better prepared to offer adequate laboratory opportunities than they were in 1915. The lack of coördination between the practical and theory departments that existed in 1915 has entirely disappeared, and if a more generous

use were made of the training school plants, there would be little to criticize.

7. In 1915 so little attention was paid to sequence of courses and so much to the student's immediate welfare that the curricula of individual students became a haphazard arrangement of miscellaneous subjects. In 1926 the courses in the curricula are prescribed in the order in which they must be taken by the student. With this plan a sequential organization is possible.

8. In 1915 students were graduated upon the presentation of the required amount of credit without regard to the degree of advancement represented. In 1926 at least forty per cent of the work must be of senior college rank.

9. In 1915 most of the schools required at least twenty-five hours of education but did not limit the amount that would be accepted. In 1926 students cannot offer more than thirty hours in education and not more than forty hours from any other department. This regulation forces a distribution of work among the departments, prevents too narrow specialization, and guarantees at least ninety hours of work in the subject matter fields.

PART V

COMPARISON OF PRESENT PRACTICES WITH THE PROPOSALS OF THE SURVEY COMMISSION, AND ADDITIONAL PROPOSALS

In this section the curricula in Missouri teachers colleges in 1926 and their administration are studied in comparison with the proposals of the survey commission.

Proposal 1.
The minimum standard of admission to all professional teaching curricula should be the requirement of graduation from an approved four-year secondary school, or its equivalent by examination; this standard should be fixed at once. Service as teacher in a public school without recognized professional training of collegiate character should be made impossible.

High school graduation is required for entrance to college classes in the teachers colleges, but it is possible for teachers to be certificated in the state without having professional training of collegiate character.

Proposal 2.

A schedule of progressive increase in residence requirements should be established. The expressed goal of this program should be, in effect, an identical residence requirement for all public school teachers from the first to the twelfth grade, urban and rural alike,—a requirement of four school years of organized professional preparation of collegiate character.

A residence requirement of at least three terms is made by all the colleges for any of the certificates. Four-year curricula are offered for teachers preparing for elementary teaching and for those preparing for secondary teaching, but it is still possible for elementary teachers to obtain life certificates at the end of the second year of the college course. Comparatively few teachers who expect to teach in the elementary school meet the requirements for degrees, because the school boards fail to recognize the advanced training; but the number is increasing and some of the city schools of the state are approaching a salary schedule which will give equal pay for equal training and service regardless of the level of the teachers' work.

Proposal 3.

In order to make possible a standard admission and residence requirement for professional curricula in the case of women, the profession of teaching should be made attractive to them throughout the state as a permanent life career. Their marriage should not be considered as a bar to such service, but rather as an added qualification.

Only a few schools in Missouri admit to the teaching corps married women and unmarried women on the same basis, and perhaps none of the school boards look upon marriage as an additional element in training. The reason most frequently assigned for the refusal to employ married women is that they no longer need employment since they have husbands to support them. This is only another way of saying that the public schools offer the city's most refined method of taking care of its charity. Training and ability to do the work should be the first considerations, and the need of employment on the part of an applicant should at all times be subordinate to them.

Proposal 4.

After a brief period of orientation and self-discovery on common ground, all professional curricula should, in the interests of the public service, have in view definitely distinguished positions, to the preparation for which their entire resources may contribute. In so far as formulated disciplines exist that clearly promote skill and power in the given position, the principle of free or group election should give place to prescriptive sequences prepared by experienced observers. In the longer curricula, where reasoned equivalence may be secured, or is a matter of indifference, option may be allowed, but the greatest possible effectiveness of the teacher in the position chosen should be the first consideration throughout.

Practically all curricula prescribe courses. Free election is the exception and not the rule.

Proposal 5.

The differentiation of curricula according to the position in view, a principle already partly recognized for primary and high school teachers, should be completely worked out, and should be applied as well to the middle and upper grades, and to the work of school administration.

This proposal is fully met by all the colleges.

Proposal 6.

Curricula of collegiate grade that have for their purpose the preparation of teachers should be professionalized throughout in the sense that every course should be chosen with specific reference to the contribution that it makes to the teacher's equipment. This would, by definition, include courses of a distinctly liberal type.

Professionalization of courses has not proceeded very far in the ten years. Perhaps the greatest accomplishment in this direction has been in the changed attitude of the faculty toward it. Nothing is in the way now for great progress along this line except the ability of the teachers to make the desired modifications in their work.

Proposal 7.

The focal characteristic of every such curriculum should be participation in the actual work of teaching; consequently the training school should be looked upon and administered as the central feature of the normal school organization.

In time allotment the training schools in Missouri teachers colleges still occupy a subordinate position in the scheme of teacher training. The attitude of the staffs toward the training school is non-critical, but the curricula do not require that a large amount of the student's time be devoted to work in which the training school plays an important part.

Proposal 8.

No professional curriculum for teachers should look exclusively toward the development of specific skill in teaching. It should aim as well to make the teacher professionally intelligent: competent to coöperate in the construction of large educational plans and policies, or at least to measure the full significance of constructive proposals. This broader aim of ensuring professional intelligence will naturally receive greater emphasis in the longer curricula, but it should find a definite expression even in the briefest preparation.

The education courses are planned with the idea of giving the student professional intelligence and are probably on a par with the best practice in the country in this respect.

Proposal 9.

The so-called "professional" courses—psychology, the history of education, principles of teaching, school management, practice teaching, and the like—should be judged not only by the extent to which they increase specific skill in classroom procedure, but also by their contribution to the broader professional intelligence and insight of the teacher. In connection with the latter aim, the claims of biology, sociology, and economics should be considered as well as those of the professional courses now recognized as such.

Catalogue descriptions, syllabi, and conferences with teachers confirm the opinion that the professional courses are rich in their "contribution to the broader professional intelligence of the teacher."

There is no evidence that biology is being given a professional treatment which makes it a serviceable course for the educational courses. As a matter of fact, it usually occurs in the curriculum after the introductory course in psychology and cannot be of any assistance to it. Sociology is generally recognized as having a more direct bearing upon the field of education than many other subject matter courses and is admitted in some of the Missouri teachers colleges as a part of an educational major.

Proposal 10.

The sequence of professional work should represent a progression from the concrete courses that deal primarily with classroom procedure to the more abstract summarizing and systematic courses. The latter consequently will appear at or near the end, and will be elaborated most fully in the longer curricula.

The education courses in the main are arranged in accordance with this principle.[56]

Proposal 11.

A general course in "pure" psychology is of doubtful value as an introduction to professional study. The introductory course should deal rather with the concrete applications of psychology to teaching (educational psychology) leaving the more abstract course in psychology until later. All courses should exemplify and expressly emphasize the psychological principles which they involve.

In only one college is pure psychology given as the introductory course in education. The other colleges require introductory courses in educational psychology, and if pure psychology is offered at all it is elective for students who do not expect to teach and is not regarded as a professional course.

Proposal 12.

A general course in the history of education is probably out of place in one-year or two-year curricula. Such a course, however, should serve an important purpose in one of the later years of the longer curricula. Most courses would gain both in force and coherence by briefly tracing the development in their own practice. These partial glimpses should then be gathered firmly into a complete picture by a systematic course in educational development as a whole.

Only one college lists a junior college course in the history of education and in none is it required for the elementary certificate. Under the terms of the conference agreement the required course which comes late as an integrating course in most of the curricula is "History and Principles of Education."

Proposal 13.

The courses generally known as principles of teaching (general method) and school management will yield the best results if associated closely with the work in participation and practice teaching.

In all of the teachers colleges courses in principles of teaching

[56] See pp. 109, 131.

immediately precede or parallel the courses in observation and practice teaching. School economy or management either appears juxtaposed with teaching or is taught as a part of the work in practice teaching.

Proposal 14.

As far as possible, the distinction between courses in "special methods of teaching" and courses in the subject matter itself should be eliminated. Every professional curriculum should embody thorough courses of distinctly collegiate character in all of the subject matter that the student proposes to teach. In these courses the specific organization of materials for elementary or secondary teaching should be fully discussed, and the approved methods of teaching should be both exemplified and justified. All teachers of the so-called academic subjects should hold a direct and responsible relationship to the training school.

The courses in Missouri teachers colleges in the subject matter departments are not professionally treated.

Proposal 15.

In each specific curriculum, a course that aims to organize and integrate the work of that field for which the curriculum prepares (primary teaching, intermediate grade teaching, junior high school teaching, and so forth) should be offered in the final year.

Three of the five colleges meet this proposal fully. The other two have courses for primary teachers of the type described but do not offer courses especially for the intermediate and upper grade teachers.

Proposal 15.

The importance of the training school in the scheme of curriculum construction above outlined suggests—

(a) Much more extensive training-school facilities than most normal schools now provide; intimate and to some extent controlling relations should be developed with the local public school system.

(b) Control by the normal school of the principal school or schools in which students serve as teachers for practice. This should not preclude a supplementary use of other schools for apprentice-teaching.

(c) A recognition of the status of the supervisor and critic teacher as equal or superior to that of the "academic" teacher.

(d) The unification of the headship of the education department with the direction of the training school and of practice teaching in one person.

(e) The safeguarding of the interests of training-school pupils by permitting not more than three-fourths and preferably not more than one-half of the teaching to be done by student-teachers.

(f) The provision of a separate school for experimental purposes, and the limitation of the training school to practice teaching and teaching for purposes of demonstration.

(g) The employment of teachers of educational theory and teachers of "academic" subjects as supervisors of teaching under the general control of the director of training.

(h) A systematic gradation of the work in observation, participation, group-teaching, and responsible room-teaching.

All of the teachers colleges in Missouri now have ample facilities for practice teaching. Two of the colleges use the local school systems to supplement the campus schools.

All of the questionnaires submitted by the teachers state that the training school staff has equal recognition with the other members of the faculty. The apparent fact that in some of the colleges the same preparation is not demanded of them as is demanded of other teachers would lead one to doubt the statements, but there is evidence that many of the training school teachers have been carried over from an older regime.

Although the most cordial relationship now exists between the departments of education and the training school staffs in all of the colleges, only one of them has lodged the headship of the department of education and the directorship of practice teaching in the same individual.

Proposal 16(a) is fully met by all of the colleges. At least a fourth of the teaching is done by trained teachers.

The training schools are limited to practice teaching and demonstration. None of the colleges are doing much work in the field of experimentation in the training schools.

In most instances all of the supervision of practice teaching is done by the critic teachers. The "academic" teachers take little or no part in it.

All of the colleges provide for the gradation of observation, participation, and practice teaching. The size of the units and the plan of the work vary in the different colleges and all of them could probably carry the gradation a few steps further with profit.

Proposal 17.

In each collegiate curriculum of two years or more, a term or a semester should be left after the period of responsible room-teaching, for the summarizing courses mentioned above.

This proposal is met as to arrangement of courses, but the final course does not always provide as well as might be desired for the summarizing of principles and the integration of all of the preceding courses.

Proposal 18.

Each prescribed professional curriculum should have in view the symmetrical development of an individual's knowledge and skill as required for an analyzed purpose. It is not a mere series of independent courses juxtaposed by title. It is rather one complex, carefully devised tool operated by different instructors to a common end. Its success depends upon the extent to which these instructors, by constant study, conference, and mutual criticism, learn to reënforce and supplement each other in the content of their teaching. Differences should be worked out in advance or omitted. Each curriculum should constitute a harmoniously interrelated body of instruction progressively directed toward a definite result that is clearly understood by all.

Although job analyses have not been made to determine the knowledge and skill required by the teacher, the curricula of the Missouri teachers colleges are arranged in accordance with generally accepted practice and probably rank among the best in the country. The complexity of the problem and the necessity for coöperation among all of the teachers who participate in the training of the student are recognized; but in practice the instruction is given more or less independently and without the interrelation which conferences and mutual criticism would indicate.

Proposal 19.

The present administration of the curricula in the Missouri normal schools is wasteful and ineffective, due to duplication of classes, to an extravagant elective system, and to the complete lack of the intercollegiate differentiation of specialized curricula. Differentiation and concentration of prescribed curricula in accordance with the previously ascertained needs of the state are suitable remedies for the existing situation.

The conditions of this proposal have been fully met by Missouri teachers colleges, so far as the work in individual institutions is concerned. The elective system is no longer an

extravagant one and differentiation and concentration of prescribed curricula are to be found in all of the colleges. There
is only incidental intercollegiate differentiation, and in the opinion
of the Conference of Educational Institutions such differentiation
is not now desirable.

The proposals resulting from this study regarding the curricula
of Missouri teachers colleges in 1926 can be grouped under three
general headings: Curricula Construction, Professional Treatment of Subject Matter, and the Training School as a Phase of
the Curricula. In the proposals concerning the future work of
the Conference of Educational Institutions in Missouri it is suggested that the Conference should devote itself unceasingly to
the problem of improving the curricula. Here attention will

TABLE LXVII

SHOWING EXTENT TO WHICH MISSOURI TEACHERS COLLEGES IN 1926 HAVE
MET THE REQUIREMENTS IN THE PROPOSALS OF THE SURVEY COMMISSION
IN 1915

Pro-posal	Subject	Page	Extent to Which It Has Been Met
1	Admission	136	Fully met
2	Residence requirement and length of course	136	Partially met
3	Married women as teachers	136	Not met
4	Differentiated curricula	137	Fully met
5	Differentiated curricula	137	Fully met
6	Professional treatment of subject matter	137	Only slightly met
7	Practice teaching	138	Partially met
8	Broad aim of professional curricula	138	Met
9	Broad educational courses and profes-sional treatment of other courses	138	Partially met
10	Sequence of courses	139	Met
11	Pure psychology omitted	139	Partially met
12	History of education	139	Fully met
13	Principles and practice	140	Met
14	Professionalized subjects	140	Only slightly met
15	Courses in different fields	140	Met
16	Training school	140	Partially met
17	Summarizing courses	142	Met
18	Faculty coöperation in curricula	142	Partially met
19	Administration of curricula	142	Fully met

be given to proposals relative to the professional treatment of subject matter and to the improved use of the training school.

Proposal 1.

All courses comprising the curricula of Missouri teachers colleges, while providing for breadth, depth, and newness of subject materials, must through the selection of content, the introduction of method, and the integration of the two provide a scholarship relevant to the adaptations in subject matter the student must make in the instruction of children, and pertinent to the functional point of view.

The principle is not new and has been subscribed to in theory by many of the teachers in Missouri teachers colleges for some time. It is our purpose to suggest a plan for the accomplishment of the desired reorganization of courses. Basic to any such plan may be stated the following principles and conditions:

1. The reorganization of the content of courses so as to emphasize the functional point of view in a teachers college must be a coöperative undertaking involving all of the departments of the college. It should, therefore, be attempted as a matter of institutional policy which has the intelligent and enthusiastic support of a large majority of the staff.

2. In the absence of textbooks and syllabi prepared from this point of view, the reorganization of courses will be a process extending over a long period of time and will depend more for its success upon the carefulness and thoroughness with which it is done than upon the speed.

3. Redundant as it seems, there is quite as much need for the professionalization of courses in education as in other departments.

4. In order to avoid duplication of work, education courses which are largely service courses should be reorganized to supplement and prepare for the professionalized subject matter courses.

5. Curricula should be arranged so as to provide a sequential relationship between education and subject matter courses and among the subject matter courses themselves.

6. The arrangement of courses must take into account the fact that professionalized subject matter courses will make use of the training school and provide for a proper distribution.

7. It is desirable to begin the working over of courses with those that are most obviously directly helpful to prospective teachers.

8. It must be understood that the treatment of subjects professionally does not weaken them in their ability to provide a broad scholarship and general culture.

9. Since the content of courses is to be determined by the actual needs

of teachers a prerequisite to their reorganization is a positive knowledge of those needs.

10. If numbers justify it classes should be differentiated for training students and those who do not have professional aim. If numbers do not justify such differentiation the presence of a few non-professional students should not modify the plans of the course in the least.

11. Professionalized courses cannot be taught by teachers of less preparation than is ordinarily considered desirable for arts courses in the same field. They should not only be specialists in their fields but, in addition, they should be masters of educational theory and practice.

12. As a corollary to the eleventh principle it should be stated that it will require the best teachers of the staff to professionalize the content and classroom presentation of their courses.

A proposed plan of procedure in the professionalization of subject matter for Missouri teachers colleges follows:

1. Appoint a committee of each faculty to assist the librarian in assembling all of the available literature on the subject.

2. Arrange for a series of faculty meetings in each college in which there will be a free discussion of the following topics: (a) An analysis of present course content. (b) Is there need for a modification of the content of courses in subject matter fields for teachers? (c) Can the subject matter needs of prospective teachers be anticipated without weakening the academic value of courses? (d) Should a reorganization of the content of courses be undertaken by the college faculty with the idea of treating them from the professional point of view?

3. Stenographic reports of the discussions of each faculty should be sent to all other faculties.

4. This discussion should continue until there is a large and enthusiastic majority of the teachers on record as heartily favoring the plan. If this cannot be accomplished there is no use to pursue the plan further.

5. Since the work is of such paramount importance, either the entire faculties of the colleges or a large representation from each should be called into a conference for the purpose of developing the principles which will control the selection of subject matter and all other elements involved in the construction of syllabi. This conference should probably last for two days. During the first morning session the issues should be presented by the best experts in the field. The afternoon should be devoted to departmental meetings for the purpose of organizing for the work and the discussion of principles. Questions growing out of these sessions should be brought together at a meeting in the evening for general discussion and the expression of expert opinion. The next day should be devoted to the perfection of the principles by departments.

6. All sets of principles should be assembled, mimeographed, and dis-

tributed to all departments and a general committee should organize them into a working whole to be presented to all of the faculties for approval.

7. In the meantime analyses of the needs of teachers in the different levels of teaching should be made. This work can be divided among the different colleges and can include an analysis of courses of study, textbooks, teachers' reported difficulties, and a study of training school classes.

8. With this body of guiding principles and the results of the analysis of the teacher's needs, each department in each school should undertake the preparation of an elaborate and detailed syllabus of its fundamental course, preferably the course required for the elementary certificate.

9. After syllabi have been completed they should be exchanged for mutual criticism, and then revised.

10. One of the most capable representatives of each group should be chosen to edit the syllabi and bring them together into a well-organized course or text. Time from other school duties should be allowed for this work.

11. The course should be taught in each of the schools by one of the best teachers on the staff and at a time when all of the members of the staff can be present. The syllabi can then be revised in the light of student reaction and expert criticism, after which they will doubtless be safe for use.

This proposed plan will take at least a full year for its completion; it will not only result in the preparation of a syllabus for the most important course in each department but it will also accomplish the following almost equally important results: (a) The work will serve as a stimulus to every member of the faculty to improve his own teaching; (b) each teacher will have a better grasp of his subject matter and method than ever before; (c) a pattern will have been provided for the professionalization of all other courses; (d) a splendid year of in-service training will have been carried on. Only slight modification would be necessary to adapt the plan to an individual school if the more general coöperation is not possible.

Since 1915 the training school facilities of all of the teachers colleges in Missouri have been improved both as to housing and in the number of students enrolled. Three schools have built and one has rebuilt training school buildings, which are models in arrangement and equipment. The fifth plans such a building in the near future and in the meantime has a satisfactory arrangement with the city schools for practice teaching. There is much evidence that these improved training facilities are not used as generally as their important part in the training plan warrants; hence the following proposals are added.

Proposal 2.

The amount of required practice teaching in the sixty-hour curriculum should be increased. This can be done by the reduction of the amount of work required in theory courses whose content can be provided for in the training school courses and the professionalized subject matter courses.

Proposal 3.

Students should begin their training school work early in the course through directed observation and participation in the more simple phases of classroom procedure, and, through the introduction of units of work, graded as to difficulty, should undertake responsible class teaching late in the course.[57]

Proposal 4.

The training school should be so administered as to make it desirable and necessary for each member of the teachers college staff to have a connection with the training school which will be of the greatest mutual benefit.

In carrying out this proposal the following suggestions grouped under six headings will be helpful:

1. Administration

   a. The director of practice teaching should be coördinate with or actually occupy the headship of the department of education.

   b. As the responsible officer of the training school he should be given full authority. He should be the chief coördinating officer among the supervisors, faculty of education, and faculty of academic subjects.

   c. Members of the teachers college faculty, who can render a distinct service in the work, should constitute an advisory council for the director of training schools. The director as chairman of the council should be the final authority in the determination of the policies of the training school.

   d. The director and his staff of supervisors are directly responsible for conducting observation courses and doing demonstration teaching.

   e. Responsibility for all phases of the work of the training school should be definitely placed in order to avoid misunderstandings and neglect.

2. Supervision

   a. All of the members of the college staff should participate in the supervision of practice teaching. The following plans are suggestive of the possibilities:

[57] Wilson, *Training Departments of Normal Schools.*

1) Subject matter teachers may be assigned a certain part of the actual supervision of the student's teaching and be held responsible for grading the student's work.

2) Conferences of students, supervisors, and college teachers may be held at intervals.

3) Subject matter teachers may be held responsible as the students' advisers regarding teaching materials and their use in the classroom.

3. Teaching

a. Members of the college instructional staffs who by temperament, training, and experience are able to do it effectively, should actually teach classes in the training school. This teaching should be for demonstration for the benefit of classes in observation, for the testing of materials and methods, or as an element in the supervision of the practice teacher.

b. Subject matter teachers may assist in planning demonstration lessons, be present when they are taught, and participate in the discussions.

4. Experimentation

a. The training school should be available for the performance of simple experiments made by teachers in connection with the professionalization of their courses.

5. Tests and Surveys

a. In connection with the professional treatment of subject matter courses tests should be given in the training school.

b. As occasion permits, subject matter teachers and their classes should participate in making surveys in the training school.

6. Curriculum Construction

a. Provision should be made for all of the teachers on the staff of the teachers college to assist in the study and construction of the curriculum of the training school.

CHAPTER V

RELATIONSHIP AMONG STATE EDUCATIONAL INSTITUTIONS

THE SITUATION IN 1915

"At the time of their establishment the responsible oversight of the state normal schools [in Missouri] was lodged with a single board of regents."[1]. The promoters of the movement "evidently thought of the work of these schools as the same throughout; duplication was resorted to for the sake of geographical convenience, but a single aim was to be defined and attained by a single management."[2] Vicissitudes came early as "serious opposition was aroused in the agitation over location."[3] Objections were raised to the single board.[4] Most of the criticism came from districts in the state which "felt that they might obtain a school more readily if all schools were locally controlled than if they had to deal with a centralized management. . . . The old plan gave way in 1874 and was followed by the present system—a board for each school consisting of the state superintendent *ex officio* and six others."[5]

The educational leaders during this early period in the history of Missouri normal schools keenly felt the desirability of educational unity among the schools, as is shown in the summary of the attempts to bring it about.

In 1874, in view of the dissolution of the central board that was just then taking place, President Baldwin of Kirksville urged a joint committee of presidents to pass upon applications for graduation,[6] doubtless with the idea that this would also help to keep the schools together. In his next report he pleads for "unity of plan, harmony of action, and hearty coöperation"[7] among all the state institutions. President Cheney of Cape Girardeau, in his report of the same year, put first among his needs "the same course or courses of study for all these schools,"

---

[1] Carnegie Bul. No. 14, p. 42.　[2] *Ibid.*, p. 42.　[3] *Ibid.*, p. 42.　[4] *Ibid.*, p. 42.
[5] *Ibid.*, p. 43.　[6] *State Report*, 1874, p. 45.　[7] *State Report*, 1875, p. 188.

and "the same conditions of graduation in all."[8]   All these
desiderata were secured by Superintendent Shannon through conference, and for ten years the joint board of presidents that
President Baldwin had suggested went from school to school as an
effective body for educational control.   The result was marked;
President Osborne of Warrensburg declared: "The value of these
measures in bringing about unity in the normal work can
scarcely be overestimated.   The tendency of a common course
of study towards this end is at once apparent"; and he saw in
it a "means of annually comparing results and thus promoting
a generous rivalry."[9]   But a union held only by this voluntary
personal tie was bound to dissolve as the individuals changed,
and the schools drifted apart.   Not until 1899 did they succeed
in bringing about another common course of study.   In 1904 they
united, with important reservations on the part of Kirksville, in
essential administrative arrangements, and corrected these again
in 1914; the important agreement of 1916 will be mentioned
later.

These occasional seasons of harmony—all voluntary and occurring only when the situation had become bad—were, however, merely incidents in long periods of marked divergence.
In fact, since 1899 attempts to unite on a curriculum have been
abandoned entirely, and each institution has been busy following the particular vision of its own leader, who calls the procedure "meeting local conditions," or "developing the genius of
the institution," or "satisfying the demands of the people," or
"upholding democracy in education," as the case may be.[10]

The members of the Carnegie survey staff in 1915 found a
"lack of unity in policies affecting the whole state" which impressed them as being worse than deplorable.   The only unify-
ing factor was the state superintendent of schools, himself an
elective officer, with little authority, and, in the opinion of some
of the incumbents of the office, isolated from the normal schools
and relatively without influence.   Each school was "a law unto
itself" and worked solely "in its own interest."   Legislative
appropriations were dependent upon the political influence of
men interested in the individual schools and money was doled

[8] *State Report*, 1875, p. 195.
[9] *State Report*, 1878, p. 283.
[10] Carnegie Bul. No. 14, p. 44.

out "where personal or sectional pressure was the greatest" and without regard to institutional problems and needs. This situation naturally created jealousy and hard feeling. It has even been claimed that one school would argue against the request for appropriations of another in order that it might succeed in accomplishing its own program. There is no positive proof of this statement, however, and it is doubtless an exaggeration, at least so far as the responsible officers of the schools were concerned. Educational diversity in terminology, standards, records, curricula content, graduation requirements, organization, and practices was great. "The real weakness in the situation," according to the Survey Commission, was "the loss to each institution of the tonic effect that would follow were it obliged to keep its practice overhauled under the critical eyes of competent outsiders either from other schools or from the state department." [11]

While this type of "rivalry" existed among the normal schools they were "relatively non-competitive by reason of their districting." [12] The disadvantages which it brought about were accentuated "in the active friction and lack of adjustment between the five normal schools on the one hand and the state university on the other." [13] This friction was usually the outgrowth of the question of recognition of credit, the university declining to accept hour for hour the work submitted by graduates of the normal schools.[14] It is not surprising, in view of these conditions, that the survey commission strongly recommended a complete reorganization of control of the state institutions based upon a principle of centralization, coördination and coöperation.

RECOMMENDATION OF THE SURVEY COMMISSION

The rather elaborate plan of reorganization involved an appointive state board of education to have control of all the state schools, a commissioner of education to be appointed by the state board with definite authoritative relationship to the state schools, and a reorganization of the university to include the normal schools as integral colleges of the university devoting their energies to the training of teachers. But the feature of the

[11] Carnegie Bul. No. 14, pp. 49-51.
[12] *Ibid.*, p. 51.
[13] *Ibid.*
[14] *University of Missouri Bulletin*, Vol. 25, No. 1, p. 31.

reorganization which concerns us here was the provision for a professional board of executives which is described in the words of the survey commission in the following paragraphs:

The plan suggested would at once make it possible to consolidate all of the state's teacher-training agencies under one educational direction, as well as under a single formal government. With this in view the affairs of these five colleges, together with the university school of education, should be placed under the direction of a new board consisting of the heads of these six units, with whom should sit also the president or chancellor of the university and the state superintendent of public schools. This board would constitute not merely the responsible authority for the management of certain institutions; it would be a board of expert men in complete charge of the preparation and supply of all teachers for the state, and the regulation of such lateral interests as the high school training classes in their professional aspects should be under its control. Its decisions would be reported to the board of curators of the university for approval, and might of course be vetoed by it. Such action, however, would certainly be rare; the habit of a competent group would be to study a measure with such thoroughness as to admit of but one conclusion before seeking final approval thereon.

A board for the purposes here indicated should be ensured the power, the responsibility, and the necessary procedure for reaching reliable results. It should nominate the personnel of instruction and administration, including the presidents and dean, in the component colleges and school of education. It should propose policies and regulations for administrative action. With the assistance of the state department of education it should study unremittingly the dimensions and character of its problem in the number and kind of teachers needed in the state. In coöperation with the several faculties, and with their approval, it should work out and revise curricula to meet these needs. It should consider and propose the creation or adaptation of material facilities with the single purpose of solving in the best possible fashion for the state the problem of teacher supply. The expert character of its members, and their relief from local and political demands, their opportunities for securing abundant accurate information, the elimination of competition, and the requirement of frequent (at least monthly) sessions for careful discussion and planning would go far toward an assurance that the ultimate solution of their problem would be correct.[15]

The members of the survey commission claimed for the proposed reorganization the following effects:

(1) The heads of the several institutions, coöperating as executives of their respective colleges under the new plan, instead of being semi-political promoters with attention divided between the local board and the legislature, would become strictly educational officers concerned solely with their individual institutions as carrying out a definite state policy framed by

[15] Carnegie Bul. No. 14, pp. 56-57.

them and for which they were responsible. Their tenure would be permanent and secure instead of biennial and precarious as now; their power in the state would be greater and their judgment surer because of constant mutual criticism and support; the position would be attractive to trained students of education and to men of first-rate ability.

(2) The teachers in the present normal schools would at once acquire full collegiate or university status; salaries, hours of work, and pension privileges, as well as qualifications of training and experience, would be regulated for all alike; there would be but one fraternity of state-employed servants in higher education. The students likewise would be relieved of invidious distinctions, both actual and alleged, between themselves and regular college or university students. In the interests of solidarity in higher education the university could well afford to welcome the alumni of the normal schools to such standing as their varying attainments might justify.

(3) Administrative differences would immediately disappear in favor of one thoroughly studied procedure worked out and applied in joint consultation. Admissions could be handled from one central office, possibly that of the state superintendent, thus securing a just and uniform treatment of credentials. A common terminology, a uniform grading and credit system, would convince both teacher and pupil that he was not a victim of local idiosyncrasy, but had received standard treatment, open to objection possibly on its merits but applied to all alike.

(4) The curricula would be unified and harmonized, and their administration placed on a rational basis. Since all schools and teachers would be of equal standing, it would make no more difference whether a certain curriculum for kindergartners or for high school teachers were given at one college or another, than it would if they were given in different buildings on the same campus. Such matters would be determined on the merits of local need and availability in view of all considerations and without institutional prejudice or jealousy. A large financial saving would certainly accrue at this point. Great advantage for the curriculum would result, too, from the increased flexibility of the staff of instruction. With intimate association of all colleges in the university, instructors could readily be assigned from one to another for special courses or lectures, thus utilizing fully each teacher's best powers. Teachers in other departments of the university would be available for the same purpose. Again, with associated administration, the school of education, which would doubtless develop primarily as a research or graduate school, would be in an admirable, in fact the only logical position to assist and be aided by the various enquiries undertaken at the five collegiate centres. Instructors in the colleges would then be in close and continual contact with this work of the graduate school, where they could perfect their training or coöperate on special problems.

(5) Outside of the institutions, the chief effect of the proposed plan would be to relieve the state of the element that most disturbs and confuses its representatives in providing for higher education. At present each separate school demands all that it dares, in the hope of finally obtaining

enough to allow it to operate and expand. Budgets are made out not on educational grounds, but with an eye to institutional success, and the arbiter as to what these various interests—some genuine, some fanciful, some real but inflated—shall receive is a legislative committee of laymen wholly uninformed except by the glowing advice of the interested local board members and presidents. By the proposed plan the budget for the training of teachers would be fully worked out jointly in the board of presidents; the chancellor and the board of curators would be responsible for its suitable incorporation in the budget of the university, and the proposals for financing the state's higher education would come as a logical whole before the state's government. With its support merged thus in the general budget, the normal school would find immediate relief from the pressure for numbers that now exercises such a baneful influence over its educational policies. Appropriations could be unspecified as to their detailed application, which would be subject to the discretion of the board of executives. It would be possible, for example, by economies in other quarters, for a central control to relieve the pressure of numbers at Springfield even on a reduced total appropriation. Such an administration would convince the state that within the general scope of its desires, its funds were being wisely distributed by those who were engaged because they knew best how to do it.

(6) To the state at large the benefit of having a single unified scheme of higher education would be manifold. The student fresh from high school and anxious about his future would receive consistent and unbiased advice at any institution and in all of the state's official educational literature, as to where he could best go for what he needed. Instead of being lured by personal and printed eulogies to help swell the roll of this or that school, he would be told candidly what each school was equipped to give him, and would be urged to get the best either within or without the state. Each school would be a stronger institution. When confronted with the alternatives, the people of Missouri prefer teachers prepared by institutions that ensure nationally recognized standards of excellence to schools that may be swayed this way and that by local pressure and that remain provincial because they lack the detached point of view that enables them to lead their communities. Furthermore, the popular effect of an orderly, harmonious scheme of education is superior to that resulting from institutional strife. Missouri has already seen partisans of the university and partisans of the normal schools lined up in opposition on questions that were not issues between the schools. This tendency is likely to increase as the normal schools grow into more and more effective rivals of the university, until wholly irrelevant decisions will be reached according as the "university vote" or the "normal school vote" can be more effectively marshalled. This outcome ought to be avoided.

(7) It is worth noting, finally, that an organization in Missouri of the nature above described, if carried through fully and in good faith, would mark a new epoch in American institutional life in this field. It would serve to seal the fast-closing breach between two groups of institutions that have stood aloof in feud-like attitude for many years. Not all states,

to be sure, are in a position to bring about such a change. States in which the normal schools are, and must long remain, chiefly secondary institutions would scarcely come within the scope of this plan. States having no state university would be confined to organizing their training agencies in a single professional group. But where there exist side by side a state university and one or more professional institutions of collegiate grade, all devoted to the same purpose, there would seem to be little question of the wisdom of incorporating all units that are functionally similar into one organic whole in so far as their direction and control are concerned.[16]

ORGANIZATION OF THE CONFERENCE OF STATE EDUCATIONAL INSTITUTIONS

The state superintendent of schools and the presidents of the state educational institutions recognized immediately the benefits to teacher training in the state in general, and to their respective institutions in particular, which would be brought about by some form of effective coöperation. They were unwilling to defer these benefits until the report could be published [17] and until legislation could be passed which would make possible the complete reorganization and necessary adjustments. Consequently, on June 22, 1916, State Superintendent of Schools Howard A. Gass called a conference of the presidents of the state schools and members of his staff in Jefferson City to consider plans for forming a working agreement. "Those present were: President A. Ross Hill, University of Missouri; President John R. Kirk, Normal School, Kirksville; President E. L. Hendricks, Normal School, Warrensburg; President W. S. Dearmont, Normal School, Cape Girardeau; President W. T. Carrington, Normal School, Springfield; President Ira Richardson, Normal School, Maryville; Hon. Howard A. Gass, State Superintendent of Public Schools; State Inspector of High School Teacher-Training Classes, M. G. Neale, acting as Secretary." [18]

A permanent, voluntary organization was effected which was known as "The Conference of the Presidents of (Missouri) State Educational Institutions and State Superintendent of Public Schools." The permanent chairman of the Conference is the state superintendent of schools and the permanent secretary is the state inspector of high school teacher-training classes. Regulations specifying conditions under which college work was

[16] Carnegie Bul. No. 17, pp. 57-59.
[17] See p. 3.
[18] Catalogue 1916, Kirksville, p. 42.

to be done were adopted.   The articles of agreement in effect in 1926 and printed here are but slight modifications of the original document.[19]

AGREEMENT OF CONFERENCE OF
STATE EDUCATIONAL INSTITUTIONS AND STATE
SUPERINTENDENT OF PUBLIC SCHOOLS [20]

ARTICLE I

In all regulations appertaining to college and secondary work, we shall conform as nearly as possible to the regulations of the North Central Association of Schools and Colleges.

ARTICLE II

Entrance Certificates: All entrance certificates shall be filed with the credentials committee on or before the opening of the semester or term, excepting that in special cases the credentials committee may for adequate reasons grant an extension of time for the filing of entrance certificates. (Pupils beginning secondary work shall file official evidence that they have completed the work of the elementary school, except persons holding teachers' certificates.)

Admission to Classes of College Rank.

A. Completion of a four-year course, with at least 15 units of credit in a first-class high school, in a fully accredited private academy, or in the secondary department of a normal school, shall be required for entrance. All parties to the agreement should adopt a uniform requirement of fifteen secondary units for admission to college work. The list of high school subjects approved by the State Superintendent of Schools shall be the list required by the institutions of the conference for entrance.

B. Students over twenty-one years of age, who are able to demonstrate their fitness to do college work may be admitted to college classes as special students, but they cannot be candidates for graduation until they have met the requirements for admission as regular students.

C. A student cannot be admitted to classes of college rank who is conditioned in more than two entrance units. All entrance conditions must be removed within one year of the date of admission. (Nine months of attendance may be considered a year.)

D. A unit is defined as a subject pursued five periods a week for at least 36 weeks, a period being 40 minutes in the clear, four units constituting a standard year's work. Excess of recitation time may accrue to the benefit of the student when sufficient limitation is placed upon the number of recitations which students may carry per week.

E. The Credentials Committee shall have final authority in all cases of evaluating credentials and classifying students as college, secondary, or special students.

[19] Catalogue 1916, Kirksville, pp. 42f.
[20] See Catalogue, Southwest Missouri State Teachers College, 1924-1926, pp. 19-26.

F. Students may be allowed secondary credits for any subject which they may have taught in high schools and which has been approved by the University of Missouri, or by the State Superintendent of Public Schools, or by similar accrediting agencies in other states.

G. Work done prior to July 1, 1917, in unclassified private educational institutions may be evaluated by the Credentials Committee of the school where credit is sought, and when approved by the visiting committee, it may be recorded by the institution concerned.

H. Any teacher who is a member of a grade or high school faculty shall be allowed to establish credit for work done only under the same conditions that apply to pupils of the school.

ARTICLE III

A. Definition of College Work. College work shall be defined as work taken by students who have met the minimum requirements for admission, in classes containing only those students who have complied with these requirements.

B. Excess and Diminished Credit. In schools where excess and diminished credit is allowed students shall not be permitted to carry for credit more than 32 semester hours per year, nor shall any student receive more than 37½ semester hours' credit per year. In schools where excess and diminished credit is not permitted students shall not be allowed to carry for credit more than 30 semester hours per year, except that, at the discretion of a committee on excess credit, students ranking among the upper thirty per cent of the student body in scholarship may be permitted to carry 33¾ hours per year and students ranking among the upper five per cent of the student body in scholarship may be permitted to carry 37½ semester hours per year. (Three quarters or two semesters shall be considered a college year.) The fact that a student carries less than 10 semester hours during one term of a school year does not give him the right to exceed 10 semester hours on another term of that year. The maximum amount of college work that may be carried by an individual student should be considered with reference to the term rather than with reference to the year, because the term is the unit in determining credits. The conditions under which excess credit may be carried by high school students shall be the same as those applied to college students. The amount of work carried by high school students shall in no case exceed 1⅔ units per term or quarter. When a student in a state teachers college which does not give excess or diminished credit according to grades, is permitted to register for more than ten hours' credit in a term, a statement should be appended to the certificate to indicate whether his rank was sufficiently high to justify this registration.

1. Excess and Diminished Credit to be Transferred. When students transfer credits from one institution to another, excess and diminished credit should be reported by institutions allowing it and should be accepted by all institutions of the Conference. If a student has earned excess

credit for college work, the amount of this excess credit shall be shown on his certificate.

C. Amount of Teaching. The maximum amount of teaching which may be done by instructors in college classes shall not exceed 18 hours per week or its equivalent in time. Two laboratory hours shall be counted as the equivalent of one recitation hour.

D. Preparation of Teachers. The minimum training of teachers of college classes shall be the equivalent of that represented by the master's degree from a standard university or college, with special preparation in the subjects taught. This requirement shall not be retroactive.

E. Late Entrance. The total credit for students who enter late shall not exceed one semester hour for each week of attendance. This rule need not be applied to students who for adequate reasons enter not more than one week late.

F. Credit for Correspondence Work.

1. At least eight lessons should be required for each semester hour of credit. A lesson should be planned so that it will require approximately five hours (sixty minutes) for its preparation.

2. A maximum of ten semester hours or two high school units may be completed in any school year.

3. No college credit shall be given for correspondence work in reading circle books.

4. A uniform fee should be charged; not less than three dollars per semester hour is recommended.

5. Copies of all lessons shall be kept on file.

G. Credit for Extension Courses.

1. Not fewer than four lecture visits by regular members of the faculty for each semester hour of credit are essential.

2. Students shall be required to do enough written work in addition to bring the standard of extension work up to that of correspondence courses mentioned above.

H. Total Amount of Extension Work. Fifty per cent of the required college work for any degree, certificate, or diploma may be completed by extension work provided that the existing requirements as to hours in residence remain unchanged. The amount of credit earned by correspondence work or extension work during one year shall not exceed ten hours.

Article IV

Records. No entry should be made on the permanent record card by any person other than the registrar and by him only in the performance of his official duties.

A. Each student's permanent record shall be kept on a grade card showing at least the following facts:

1. The credit accepted from other institutions, with the name of institution or institutions, and the date or dates on which the advanced standing was granted.

2. Name of courses for which student registers.

3. Catalogue number. In all records, courses shall be designated as' follows: (a) In secondary courses, the name of the subject, together with a Roman numeral indicating the year of secondary work shall be used. (b) In the freshman and sophomore college years, the name of the subject together with an Arabic numeral from 1 to 99 shall be used. (c) In the junior and senior college years the name of the subject together with an Arabic numeral from 100 to 199 shall be used. (d) Where a course is divided into terms or semesters, the letters a, b, and c shall be affixed to the course number to indicate the first, the second, and the third terms, respectively; and the letters a and b shall be affixed to the course number to indicate the first and the second semesters respectively.

4. Number of hours' credit.

5. Term in which taken.

6. Grade.

7. Classification of student.

8. Conditions specified in red ink.

B. Each student's daily program card or study cards shall show at least the following facts:

1. Names of courses for which student registers.

2. Catalogue numbers of these courses.

3. Number of hours' credit for which the student is registered in each course.

4. Term or semester in which the work is taken.

Article V

Advanced Standing. All advanced standing, either secondary or college, for work done in other institutions shall be recorded in the first term or semester during which the student is in attendance. In certifying credits from one institution to another, the institution certifying the credits shall furnish a chronological transcript of the student's work. On the transcript secondary work and college work respectively shall be clearly indicated by the phrases "secondary work" and "college work." The exact nature of each course shall be indicated by the title given on the transcript.

A. From standard institutions of high school and college rank.

1. Students entering from classified high schools shall be given credit according to the rating given by the State Superintendent of Public Schools. Certificates accepted for secondary school work shall indicate the amount of time spent in earning the credits and the years respectively in which the credits were earned.

2. Advanced standing may be given on certificate for work completed in accredited standard junior colleges. Irregularities in junior colleges shall be reported to the junior college committee by registrars of the colleges.

B. From other institutions.

1. Secondary credit.

(a) For work completed in an unclassified secondary school, credit may be given to the amount indicated by the State Superintendent's rating for this school. Students claiming more credit for work done in either classified or unclassified secondary schools than is recommended by the State Superintendent's rating shall be given this credit by examination only.

(b) In no case shall entrance examinations be given for more than four units for each year spent in school.

(c) The entrance examinations shall be given by a committee of the faculty.

(d) The questions shall be set and the papers graded by the department in which the applicant seeks credit.

(e) Entrance examinations shall be held not later than the first week of each term.

(f) The time of the examination in each subject shall be stated in the catalogue.

(g) The examination questions and papers shall be deposited with the chairman of the examining committee and kept on file for at least one year. The examiner's reports and all certificates and documents pertaining to the entrance and advanced standing of each student shall be kept in a permanent file.

(h) No credit by examination shall be given after a student has completed one year of work in the school, nor after an advanced course in the subject has been completed. This applies to students entering institutions since this agreement was made. Three quarters or two semesters shall be considered a school year.

(i) Students shall not be admitted to examination for advanced secondary standing unless they produce evidence showing that they have made systematic preparation in the work for which this advanced standing is claimed.

(j) Where college credit is substituted to make up a deficiency in secondary credits, five hours of college credit shall be counted the equivalent of one unit of secondary credit.

(k) "Systematic preparation" as used in Article V, Section B, division (i) as applied to secondary credit shall be left to the judgment of the Visiting Committee.

2. College Credit. Credit from institutions other than those mentioned in Article V, Section A shall be given only on the basis of examinations except as provided for in Article VI, Section B. The method of giving the examinations shall be that designated in Article V, Section B. In the case of examination for college credit a student shall be considered to have had "systematic preparation" only in case he has made preparation under the direction of a qualified teacher.

C. No advanced standing of college rank shall be given for postgraduate work in a high school unless such high school is properly equipped and definitely organized to do work of college rank, and graduate courses are restricted entirely to students who have completed a four-year secondary course and the teachers have the qualifications set forth for teachers of college subjects.

D. No credit shall be given for teaching experience gained as a teacher receiving a salary. If it seems probable that an experienced teacher cannot take with profit any required courses in observation or practice teaching, he should be excused from such courses and required to elect an equal amount of academic or professional work.

E. No advanced standing for college credit shall be given for grades on state or county certificates when such grades have been secured by examination. Work shall not be accepted from technical schools except by examination.

ARTICLE VI

A. Visiting Committee. A Committee of three shall be selected to visit each of the state institutions, and report to the conference at such times as the conference may designate, the workings of each of the state institutions with reference to each of the foregoing propositions.

1. Composition. The committee shall be composed of one representative of the University, one of the Teachers Colleges, and one of the State Department of Education.

2. Selection. The representative of the State Department of Education shall be appointed by the State Superintendent of Public Schools and shall be chairman of the committee. The representative of the University shall be chosen by the faculty and president of the University. The representative of the Teachers Colleges in rotation, beginning with Teachers College No. 1.

3. Tenure. The members of this committee shall serve for a period of one year, beginning July 1.

B. Unclassified Colleges and Schools. The work of unclassified colleges and schools shall be accepted as determined by the University of Missouri or the State Superintendent of Public Schools. It shall be the duty of the State Superintendent of Public Schools to call the attention of these colleges and schools * to this plan.

ARTICLE VII

A. The Professional Degree. The professional degree for the completion of the 120-hour course given in the Teachers Colleges and the School of Education of the University of Missouri shall be the degree of Bachelor of Science in Education.

B. Uniform Minimum Requirements for the Professional Degree. For the degree of B. S. in Education and the 120-hour Life Certificate the following courses shall be required:

1. Educational Psychology—2.5 hours, to be preceded, when possible, by a course in general psychology or biological science. (It is recommended that courses in general psychology be not counted as education.)

2. Principles of Teaching—2.5 hours, to be preceded by Educational Psychology.

3. School Economy—2 hours, to include a study of building and grounds, school law, classroom management, professional ethics, relation of the school to the community, and extra-curricular activities.

* See Appendix for reports of committee.

4. Practice Teaching—Enough to demonstrate the candidate's ability to teach (at least one term). Exemption may be granted as set out in the Conference Agreement. This requirement is not to apply when the diploma is not a license to teach.

5. History and Principles of Education—2.5 hours, to be given as late as possible in the student's course.

6. English, preferably English Composition—5 hours.

7. A major of at least 15 hours and a minor of at least 10 hours in academic or technical subjects, to be selected in consultation with an adviser, preferably in the department in which the major is chosen. Exception may be made in case of students pursuing fixed curricula in vocational subjects.

C. Additional Recommendations Concerning the Degree and the 120-hour Life Certificate.

1. A course of at least 2 hours in Hygiene with special reference to the health of the school is desirable.

2. The 120 hours required for the degree shall not include any credit for physical exercise.

3. The minimum requirement in Education is 24 hours.

4. The maximum credit to be given in Education should be 30 hours.

D. Junior and Senior College Courses. So far as possible, freshman and sophomore students should be scheduled only in classes of junior college rank; junior and senior students should be scheduled only in classes of senior college rank.

E. Multiplicity of Courses. Courses offered in the several departments should not be unnecessarily multiplied.

F. Departments in the several colleges which give courses required for certificates and degrees shall be asked to prepare and exchange syllabi of these courses.

ARTICLE VIII

Residence Requirements and Recommendations Concerning the 60-hour Certificate and the Regents' Certificate.

A. Residence Requirements. No elementary Certificate shall be granted by any of the institutions represented in this conference, with less than two terms in residence and no diploma shall be granted on less than three terms in residence.

B. Uniform Minimum Requirements for the 60-hour Certificate.

1. Education—All the courses required for the degree, except History and Principles of Education; namely, Educational Psychology, School Economy, Principles of Teaching, and Practice Teaching.

2. English, preferably English Composition—5 hours.

3. Other academic or technical subjects, at least five hours in each of 3 subjects in addition to Education and English.

C. Uniform Minimum Requirements for the Regents' Certificate. These subjects shall be required for the Regents' Certificate:

1. Elementary Education—5 hours. This course is to include such

topics as the selection, organization, and presentation of the subject matter in the elementary school subjects, and also classroom management.

2. Observation and Teaching—2.5 hours.

3. English, preferably English Composition—5 hours.

ARTICLE IX

Life Certificates. It is the aim of the Conference at the earliest expedient date to base the elementary certificate of the Teachers Colleges upon 60 semester hours of credit and to base the life diploma upon 120 hours of credit.

ARTICLE X

When this conference finds that the conditions named in this report have been fully met, college work done in any of the institutions shall be accepted hour for hour in the other institutions, and graduates of the 120-hour course shall be admitted to the graduate school of the University of Missouri.

ARTICLE XI

Present conditions for accepting college work from other institutions.

A. College work done in any of the institutions of the conference agreement by students who have regularly enrolled for the first time since September 1, 1916, shall be accepted by the other institutions hour for hour and such students finishing the 120-hour course shall be admitted to the graduate school of the University of Missouri.

B. College work done by students regularly enrolled before September 1, 1916, and in attendance not less than one term, since September 1, 1916, shall be accepted on the same basis as the above, provided satisfactory evidence is produced showing the entrance requirements have been met, and provided further the college credit granted in any year does not exceed the maximum amount provided for in the conference agreement.

C. College work done by students enrolled before September 1, 1916, and not in attendance one term since September 1, 1916, shall be accepted in accordance with the provisions under B, with the understanding that each case will be dealt with according to its particular merit and that each school accepting such credit, shall be the judge of the amount of credit granted.

ARTICLE XII

A. Publication and Terminology. The Articles of Agreement should be published in the catalogues of all institutions that are parties to the agreement.

B. Uniform Terminology:

Secondary Courses in Education.

1. Elementary Psychology.

2. Rural life problems.

3. Rural school management.

4. Rural school methods.
5. Subject matter and method in ————————

College Courses in Education.
   I. Psychology.
      1. Psychology.
      2. Educational psychology.
   II. Administration of Education.
      1. School economy.
      2. Supervision of instruction.
      3. Rural school administration and supervision.
      4. High school problems.
      5. Educational administration (for senior college students).
      6. Mental tests.
      7. Educational tests and measurements.
   III. Methods in Education.
      1. Principles of teaching (primarily for junior college students).
      2. Principles of education (primarily for senior college students).
      3. Teaching of ———————— in the elementary schools.
      4. Teaching of ———————— in the high schools.
      5. Primary and kindergarten methods.
      6. Elementary education.
   IV. History of Education.
      1. History and principles of education.
      2. History of modern elementary education.
      3. Modern school systems (senior college students).
      4. History of education in the United States.
   V. Teaching.
      1. Teaching in the elementary school.
      2. Teaching in the high school.

C. Conference Meetings. Each of the six teachers colleges and the State Department of Education shall have two votes in the conference meetings.*

The articles of agreement are complete enough in their statement to make clear the way in which the Conference operates. Meetings are called by the state superintendent of schools as need arises. They are usually held in connection with some other state meeting, the state teachers' association or the annual meeting of city superintendents which is held at the state university, although one or two meetings are called at other times during the year. The meetings are attended by the state superintendent of schools, the state inspector of teacher training, and the presidents and deans of the institutions. Any matters pertaining to the state's program of teacher training or to the welfare of the institutions belonging may be considered by the Con-

———————
* See Appendix for minutes of the Conference.

ference. The Conference is without legal authority. Its proceedings are subject to review by the boards of the respective schools, but there has not been a single instance in the ten years of its existence when a board of regents has failed to approve and adopt the recommendations of the Conference.

Perhaps the most important single agency of the Conference is the visiting committee described in Article VI.[21] The committee makes visits to each institution annually and determines to what extent the individual institutions are complying with the Conference Agreements. They report to the Conference, and if occasion demands, the institutions must justify their departure from the regulations. The Conference has no legal power to enforce its ruling, but it exerts a great and powerful moral force which makes the violation of its standards unthinkable. Not only is the professional reputation of the officers of the colleges who fail to abide by the rulings of the Conference involved, but the educational, professional, and ethical standing of the colleges themselves would seriously suffer.

In order to expedite its work the visiting committee is supplemented by a credentials committee composed of the registrars or chairmen of the entrance and advanced standing committees of the several colleges. This committee meets annually, or oftener when there is business to transact, in the office of the state superintendent of schools. All cases of admission or advanced standing which under the rules must be presented to the Conference, are passed upon by this committee. In practice its action is final, although any member may bring its case to the Conference if there is a difference of opinion.

ACCOMPLISHMENTS OF THE CONFERENCE

Among the outstanding accomplishments of the Conference may be listed the following:

1. It has promoted understanding and good will among the teachers colleges. Unwholesome rivalry has ceased to exist. As an illustration of the harmony that exists, one needs only to cite the fact that the needs of all the teachers colleges were presented to the appropriations committee of the Fifty-third General Assembly in 1925 at a single hearing by a member of the board of regents of one of the schools.

[21] See p. 101. See also Appendix D.

2. It has developed mutual respect and trust on the part of the university on the one hand and the teachers colleges on the other. Credit is accepted hour for hour by the university and all of the teachers colleges.[22]

3. Uniformity of administrative practice has been effected along the following lines:

    a. Admission requirements have been standardized and are administered uniformly at all the teachers colleges and the university.

    b. Minimum requirements are identical for work of college rank.

    c. There is a uniform plan of credit assignment.

    d. The minimum training of teachers of college classes is identical.

    e. Maximum teaching loads are the same.

    f. A student's program, the amount of work a student may carry, is prescribed for all schools by the Conference.

    g. Correspondence and extension work and credit for such work are governed by uniform regulations.

    h. Records are kept under the same regulations at all of the schools. Blanks for the transfer of credit are uniform, and permanent record blanks are as nearly so as varying conditions will permit.

    i. Advanced standing from other institutions is evaluated on the same basis at all of the schools.

    j. A uniform terminology for required courses in education has been adopted.

4. The visiting committee and the Conference discussions have forced each school "to keep its practice overhauled under the critical eyes of competent outsiders." [23]

5. Uniform minimum curriculum requirements for all certificates, diplomas, and the professional degree have been prescribed.

6. A sharp differentiation between the amount of work of junior college rank and senior college rank which can be accepted for the degree has been made.

7. Multiplicity of courses has been discouraged.

---

[22] See Catalogue, University of Missouri, 1924, p. 31.
[23] Carnegie Bul. No. 14, p. 50.

8. Exchange of syllabi of courses required for certificates has been encouraged.

9. Conditions for the acceptance of credit among the colleges for work done before the conference agreement went into effect have been clearly stated and misunderstandings on the part of colleges and individual students eliminated.[24]

Dr. Robert J. Leonard in his study of voluntary organizations of this kind, made in 1922, says of the Missouri Conference:

In 1916, an attempt of an entirely different sort from any of those thus far mentioned was made in Missouri in an effort to establish closer working relationships among the institutions in this state. A state educational conference was organized composed of representatives from the state department of education, the state university and the state normal schools. The conference was entirely unofficial, and had no legal status. It was a movement arising out of the necessities of the situation, and supported, at least nominally, by all of the institutions. The problems brought before the conference related to standards for faculties, definitions of units and credits, the transfer of students from one school to another, and other like questions. While larger questions of institutional policies have not come before this body, at least up to the summer of 1922, it represents a sincere effort on the part of certain officers and instructors in the institutions to foster harmony and coöperation.[25]

As further evidence of its accomplishments the opinions of the men who have been associated with the Conference during its existence are quoted.

Dr. Jesse H. Coursault, Professor of Education, formerly Dean of the School of Education, University of Missouri:

In my opinion, the Conference including representatives of the five Missouri State Teachers Colleges, the State Department of Education, and the University of Missouri, has been highly successful in bringing about a more desirable relationship among the institutions concerned, and in improving the standards and quality of work in the training of teachers. This Conference is one of the big steps towards the improvement of education in Missouri.

In the improvement of the relationship among the institutions concerned, the spirit of individual competition has given way to that of coöperative action. Representatives of the several institutions meeting to consider problems common to all have had the advantages of sympathetic personal relationships, which were taken by them to their respective institutions.

[24] Catalogue, University of Missouri, 1924, p. 31.
[25] Leonard, R. J., *The Coördination of State Institutions for Higher Education Through Supplementary Curricular Boards*, pp. 14 and 15.

The Conference has been free, frank, and friendly in its discussions. Although the teachers colleges have five times as many votes in the Conference as does the university, decisions have been controlled in a democratic way by the cogency of ideas rather than by the force of votes representing mere self-interest. When the university desired a large expansion of its graduate work in education, the presidents of all the teachers colleges, without exception, wrote opinions strongly indorsing this project, with permission that these opinions be given wide publicity. An important factor in creating friendly relationships was the Conference Visiting Committee, composed of a representative of the teachers colleges, a representative of the State Department of Education, and a representative of the university. Because the detailed regulations in the Conference Agreement could not be stated with the precision necessary for identical interpretations by all concerned, this committee was provided for by the Conference to investigate the administration of these regulations by the several institutions. Each teachers college was represented in turn on this Visiting Committee. With mutual confidence, this committee, during its visits, has always been given the freest access to the scholastic records of the institutions, has met cordial responses in answer to its questions, and as representing coöperating institutions has been shown special courtesies. Furthermore, the work of the Visiting Committee has brought into close personal relationship representative members from the several institutions, who carry in some degree to their respective institutions the favorable results of this relationship.

The first and most important step towards the improvement of scholarship is the Conference Agreement, which has set higher minimum standards for the training of teachers, and has brought the teacher-training institutions of the state into closer relationship with the State Department of Education. This department, through issuing teachers' certificates and classifying schools, has large control in regulating standards for teachers. The obligation to maintain standards agreed upon by all the institutions concerned, opposed any natural temptation to lower requirements in competing for larger enrollments, or to add to the faculties, for financial or other reasons, instructors with qualifications lower than those set forth in the agreement. The Visiting Committee in its inspections found new ways for improvement not provided for in the agreement, and from time to time made to the Conference recommendations which were readily accepted. The obligation of this committee to present worthwhile reports naturally made it critical. As the result of an action by the Conference, furthermore, the deans of the institutions met in the interest of improving requirements. All the recommendations agreed upon by the deans were later adopted by the Conference with one motion. A committee provided for by the Conference to evaluate all irregular credits offered for admission or for advanced standing, has found in its work some ways of improving standards. Furthermore, the uniform blank adopted for the transcript of credits when a student transfers from one institution to another, provides in detail for all the important items needed for intelligent classification.

In brief, the Conference has taken an important step in organizing the work of the state in the higher training of teachers, in maintaining good will and a spirit of coöperation in this work, in improving educational standards, and in making an easier and more attractive pathway from undergraduate work to that of the graduate school.

Dean M. G. Neale, School of Education, University of Missouri, formerly State Supervisor of Teacher Training:

In my judgment the Missouri Conference of Educational Institutions has been a very valuable agency in bringing about a better understanding among our state-supported institutions of higher learning. As I saw the problem when we first began to talk over the matter of such an association there was a great deal of unnecessary distrust. There were, of course, conditions that needed to be corrected and standards that needed to be established in order that a clear-cut definition of college work might be made which would make it possible for one institution to accept without misgivings college credits reported from another. The organization grew out of a very distinct feeling of need. It was almost inevitable.

Knowing as I do the conditions that existed before and after this association began its work, I have no hesitation in saying that it has accomplished some very valuable things. We do not have the bickering over credits and the dissatisfaction among students that we formerly had. I think it increases the respect of students for all the state institutions.

In my judgment many of the improvements would have come about without the organization. They simply had to come. The organization made their coming more pleasant and it has resulted in a uniformity of terminology with respect to credits and a uniformity in reporting transfers of credit which save a tremendous amount of time. One of the out growths of this organization is the Evaluating Committee which makes possible the adjustment of old and irregular credits in such a way as to insure the acceptance of these credits by all the state institutions.

Dr. E. L. Hendricks, President, Warrensburg State Teachers College, and President of Missouri State Teachers Association:

Following are some of the things which in my judgment the Educational Conference in Missouri has secured. Keep in mind the fact that the Conference is made up of the Superintendent of Public Instruction as chairman, and his assistant as secretary, together with the President and Dean of the University and the Presidents and Deans of the Teachers Colleges of the state. Let me suggest first the efficiency of coöperation which must result from such an organization. This coöperation is obvious when we appear before the legislature for our respective appropriations. Before the conference was formed each institution was under obligation to secure all that it could in appropriations. Now the several institutions in Conference agree upon the needs of the respective institutions. Our several interests are pooled by the Conference and by mutual agreement one representative presents the needs of all to the legislature.

The Conference has secured use of uniform records and of credit requirements. It has a visitation committee which visits the several institutions and points out items wherein the school visited failed to reach the highest standard set up for teacher-training work. The Conference has an evaluation committee which passes upon questionable credits presented to either of the institutions, and the decisions of this evaluation committee are thereafter the decisions of each of the institutions. The Conference has also taken steps toward a universal policy on the matter of certification of teachers. Progress has been made and further steps will be taken for the improvement of our certification system. The Conference has done away with the solicitation of students from adjoining districts. Each teachers college now recognizes that it is only a part of a system designed to serve the state. Attention is given to character of work presented students rather than numbers in attendance. The Educational Conference has secured a more nearly adequate and more nearly uniform salary for the several teachers college faculties. And the Conference has also secured uniform terminology.

At the time of the organization of the Educational Conference in Missouri the only objection presented was that the teachers colleges and the university could not work in harmony. It was stated that their interests were so divergent that they could not be harmonized. And they, on the other hand, like Eugene Field's "Gingham Dog and Calico Cat" would eat each other up. No such dire consequence has resulted. Missouri has had most happy results from her Educational Conference. All the more effective possibly because it has been voluntary.

Dr. Eugene Fair, President, State Teachers College, Kirksville, Missouri:

I believe so strongly in the Conference that I think we can do almost anything if we agree on a program and stand together. The voluntary aspect of it appeals to me very much and from what little I know, from the beginning of the Conference, it has surely made creditable progress in Missouri, especially in cementing the close relations among the several teachers colleges.

Dr. Uel W. Lamkin, President, Northwest Missouri State Teachers College, Maryville, Missouri:

The Conference of Missouri Educational Institutions has brought about the most desirable relationship between the six educational institutions; namely, the University of Missouri and the five State Teachers Colleges. From the time of the first agreement until now there has been a closer relationship, misunderstandings have been avoided, the same standards for entrance and graduation have been established and maintained. The Conference has made for more efficient faculty in all of the institutions. In fact, the entire result has been more than satisfactory to educational interests of Missouri.

Dr. Joseph A. Serena, President, Southeast Missouri State Teachers College, Cape Girardeau, Missouri:

The Missouri Conference of state institutions has done and is doing wonders in stabilizing higher education in this state by thoroughly evaluating all entrance statements, and in frequent conferences outlining safe educational procedure. The Missouri Conference is proving a valuable adjunct to education in this commonwealth. Each year it seems to discover additional functions that are telling for its efficiency. Personally I do not see how we could get along without it.

Dr. W. S. Dearmont, President, Cape Girardeau State Teachers College (1899-1921):

I regard the Conference as invaluable for the purpose of bringing about more desirable relations among the state schools and in establishing standards in the state colleges. It is the only right way, in my opinion, to accomplish these results. As I view the matter, there has been too much attempt in the various states in recent years to regulate the relationships among state schools by rigid statutory enactments and to establish standards in the same way. Hardly less objectionable have been the activities of state boards and state departments of education in their attempts to hand down from above to these institutions regulations fixing their relations and fixing standards of work in these institutions. I feel that reason and common sense, as well as experience, prove that these two methods of regulation relations among state institutions and establishing standards are unwise. The Missouri plan is theoretically right and during the years that I was at the head of one of the state colleges of Missouri while this plan was in operation, there was every evidence that the plan was working well in practice.

The organization by the institutions of a state of a conference somewhat on the plan of the Missouri educational institutions, is the ideal way through which the institutions will coöperate and through which they will coördinate their activities and lay out the lines of their relations. I believe that such a conference will recognize and make effective all vital and necessary relations and coöperative activities and, at the same time, the conference will bring to each institution a knowledge of the best results accomplished in any one institution. On the whole, all desirable uniformities among these institutions can be brought into existence through this conference and all necessary differences in the work of the several institutions can be and will be best agreed upon by such an agency as the Missouri Conference.

At the beginning of this chapter a brief statement of the proposed reorganization of the higher educational institutions of the state of Missouri was made. Among other things a pro-

TABLE LXVIII

EFFECTS TO BE PRODUCED BY PROFESSIONAL BOARD OF EXECUTIVES AS STATED IN 1915 [1]	WHAT HAS ACTUALLY BEEN ACCOMPLISHED BY THE CONFERENCE OF STATE EDUCATIONAL INSTITUTIONS IN TEN YEARS [2]
1. Normal school teachers would acquire collegiate status, salaries, and hours of work.	1. Teachers college teachers have collegiate status, and hours of work. The median annual salary at the university is $3370. At the teachers colleges it is $2340.
2. Qualifications of training and experience would be regulated for all alike.	2. The minimum qualifications for college teaching are the same for all alike.
3. Normal students would be relieved of invidious distinctions between themselves and university students.	3. Teachers college students receive credit hour for hour and graduates are admitted to the graduate school of the university.[3]
4. Administrative differences would disappear in favor of one thoroughly studied procedure worked out and applied in joint consultation.	4. Some administrative differences exist but important features of administration are the result of the joint consultation of the state conference.
5. Admissions would be uniform.	5. Admissions are uniform.
6. There would be a common terminology, a uniform grading and credit system.	6. Common terminology, uniform grading and credit systems are employed.
7. Curricula would be unified, harmonized, and rationally administered.	7. Curricula are unified, harmonized, and rationally administered.
8. Normal schools could specialize in types of training offered.	8. There has been no effort for the teachers colleges to specialize in types of training offered although it has been considered by the Conference.
9. Instructors could be assigned from one school to another for special courses.	9. Present organization does not admit of exchange of teachers, although lecturers are exchanged.
10. The school of education would develop into a graduate school.	10. The school of education is developing rapidly into a graduate school, many of whose students are graduates of teachers colleges.[4]
11. Confusion in making appropriations for higher education would be avoided.	11. The teachers colleges present their requests jointly.

TABLE LXVIII (*Continued*)

EFFECTS TO BE PRODUCED BY PROFESSIONAL BOARD OF EXECUTIVES AS STATED IN 1915 [1]	WHAT HAS ACTUALLY BEEN ACCOMPLISHED BY THE CONFERENCE OF STATE EDUCATIONAL INSTITUTIONS IN TEN YEARS [2]
12. Budgets would be worked out jointly by presidents.	12. The teachers college presidents and a representative of each board of regents met in Kansas City in September, 1924, and prepared jointly the budgets for the several schools.
13. Pressure for numbers in the normal schools would cease to exist.	13. No teachers college in Missouri is at the present time using any means except quality of work to attract students.
14. High school graduates would receive unbiased advice at any institution as to where he could best go for what he needed.	14. Senior college students are advised to enter the professional schools of the university if they do not expect to teach.
15. Institutions would have nationally recognized standards and not be swayed by local pressure.	15. All the schools work under the standards and are approved by the North Central Association of Colleges and Secondary Schools.
16. It would seal the breach between the two groups of institutions and make for a harmonious scheme of higher education.	16. There is no evidence of a breach existing between the university and the teachers colleges. The scheme of teacher training is harmonious.
17. The plan would be imitated by other states and mark a new epoch in American education.	17. Several states have coöperative plans among the higher educational institutions, but the influence of the Missouri Conference in their formation is unknown.

[1] See pp. 152-55.
[2] See Articles of Agreement, pp. 156 ff.
[3] See University of Missouri Catalogue, 1924, p. 31.
[4] See Leonard, R. J. *Coördination of State Institutions for Higher Education Through Supplementary Curricular Boards.*

fessional board of executives was recommended. The reorganization was never made, but a voluntary conference of executives was formed to function as an unofficial professional board. Its organization and the conference agreements have been described. By way of summary Table LXVIII compares the accomplishments of this conference with the claims made for the professional board of executives recommended by the survey commission.

PROPOSALS RELATING TO THE FUTURE WORK OF THE CONFERENCE

1. The Conference should continue to function in all of the lines of activity upon which it has embarked.

2. So long as the Conference continues to operate with its present effectiveness and fine spirit of coöperation, it should not seek legal status and mandatory authority. The coöperative plan has all of the advantages which come from local autonomy and centralized control in the determination of the educational policies of the colleges. Its influence is exerted not because of its power to put its mandates into operation but because of its ability to suggest the best solutions for the problems of teacher training in the state. The fact that its recommendations are subject to the review of the several boards of control is an element of strength in that it is a constant check which forces thorough consideration of all issues. Its history has demonstrated its ability to exert far-reaching influence through the merits of its rulings.

3. The Conference should assume responsibility for, initiate and continue constantly, scientific studies of the state's demands for trained teachers. It should sponsor and plan such studies under competent direction. They should be state wide in scope and should make use of the talent available in all of the colleges in the work.

4. The Conference should conduct surveys to determine the state's ability to train teachers to meet the demand. These surveys should include the training of teachers for all levels of the teaching service and the special fields of teaching. Care should be taken to avoid comparisons among the colleges in any line of work by approaching the problems as state-wide studies.

5. The Conference should direct in coöperation with the authorized agencies of the several faculties scientific studies of curricula for the training of teachers. This type of investigation should proceed without interruption. Reports of progress should be made to the Conference for its consideration from time to time.

6. The Conference should study the "marketing of the product of the teachers colleges" to the end of being of the greatest service to the schools of the state, and to the students, in the proper placement of the graduates.

7. The data gathered in connection with the studies suggested should be considered at all times with the view to the determination and modification of major and service lines for the individual colleges.

8. The collection of data of the kind suggested will indicate the state's need for additional teacher-training facilities either through the enlargement of the plants of the colleges now in existence or by the establishment of other schools.

9. The Conference should make scientific studies of taxation especially with reference to sources of revenue and plans for financing higher education. In the absence of other state agencies for the purpose, the Conference should be in position to furnish the legislature with authoritative and scientific information on the subject.

10. The Conference should make scientific, comparative studies of student costs. These should be made for the state as a whole, leaving it to individual institutions to make comparisons of its own costs with those of the other individual schools and the state as a whole. This information will not only serve as a check on the individual colleges, but will be valuable in defense of the state's teacher-training budget.

11. The Conference, augmented by representatives of the respective boards of regents, should discuss and agree upon the budgets of the individual colleges to be presented to the legislature. It should arrange for the joint presentation of the requests and thus avoid the possibility of creating the impression of unwholesome rivalry.

12. The expense of conducting the proposed investigations should be prorated among the colleges until such time as legislative appropriations can be secured for the purpose.

CHAPTER VI

CONCLUSIONS AND PROPOSALS

The preceding chapters in this study have contained detailed statements of the progress made in Missouri teachers colleges during the decade from 1915 to 1926. Changes in student personnel, teacher personnel, curricula, and the relationship among the higher educational institutions of the state have been considered. The extent to which the colleges have developed in harmony with the proposals of the Carnegie Survey Commission has been pointed out and proposals for the next steps in their development have been made. In this chapter will be found a general summary of the study and a proposed program for the continued improvement of the Missouri teachers colleges. The findings of the recent surveys of the teacher-training programs of a number of the states would suggest that the experience of Missouri in attempting to supply an adequate number of trained teachers for her elementary and secondary schools, has not been unique. Although this study is confined to the colleges of a single state, it is hoped that the conditions are sufficiently typical and the recommendations of sufficient merit that they will prove more or less generally helpful.

TENTATIVE STANDARDS OF AMERICAN ASSOCIATION OF TEACHERS COLLEGES APPLIED TO NORMAL SCHOOLS OF 1915 AND TEACHERS COLLEGES OF 1926

In order to bring together the significant characteristics of the Missouri normal schools at the beginning and at · the close of the decade, on pages 177-179 are given the tentative standards for admission to the American Association of Teachers Colleges [1] applied to the schools as they were in 1915 and as they are in 1926. The standards referring to the four-year course and those relating to the items which have been considered in this study are used.

[1] See Appendix G.

	Standards of the American Associa- tion of Teachers Colleges [1]	Missouri Normal Schools in 1915	Missouri Teachers Colleges in 1926
Admission require- ments	A. 15 H. S. Units B. May be estab- lished by ex- amination C. No credit al- lowed for teaching ex- perience	A. 15 Units. Many excep- tions B. No examina- tion required C. Credit allow- ed for teach- ing experience	A. 15 Units. No exceptions B. Examination under strict regulations C. No credit al- lowed for teaching experience
Standards of Gradu- ation	A. 120 semester hours B. 60 semester hours for 2- yr. curriculum	A. 120 semester hours B. 60 semester hours for 2- yr. curriculum	A. 120 semester hours B. 60 semester hours for 2-yr. curriculum
Size of Faculty	A. College de- partment one teacher to 20 students B. Training school 1 to 18	A. One teacher to 21 students standard en- rollment B. No data	A. One to 19 standard en- rollment B. Median for four schools 1 to 12
Preparation of Fac- ulty [2]	A. Minimum for training school B. S. B. Minimum for college teach- ers A. M.	A. 27 per cent met require- ment B. 30 per cent met require- ment	A. 92 per cent meet require- ment B. 69 per cent meet require- ment
Teaching Load	A. Sixteen class periods a week	A. Median was between 20 and 24	A. Median is 16
Training School and Student Teaching ..	A. Training school under control of col- lege	A. Requirement met	A. Requirement met

[1] *American Association of Teachers Colleges, Yearbook*, 1924. See also Appendix G.
[2] Exceptions to requirements are not considered.

	Standards of the American Association of Teachers Colleges [1]	Missouri Normal Schools in 1915	Missouri Teachers Colleges in 1926
Training School and Student Teaching .. (*Continued*)	B. Children's interests protected	B. Requirement met	B. Requirement met
	C. Not more than 40 children for each supervisor	C. Requirement met	C. Requirement met
	D. 120 hours supervised teaching required for degree	D. Partially met	D. From 120 to 180 hours are required
	E. Thirty children for 12 students teaching 180 hours each	E. Catalogues indicate equivalent of 18	E. Enrollment reports show equivalent of 29
	F. Amount of supervision limited to 12 students of 180 hrs. each or equivalent	F. No data	F. Equivalent generally met in Missouri teachers colleges
	G. Competent supervision in case of off-campus training schools	G. Requirement met	G. Requirement met
	H. Two-fifths of teaching in training schools by supervisors	H. No definite standard	H. Requirement met
Organization of the Curriculum	A. Sequential	A. No requirement	A. Requirement met
	B. Senior college courses not open to freshmen	B. No requirement	B. Requirement of all colleges

[1] *American Association of Teachers Colleges, Yearbook*, 1924. See also Appendix G.

	STANDARDS OF THE AMERICAN ASSOCIATION OF TEACHERS COLLEGES[1]	MISSOURI NORMAL SCHOOLS IN 1915	MISSOURI TEACHERS COLLEGES IN 1926
Organization of the Curriculum......... (*Continued*)	C. 50 per cent of courses of senior college rank	C. No requirement	C. Minimum of 40 per cent senior college courses absolute requirement
Limits of Registration of Students	A. At least 200 students B. 15 per cent of senior college rank	A. Requirement met B. No definite data. Reports indicate not met	A. Requirement met B. Requirement met

[1] *American Association of Teachers Colleges, Yearbook*, 1924. See also Appendix G.

A. CONCLUSIONS AND PROPOSALS RELATING TO STUDENT PERSONNEL

I. *Students Without Professional Aim.* (See Chapter II, p. 41.)

a. Under present conditions Missouri teachers colleges are not justified in offering courses designed to attract students who do not expect to teach.

b. If it becomes a state policy to offer courses in the teachers colleges leading to non-professional degrees, or if pre-professional courses of junior college rank are offered for students who will not teach, the organization of the work should not divert the professional courses from their purposes.

c. If the Missouri teachers colleges are to undertake more extensive work than that of teacher training, the state should recognize the multiple purposes of the colleges by making appropriations accordingly.

II. *The Selection of Students.* (See Chapter II, p. 41.)

a. To avoid an investment by the state in the training of students who will be unsuited to the teaching profession either because of constitutional unfitness, or because of training for work unsuited to their tastes or abilities, each college should maintain a bureau of vocational guidance to give students expert direction in the selection of curricula and colleges.

b. After sufficient information has been obtained by the use of intelligence tests, teachers' marks, and expert opinion to justify the procedure, students who are of less than average ability should be dropped, on the grounds that people of less than average ability should not prepare to teach.

c. In order to prevent the graduation and certification of students who are indifferent or who lack the attitudes ordinarily regarded as essential in the teacher's equipment, a system of honor points should be installed in each college. A number of honor points in addition to hours of credit should be required for graduation.[1]

III. *Certification of Teachers.*

a. Permanent certificates should not be granted to teachers who have not demonstrated to competent judges their ability to do independent teaching in their own classrooms.

b. The teachers colleges should, in coöperation with the state superintendent of schools, seek to bring about reforms in the certification of teachers in the state which will be in harmony with the best practice to be found. The plans should especially provide for a minimum, initial collegiate training and stimulate the greatest amount of in-service growth on the part of the teachers of the state.

IV. *Needed Research.* (See Chapter II, p. 42.)

a. To determine the feasibility and desirability of a state policy of carrying on junior college work at the teachers colleges for students without professional aim or for those who are preparing for other professional study.

b. To determine the effect upon the professional spirit of the teachers college of the presence of students who expect to teach only a short time while making preparation for business or other professions and who meet minimum requirements in teacher-training courses and do a maximum of work in non-professional courses.

c. To determine the quality of teaching done by men who are well educated but who are using the teaching profession as a steppingstone to better paying professions.

B. Conclusions and Proposals Relating to Teacher Personnel

I. *Organization of the Faculty.* (See Chapter III, p. 81.)

a. Teachers college faculties should be organized on the basis of professional rank with definite requirements for promotion from one rank to another.

b. Members of the teaching staffs of teachers colleges should not devote an undue amount of their time and energy to administrative work. An adequate clerical staff should be provided and teachers should not permit any other work to interfere with their classroom teaching.

c. In order to recruit the faculties by the addition of young men and women of adequate and desirable training it is obvious that many

[1] Kelly, F. J., *The American Arts College*, p. 120.

of them will have had limited opportunity for previous experience in college teaching. The importance, therefore, of systematic in-service training cannot be overemphasized.

d. For the purpose of coördinating the work of the colleges and in order that the best thought in any of the faculties may be made available for all of them, departmental or faculty intercollegiate conferences should be held.

e. First-hand acquaintance with and continued coöperative interest in the public schools of the state are essential elements in the equipment of the teachers in teachers colleges. Administrative plans should provide for desirable, mutually helpful contacts with the public schools of the state for all of the members of the teaching staffs to the end of promoting acquaintance and synergetic relationship.

f. The administrative policy of the training school should be such as to bring each teacher into vital contact with it in the way in which his particular talents will make the relationship most profitable. (See p. 48.)

II. *Salaries of the Faculty.* (See Chapter III, p. 82.)

a. Definite salary schedules based upon professional rank and service to the college should be adopted. They should indicate salary ranges, but should not necessarily be uniform or automatic in their operation.

b. In order to secure desirable permanency on the part of the teaching staff, to attract the services of men and women of the best training, and to obtain and retain the respect of the colleges and universities, teachers in teachers colleges should receive as large, if not larger, salaries than members of the faculty of the state university.

III. *Preparation of the Faculty.* (See Chapter III, p. 81.)

a. The Master's degree should not be considered as adequate training for teachers in Missouri teachers colleges. Additional training of at least two years of graduate study rewarded usually with the Doctor's degree should be considered the ultimate minimum.

b. The kind of training a teacher has had is of equal if not of more importance than the amount. Assuming adequate higher training, desirable personal qualities, and teaching ability the student experience of a prospective teacher in a teachers college should be of a variety and character most likely to produce the right attitude toward the work to be done. (See p. 85.)

c. In order to guarantee a supply of teachers trained to meet the requirements necessary for the proper development of the teachers colleges, the needs should be anticipated and promising young men and women should be encouraged to pursue directed courses of training to satisfy these needs. (See p. 85.)

IV. *Needed Research.*

    a. Collegiate enrollment is increasing much more rapidly than fiscal support. College teachers are confronted with large classes. Limited registration is possible in some schools, but in a majority it is not. The solution of the problem lies in the development of a technique of teaching college classes of large size with as much satisfaction to the teacher and the student as our present classes, limited to a small enrollment, afford.

    b. A technique for the determination of the teaching load would be most helpful.

C. Conclusions and Proposals Relating to Curricula

I. *The Professional Treatment of Subject Matter.* (See Chapter IV, p. 145.)

    a. All courses in the curricula of Missouri teachers colleges must provide for breadth, depth, and newness of subject matter. At the same time through the selection of material, the selection of methods, and the integration of the two, the courses must provide a scholarship of direct professional benefit to the teacher.

    b. In the professional treatment of subject matter the following conditions and limitations must be observed (see pp. 144 and 145):

        1. All of the courses required as a part of the professional curricula should be "professionalized." This implies the enthusiastic cooperation of the entire staff.

        2. The difficulty of the process and its importance make it necessary to assign plenty of time for the initial part of the work. The process is continuous.

        3. Education courses should be reorganized in accordance with the principles of professionalization and in order that they may more effectively function as service courses.

        4. The training school should be considered as an element in the professional treatment of subject matter.

        5. Attention at first should be given to the professional treatment of the subject matter courses which are obviously of direct help to the teacher.

        6. Broad scholarship and general culture are not subordinated as aims in professionalized subject matter courses.

        7. Teachers of broad and intensive training in subject matter and the principles of education are required for professionalized subject matter courses.

    c. The Missouri teachers colleges should undertake the reorganization of the content of courses as an intercollegiate enterprise according to a systematic scheme. (See pp. 145 and 146.)

II. *The Administration of the Training School and Practice Teaching.* (See Chapter IV, pp. 147 and 148.)

    a. The amount of required practice teaching should be increased to ten semester hours for the sixty-hour curricula, and the theory courses in education reduced accordingly.

b. Gradated participation and practice teaching should start with the simpler phases of general participation and progress to independent, responsible class teaching which should come late in the course.

c. The administrative policy of the training school should definitely provide for the enlarged use of the training school and should promote its direct relationship to all of the departments of the college. The details of plans for this purpose are to be found on page 100. (See proposal B, I, f, p. 181.)

III. *Needed Research.*

a. Textbooks and syllabi of courses in which subject matter is given a professional treatment on the collegiate level are much needed.

b. Careful analyses of the subject matter needs of teachers in the different fields would be helpful in providing the proper content in teacher-training courses.

c. Conclusive studies regarding the relative merits of distributed and concentrated practice teaching would assist in the administration of the work.

d. The effect of a large amount of demonstration teaching, for purposes of illustrating various types of teaching method, upon the progress of the children should be determined.

D. PROPOSALS RELATING TO THE CONFERENCE OF EDUCATIONAL INSTITUTIONS

I. *Present Activities.* (See Chapter V, pp. 164 and 165.)

a. The Conference of State Educational Institutions in Missouri should continue to function in all lines of activity now embraced in its program.

II. *Intercollegiate Relationship.*

a. In order that the desirable intercollegiate relationship which now exists may be maintained, no college should enlarge its field of work except in accordance with a general policy adopted by the Conference. This proposal relates especially to work of a graduate character which is, and for many years should be, the exclusive right of the state university.

III. *Perpetuation.*

a. So long as the Conference continues to operate with its present effectiveness and splendid spirit of coöperation, it should continue as a voluntary organization. Its present status has all of the practical advantages of a legalized coördinating agency with none of its possible objectionable features.

b. If conditions should ever be such that the necessity of legal authority to enforce its regulations should be felt, the history of accomplishment points to the Conference as the most desirable agency for bringing about a coördination of the state's higher educational institutions on a professional basis.

c. The possibility of veto by any one of the several boards of control of the colleges is one of the chief elements of strength in the present plan.

IV. *Future Activities Relating to Professional Development.*

a. The Conference should establish and maintain a research division for the purpose of conducting and directing studies needed in the determination of the state's policy of teacher training.

b. Typical problems for which the Conference should assume responsibility are here listed.

1. In coöperation with the research departments of the institutions the Conference should constantly study curricula for the training of teachers. Their findings should be reported to the Conference and should be the basis of its curriculum policy.

2. The Conference research division should study at all times the state's demand and supply of trained teachers.

3. Surveys should be made to determine scientifically the state's ability to train an adequate supply of teachers. Reliable information concerning the need for such agencies as teacher-training classes in high schools should be included in the program.

4. Comparative studies designed to afford a measure of the work of Missouri colleges in comparison with other states to the end of improving the Missouri colleges should be undertaken by the Conference.

c. The activities of the Conference should be limited to those aspects of the teacher-training problems which are common to all of the colleges holding membership in the Conference. It should never be the policy of the Conference to interfere with the policies and practices of an individual school except as its conduct may affect the general policy of teacher training in the state.

V. *Future Activities Relating to Major and Service Lines.*

a. In the light of the investigations that have been proposed, there should be a constant redetermination and modification of the major and service lines of all of the colleges.

b. Intercollegiate specialization should be undertaken only as a result of the Conference recommendations. Otherwise, there can be no assurance of a well-balanced development of the state's program.

VI. *Future Activities Relating to Fiscal Support.*

a. Scientific comparative studies should be made of student costs of teacher training. Such studies will serve as a check on individual colleges and will help to justify the teacher-training budget of the state.

b. Budgets for the individual institutions should be discussed and agreed upon finally by the Conference, in conjunction with representatives of the several boards.

c. The Conference should present to the proper committee of the legislature the claims of all of the schools for appropriations.

d. In the absence of any other agency in the state for the purpose, the Conference should make scientific studies of sources of revenue and plans for financing the state's program of higher education. This information should be made available to the legislative bodies of the state.

e. The Conference should have definite information supported by all relevant facts in justification of any proposed enlargement of the state's facilities for the training of teachers.

VII. *Student Placement.*

a. The Conference should study the "marketing of the product of the teachers colleges" to the end of being of the greatest service to the schools of the state and to the students, in the proper placement of the graduates.

APPENDIX A
DATA SHEET RELATING TO STUDENTS

DATA RELATING TO STUDENTS
OF THE
STATE NORMAL SCHOOL OR TEACHERS COLLEGE LOCATED AT_____
CITY   STATE

The information you are giving will be used in tabulations in impersonal ways. No names will be used in the reports made from this study. It is desirable to have your name in case further correspondence is necessary. The facts are important, however, and the name may be omitted if desired. No question is asked without a good reason. All of your replies will be held as strictly confidential matter. Be as accurate as possible.

1. Your name (last name first)_____
Mr.
Miss
Mrs.
(Check)

2. Of what descent (Irish, German, or what) was your father? _____
   a. Was he born in the United States?_____
   b. If not, in what foreign country was he born?_____

3. Of what descent was your mother?_____ a. Born in the United States?_____ b. If not, in what foreign country was she born?_____

4. Is your father living?_____ Mother living?_____

5. What is (or was) your father's occupation? _____

6. In what state or foreign country were you born?_____

7. How many children did your parents have?_____

8. In order of age state your place among the children of your parents_____

9. How many of you still make your home with your parents?_____

10. State approximately in one sum the total annual income of all the family living at home at the time you entered the normal school or teachers college. About $_____annually

11. How many of the family contribute to that sum to support the whole family?_____

12. Have you brothers or sisters who have taught or are now teaching?_____ How many?_____

13. Your age when you entered normal school or teachers college?_____years and_____months.

14. From what high school did you graduate?_____

15. How many years in the course beyond the eighth grade?_____

16. If not a high school graduate, how many years of high school work did you have beyond the eighth grade?_____

17. State in "units" what your high school course consisted of. (A unit is a subject with five recitation periods per week through a year of approximately 36 weeks.) Express fractions of units as ¼, ½, ¾, etc.

Latin				Civics
Spanish	Gen. Science	Arithmetic		Sociology
French		Algebra		Economics
German	Biology	Geometry		
Italian	Botany	Trigonometry		Home economics subjects
	Zoology			Manual training subjects
English Lit.	Chemistry			Business course subjects
English Comp.	Physics	American history		Music
English grammar		Other history		Art courses

Total units_____

18. Did you teach between the completion of the eighth grade and the beginning of your high school course?_____ If so, how many months?_____

19. Did you teach between the completion of your high school course and your entrance into the normal school or teachers college? _____. If so, how many months?_____

20. Place a check in the blank (or blanks) applying to you. Is your home:
   a. On a farm?_____
   b. In a community of less than 1000 inhabitants?_____
   c. In a community of 1000 to 2500 inhabitants?_____
   d. In a community of 2500 to 5000 inhabitants?_____
   e. In a community of 5000 to 25000 inhabitants?_____
   f. In a community of more than 25000 inhabitants?_____

21. About what per cent of the money you are using to pay your school expenses this year comes from the following sources?
   a. Father or mother_____   f. By working while in college_____
   b. Borrowing_____   g. Other sources (please specify)_____
   c. Your own savings_____
   d. Brother or sister_____
   e. Scholarship_____

22. Check the type of teaching you expect (or hope) to do after completing your preparation:
   a. Kindergarten_____   d. Fifth or sixth grade?_____
   b. First or second grade?_____   e. Junior high school (seventh, eighth, or ninth grade)?_____
   c. Third or fourth grade?_____   f. Senior high school. What subject?_____
   g. Special elementary school subject. What subject?_____

23. Indicate below about how many years you expect to teach. It is possible that marriage or change of occupation may terminate your teaching. Please be quite frank about it and make your best estimate in years at what your teaching life will be if you can realize your wishes. _____years.

187

DATA SHEET RELATING TO STUDENTS (*Cont'd*)

II. GENERAL EDUCATION AND PROFESSIONAL TRAINING

1. (Under "kind of school" indicate whether public, private or parochial:

School	Name and Location of Institutions	Kind of School	Number of Years Attended	Nature of Course Completed	Year Graduated	Degree or Diploma
Elementary, Rural						
Elementary, Graded						
High School						
Normal School						
College or University						
Special Schools						
Summer Schools. Number of Weeks of Each			(Weeks)			
			(Weeks)			
			(Weeks)			
			(Weeks)			
Extension Courses						
Other Preparation For Present Work						

SUMMARY OF PREPARATION

2. Elementary school...years
   Secondary school...years   Summer school, total _____weeks
   Normal school (T. C.)..years   Amount of extension work_____
   College or university..years   _____
   Total (exclusive of extension
   and summer sessions).....................years

3. List below, with name of institution, any courses you are now taking either in your own school or other institutions:

   _____   _____
   _____   _____

4. List below any extension courses you are now taking. Include name of institution:

   _____   _____
   _____   _____

DATA SHEET RELATING TO STUDENTS (*Cont'd*)

III. EDUCATIONAL EXPERIENCE

Name and Location of Schools	Nature of Position State also Subjects or Grades	Kind of School Public or Private	Number Years Served	Annual Salary

SUMMARY OF EXPERIENCE

2. Number of years' service before entering the present school:

	Elementary Rural	Graded	Secondary	Normal School	College	University
Teacher						
Supervisor						
Principal						
City Sup't.						
County Sup't.						
State Sup't.						

3. Date of beginning work in this school_____. How many years, including this year have you served in this school in each of the following capacities?

Instructor.._____years
Supervisor.._____years
Critic teacher.._____years
_____years
_____years

4. Total number of years' experience in educational work in all institutions, including the present year..........years

IV. PRESENT WORK

1. List below the classes you now teach, number of students, etc :

Class Title (e. g. Principles of Education.)	Number of Students in Class	Number Periods Class Instr. Weekly	Length of Each Period in Minutes	Number Laboratory Periods Weekly	Length of Laboratory Period in Minutes	Nature of Class work (e. g. Lecture, Recitation.)
Extension Courses						
Correspondence Courses						

DATA SHEET RELATING TO STUDENTS (*Cont'd*)

2. How many clock hours weekly do you spend in each of the following:

Supervision of student teachers.._____clock hours
Group conferences with students.. "   "
Individual conferences with students.. "   "
Teaching children.. "   "
Correcting papers.. "   "
Making out reports and records.. "   "
Conferences with parents and visitors... "   "
      Total... "   "

3. Describe below any assistance you now have; e. g. room teacher, clerical or secretarial help, student assistant. Do not include practice teachers:

Title of Assistant	Character of Help Given	Number Hours Weekly

4. List below your participation in extra-curricular student activities, during the present academic year; e. g. athletics, debating, literary societies, etc.:

Type of Activity	Capacity in Which You Serve	Number of Students Involved	Total Hours to Date this Year	Probable Total Hours for the Remainder of Year

5. List below the faculty committees of which you are a member:

	Name of Committee	Capacity in which You Serve	Is it a Standing Committee?	Average Hours Weekly You Give
Academic Dep't.				
Training Dep't.				

6. In the above table, star the committees, the work of which you feel is of professional value to you. About what percentage of the total time you give to committee work is beneficial to you professionally?_____%

V. OPPORTUNITIES FOR PROFESSIONAL GROWTH

1. How many hours monthly do you spend in faculty meetings?_____. How many hours monthly in departmental meetings?_____

2. How many faculty meetings does your staff have yearly, on the average?_____ What percentage of the total time of these faculty meetings is devoted to each of the following matters?

Matters of educational policy.._____%
Details of administration.._____%
Professional improvement of the staff..._____%
Other matters (Please specify).._____%
...._____%

DATA SHEET RELATING TO STUDENTS (*Cont'd*)

3. In your opinion do you and your colleagues participate to a desirable extent in the determination of the educational policies of your school?_____ Make any comments here:

_____

_____

4. Do you have a satisfactory degree of freedom in your teaching and in the conduct of your classroom?_____

5. Is there any supervision of your instruction?_____ By whom?_____
How many visits have you received from this supervisor or supervisors so far during the present academic year?_____ How many of these visits have been followed by conferences?_____

6. Do you find this supervision helpful?_____ Would you prefer a different sort of supervision?_____ If you are not supervised, would you like supervision? _____ By whom?_____

7. Describe briefly any collective investigations or experiments which the members of your staff have recently engaged in. Mention the nature of your participation.

_____

_____

_____

8. Do you feel that the institution which you serve stimulates and expects professional growth on your part? _____ Why?_____

VI. PROFESSIONAL ACTIVITY

1. How much time do you give weekly to students in discussing personal problems not listed under individual conferences above?_____ _____hrs.

2. How much time on the average do you devote to direct preparation for your classes?_____hrs.

3. How much time are you able to devote weekly to professional reading, other than that in direct preparation for class work?_____hrs.
List the books which you have read in the past two or three years that have helped you most in your work:

_____   _____

_____   _____

_____   _____

4. List the magazines and journals that you find most helpful professionally:

_____   _____

_____   _____

_____   _____

5. How much time are you able to devote to general reading weekly?_____hrs.

6. How much time are you able to devote to recreation, other than reading, weekly?_____hrs.

DATA SHEET RELATING TO STUDENTS (*Cont'd*)

7. List the titles, dates and publishers of books you have published:

8. List the titles of articles you have published, with magazine and date:

9. List anything else you have published (syllabi, tests, etc.):

10. What experience have you had in constructing courses of study (excluding class problems):
    For this institution?   For other institution?

11. What addresses, lectures, papers, etc., have you delivered in the past year outside your own school:
    (a) Before educational bodies (institutes, conventions, etc.)?   (b) Before lay bodies (business clubs, mothers' clubs)?

12. List educational organizations of which you are a member:

Organization (e. g. N. E. A.; Amer. Hist. Ass'n.; Nat'l. Council Teachers Eng.)	If Officer please Designate (Sec'y., etc.)	Member of which Committees?	Date of last Meeting Attended	Cost to you of this Attendance	Were you on the Program at the last Meeting?

13. Does your school encourage attendance at these meetings?_____
    How?_____

14. List any leaves of absence you have ever had:

Date	Length of Leave	Institution Giving Leave	How Spent?	Was the leave with full, partial or no salary?

15. List any traveling you have done:

Continents, Countries or parts of U. S. visited	Approximate Date	Number months actually Traveling	If on leave, from what Institution?	Did your school recognize this travel in any way? How? (e. g. by promotion, salary inc.)

DATA SHEET RELATING TO STUDENTS (*Cont'd*)

16. Are you now carrying on any experiments or research in education, not listed above under group projects? If so, of what nature?

_____

_____

17. Have you recently completed any such research? When? Of what nature?

_____

_____

18. Have you recently organized and presented any new courses? Please list, with dates:

_____

_____

19. How many class periods (class sessions) of other instructors, not in the training school, have you visited in the past year for the purpose of analyzing or comparing the methods of instruction used?_____.

20. How many class periods in the training school have you visited in the past year?_____.

21. List below any measures you have taken to promote your own professional fitness that have not been mentioned above:

_____

_____

_____

22. Suggest changes, of any nature, that would enable you to teach more effectively

_____

_____

_____

STATUS OF CRITIC TEACHERS

1. Do the members of the faculty consider critic teachers of equal professional rank with the other members of the staff?_____.

2. Do the two groups have the same social status:
   In the life of the normal school? _____.
   In the life of the community?_____.

3. Do critic teachers participate on equal terms with other members of the staff in determining the policies of the normal school as a whole:
   By active membership in committees?_____.
   By active part in discussions in faculty meetings?_____.
   By conference with the principal of the normal school?_____.

DATA SHEET RELATING TO STUDENTS (*Cont'd*)

TO BE FILLED OUT BY CRITIC TEACHERS
IN ADDITION TO ACCOMPANYING SHEETS

A critic teacher is an instructor who is responsible for a definite group of children and also for a group of students who are teaching these children under his or her supervision.

NAME OF SCHOOL_____

I. Work you are doing in the **training department:**

    A. Are you doing supervisory work in the practice or observation school affiliated with the normal school or in the city schools?_____.

    B. In what grade or grades are you teaching?_____.

    C. What subjects are you teaching?_____

    D. For how many children are you directly responsible now?_____.

    E. Distribution of time for the past week (Indicate in clock hours):   **Clock Hrs.**

        1. In teaching children for demonstration purposes................................._____

        2. In teaching or supervising children but not for demonstration purposes........._____

        3. In supervising student teachers..._____

        4. In group conferences with student teachers.................................._____

        5. In individual conferences with student teachers............................._____

        6. In the making out of reports.._____

        7. In conferences with parents ...._____

        8. In conferences with other visitors.._____

        9. List below any other activities connected with your work but not included in any of the above:

        _____

        _____

        _____

        _____

        _____

        TOTAL number of hours spent in the past week in all the above activities.........._____

    F. Please give below in proper columns by terms and for years indicated the number of student teachers you supervised:

TERMS	1921-22	1922-23	1923-24	1924-25
First Term				
Second Term				
Third Term				
Fourth Term				

    G. For how many weeks is each student teacher assigned to you for supervision_____.
        For how many hours a week?_____

II. Distribution of time spent last month in attendance at meetings called by: **Clock hrs.**

    A. Principal (President) of the normal school.._____

    B. Director or principal of the practice or training department........................_____

    C. Any other members of the normal school faculty..................................._____

    D. Principal of the school building in which you are doing your work. (Do not give this data if it is included in data given in answer to questions A.-C.)......................_____

    E. Superintendent of city schools ...._____

    F. Supervisors of the city schools..._____

        TOTAL number of hours..._____

APPENDIX B

DATA SHEET FOR MEMBERS OF THE INSTRUCTIONAL STAFFS OF NORMAL SCHOOLS OR TEACHERS COLLEGES

DATA SHEET FOR MEMBERS OF THE INSTRUCTIONAL STAFFS OF
NORMAL SCHOOLS OR TEACHERS COLLEGES

NOTE:—Please furnish as fully as possible the information asked for in the following questions. In constructing an adequate picture of the normal school situation it is necessary to have facts that can be secured only by the voluntary cooperation of the members of the instructional staffs of the several schools. Please remember that all information of a personal character will be treated in the strictest confidence and will be published only in group compilations from which it will be impossible to identify individuals. The name Normal School, instead of Teachers College, is used throughout.

NAME OF SCHOOL_____

I. PERSONAL DATA

1. Name_____ Age (nearest birthday)_____
    (Name may be omitted if desired)

2. Birthplace_____. Sex: Male, Female. Single, Married, Widowed.
                          (underline)   (underline)

3. Birthplace of father (Name of state or foreign country)_____of mother_____

4. How many persons, besides yourself, are wholly dependent upon you for support?_____ How many are partially dependent?_____

5. What was the principal occupation of your father or guardian during the time you were in high school?_____. How many children were there in the family then?_____.

6. How many other members of your immediate family are or have been teachers?_____

7. At what age did you begin teaching?_____. Did you teach between your high school course and your normal school or college course?_____. If so, how long?_____.

8. If you had an opportunity now to choose a vocation, would you choose teaching?_____. Give reasons for your answer_____
    _____
    _____
    _____

9. What is your present annual salary, excluding summer school work? $_____. For how many weeks teaching is this salary paid?_____.

10. Do you regularly augment this salary by summer school teaching?_____. To what extent? $_____

11. Extra compensation annually from extension classes: $_____. From correspondence courses: $_____. From tutoring: $_____.

12. Do you find it necessary to augment your salary by other (non-educational) work?_____. Of what nature?_____. To what extent? $_____.

13. Annual income from other sources, such as interest from bonds: $_____

14. Amount saved during the past year:
    (a) Life insurance (total of premiums) $_____
    (b) Pension or retirement fund_____$_____
    (c) Other savings_____$_____

APPENDIX C

REPORT TO VISITING COMMITTEE APPOINTED IN ACCORDANCE
WITH ARTICLES OF AGREEMENT ADOPTED IN CONFERENCE OF
PRESIDENTS OF STATE EDUCATIONAL INSTITUTIONS AND
STATE SUPERINTENDENT OF PUBLIC SCHOOLS

Name of institution..................... Date ....

GENERAL DATA

Number of secondary pupils enrolled.............
Number of college students enrolled..............
     Total enrollment   ....
Number of college and high school teachers, including student assistants
who conduct class work..............

ARTICLE II

A. Number of students admitted to college work on not less than 15 units of credit in a first-class high school, a fully accredited private academy, or the secondary department of a state normal school .... Number of cases (included in class above) in which secondary school records are not on file...........

B. Number of special students not less than 21 years of age who have been admitted to college classes..............

C. Number of students admitted conditionally to college work who are conditioned in not more than two entrance units.............. Number of students admitted conditionally to college work who are conditioned in more than two entrance units..............

D. Are all students required to remove entrance conditions within one year of date of admission?...............

E. Does the credentials committee have final authority in all cases of evaluating credentials and classifying students as college, secondary or special students?...............

F. Are college and secondary students in any cases instructed together in the same class? If so, specify the classes..............

G. Do the same teachers in any case teach both college and secondary

196

classes? If so, specify in each case the name of the teacher and the classes he teaches....................

H. What is the maximum number of units that may be carried each term or semester by a secondary pupil?..............How many secondary pupils are carrying this maximum?..............

ARTICLE III

A. If excess and diminished credit is allowed, number of students carrying work at the rate of more than 32 hours per year .... Does any student receive more than 37½ hours credit in one year? ....

B. If excess and diminished credit is not allowed, number of students carrying work at the rate of 30 hours per year ....; 33¾ ....; 37½ ....

How are students selected who carry excess work?

C. Number of college teachers having 18 or less hours of teaching per week .... Number having more than 18 hours of teaching per week ....

D. Number college teachers having degree of Ph.D. ....
Number of college teachers having master's degree or equivalent ....
Number of college teachers not having master's degree or equivalent..........................
Number of college teachers employed this year for first time not having master's degree or equivalent ....
Number of students entering more than one week late who are registered for more semester hours' credit than there are weeks in the period for which they are registered............

E. & F. Are all correspondence and extension courses given in accordance with agreement? ....
If not given as per agreement, in what respects do they differ?
....

ARTICLE IV

A. Is all entering of credit done by the registrar? ....
(a) Does each student's permanent record card show the following facts:
1. The credit which has been accepted from other institutions with the name of institution and the date on which the advanced standing was granted ....
2. Name of courses for which students register ....
3. Catalogue number ....
4. Are all secondary courses indicated by Roman numerals? ....
5. Are all freshmen and sophomore college year courses indicated by Arabic numerals from 1 to 99? ....

6. Are all junior and senior college courses indicated by Arabic numerals from 1 to 99? ....

7. Are the letters a and b used to designate the first and second semesters, respectively, and the letters a, b, and c used to designate the first, second, and third terms, respectively? ....

8. Number of hours' credit ....

9. Term in which taken...........

10. Grade ....

11. Classification of student ....

12. Are conditions specified in red ink? ....

(b) Does each student's daily program card or study card show the following facts:

1. Name of courses for which student registers ....

2. Catalogue number of these courses ....

3. Number of hours' credit for which the student is registered in each course ....

4. Term or semester in which the work is taken ....

ARTICLE V

Is all advanced standing from other institutions recorded in the first term or semester during which the student is in attendance?

(a) 1. Have all students coming from classified high schools been given credit according to the rating given by the State Superintendent of Schools? ....

2. Has advanced standing for more than 64 hours' credit been given to students coming from junior colleges? ....

(b) 1. (a) Have pupils from unclassified secondary schools been given credit according to the rating of the State Superintendent of Schools for such schools? ....

(b) Have all students who claimed credit for work from unclassified schools been required to pass examinations in the work for which credit is claimed in excess of that recommended by the State Superintendent? ....

(c) Have entrance examinations been given for more than four units for each year spent in school by such pupils? ....

(d) Have entrance examinations been given by the committee of the faculty? ....

(e) Have entrance questions been set and papers graded by the department in which the applicants have sought credit? ....

(f) Have examinations been given later than the first week of each term? ....

(g) Are the times for examination stated in the catalogue? ....

(h) Are all examination questions and papers deposited with the chairman of the examining committee and kept on file for at least one year? ....

(i) Has credit by examination been given after a student has completed one year of work in the school, or after an advanced course has been taken in the subject for which credit is asked? ....

(j) Have students been admitted to examination for advanced standing without having produced evidence that systematic preparation had been made for such work? ....

(k) In substituting college credit to make up a deficiency in secondary credit is five hours of college work counted as the equivalent of one secondary credit? ....

(l) Has high school credit been allowed on the basis of courses where the applicants teaching in the high school have been approved by the State Department of Education or the university visitor? ....

(m) Has credit without examination been given from institutions other than standard institutions of high school and college rank? ....

(n) Has any advanced standing of college rank been given for post-graduate work done in a high school that is not properly equipped and definitely organized to do work of college rank and does not restrict such advanced work entirely to students who have completed a four-year secondary course, and who are taught by teachers having the qualifications set forth in the Articles of Agreement for teachers of college subjects? ....

(o) Has credit been given in the last year for experience gained as a teacher receiving a salary? ....

(p) Has advanced college standing been granted in the last year for grades on state or county certificates when such grades have been secured by examination? ....

Article VI

(a) Has any elementary certificate been given in the last year on the basis of less than two terms of residence? ....

(b) Has any diploma been granted in the last year on the basis of less than three terms of residence? ....

(c) Is the regulation that no special student be permitted to graduate rigidly enforced? ....

Signed by ....
Official position:

STATEMENT BY DEAN M. G. NEALE

Part of a letter from Dean M. G. Neale of the School of Education, Missouri University:

In answering your second question I may say that it is the policy of the University of Missouri to devote more and more of its energy to graduate departments. This is particularly true of the School of Education. We have cut our undergraduate offerings in the field of education to the very minimum in order that members of our faculty may have more time for graduate courses. I do not have available now exact figures on the increase of graduate work or the increase in graduate enrollment in the University. I do know that this semester we have 295 graduate students, an increase of about 40 per cent over the registration in the graduate school for 1924-25.

I can give you definite figures for the summer sessions. In 1920 there were 63 graduate students registered for summer session work. In the summer of 1924 there were 272, and in 1925, 410. In other words, there were almost seven times as many graduate students registered in the summer of 1925 as there were in the summer of 1920. In 1920 there were nine summer session students devoting their time entirely to education courses. In 1924 there were 95, and in 1925, 180. In the summer session of 1920 graduate students took 294 semester hours of graduate work. In 1924 they took 1511 hours, and in 1925, 2205.

The increase in the attention paid by graduate students to professional education courses may be seen from the fact that in the summer of 1920 graduate students took only 65 semester hours of work in professional education courses. In the summer session of 1924 they took 691 semester hours and in the summer of 1925, 1118. In other words, in 1920 only a little more than one-fourth of all the graduate work was in Education. In the summer of 1925 over one-half of the graduate work was in that field.

The extent to which graduate work in Education is emphasized during the summer session may be indicated by the fact that of the 78 professional education courses offered during the summer session of 1926, 28 will be for graduate students only, 35 for both graduates and undergraduates, leaving only 15 courses of purely undergraduate character. Most of these 15 courses are on the teaching of various high school subjects.

REPORT OF CONFERENCE OF STATE EDUCATIONAL INSTITUTIONS AND STATE SUPERINTENDENT OF SCHOOLS, AT COLUMBIA, MISSOURI, JANUARY 29, 1925

The Conference met in the University Men's Faculty Room [University of Missouri] with the following members present: Supt. Chas. A. Lee, presiding. President Stratton D. Brooks and Dean M. G. Neale of the University, President Jos. A. Serena and Dean R. S. Douglass of Cape Girardeau, President E. L. Hendricks and Dean W. W. Parker of Warrensburg, President Clyde M. Hill and Professor M. A. O'Rear of Springfield, President Uel W. Lamkin and Dean Geo. W. Colbert of Maryville, Dean W. H. Ziegel of Kirksville, and John B. Boyd of the State Department of Education.

The minutes for January 10, 1924, and for November 12 and 13, 1924, were read and approved. The reports of the committees were then considered.

President Hill reported that his committee had revised and codified the Articles of the Agreement and that the same had been printed in the 1925 Catalogue of the Southwest Missouri State Teachers College.

The Committee of Deans made its report and the following recommendations were adopted:

a. After September 1, 1926, fifteen units shall be required for admission to college and no conditions shall be granted. Motion—Dean Douglas.

b. The maximum credit for correspondence work or extension work or both shall not exceed one-third of the requirement for the course pursued. Motion—President Hill.

c. The maximum credit for correspondence or extension work in a single year shall be retained at ten hours or two high school units, but exceptional cases may be dealt with by each institution and additional work permitted up to a maximum of twenty hours or three high school units. Motion—President Hendricks.

d. For the purpose of determining teaching load extension work shall be counted credit hour for credit hour. Motion—Dean Douglas.

e. In determining teaching load twenty-five active correspondence students shall be considered as equivalent to a class in residence. Motion—Dean Douglas.

f. Uniform blanks for transcript of credits recommended by Dr. Coursault shall be used by all the state institutions. Motion—Dean Douglas.

The following men were appointed on the Evaluating Committee: J. H. Coursault, Eugene Fair, R. S. Douglas, W. W. Parker, Norman Freudenberger, Geo. W. Colbert, and John B. Boyd, and it was agreed that the Committee should meet at an early date.

President Lamkin presented a letter from a committee of his faculty setting forth certain limitations of the present program of extension service and asking joint consideration of certain recommendations. The matter was referred to a committee of representatives of the state institutions to be appointed by the presidents. The University representative is to serve as Chairman.

The Conference adjourned.

APPENDIX D

TYPICAL REPORT OF THE VISITING COMMITTEE OF THE
CONFERENCE OF HIGHER EDUCATIONAL INSTITUTIONS

To the Conference of State Educational Institutions and State
Superintendent of Public Schools
January 10, 1924

Your Committee visited all of the institutions of the Conference during
the week December 17-22, and herewith submits a report of each school
and makes the following recommendations for your consideration:

1. All certificates of credits should be on official blanks showing certain
essential data, such as year and school in which each credit was made, date
of entrance and date of graduation, or attendance, classification of the
school, date of birth of student, and signature of proper official filling out
blank.

2. It appears essential that a committee, the Deans, be appointed to
prepare a blank for transcript of credits giving the minimum essentials,
with the understanding that each institution may so modify the blank as
to secure special information desired.

3. In the case of certificates of credits from schools of other states the
basis of evaluation should be written on the blank by the evaluating agent
of the institution accepting the credit.

4. We suggest an amendment of Art. II, Sec. A, of the Conference Agreement by adding the words: "and the maximum and minimum credits prescribed by the State Superintendent shall be observed."

5. We recommend that secondary credit made before 1913 be evaluated
on the basis of classification given by the State Department or by the
State University.

6. We recommend that there be added to Art. V, Sec. B, Subdivision 1,
(k) the following statement: "No secondary credit shall be given for
grades on State or County Certificates."

7. We recommend that Art. III, Sec. C, be amended by adding the following words to the first sentence: "including correspondence and extension
work." We also suggest that we come to an understanding as to the
amount of correspondence or extension work that is equivalent to an hour
of classroom work.

8. We recommend that in the acceptance of credit from institutions not
in the Conference evaluation of both secondary and college credit be made
in accordance with the provisions of the Conference Agreement. For
example, if a college of the Missouri College Union accepts secondary or
college credit from an unaccredited institution, a member of the Conference should not accept evaluations of credits made by this college.

9. We recommend to the Conference the following definition of *"Systematic preparation"* as used in Art. V, Sec. B, Subdivision 1, (k): "Systematic

202

preparation consists (a) of the study and completion of a course or courses in an unaccredited school, or (b) of an equivalent amount of study under a private teacher who meets the requirements of the State Department of Education for teachers of the subjects taught, or (c) of teaching a subject in an unaccredited school.

10. We request an interpretation of Art. V, Sec. B, Subdivision 1, (h), of the Agreement and submit the case of Mr. Rolla H. Wybrant, concerning which there is a difference of opinion.

SPECIAL RECOMMENDATIONS

11. We recommend that the teachers colleges offer curricula leading only to the degree of B. S. in Education.

12. We urgently recommend that a committee be appointed to revise the articles of the Agreement of this Conference on the basis of our present understanding with a view especially to a better organization of its various provisions, and furthermore that said committee prepare a statement of provisions of special importance to students with a view to having this abbreviated statement published in the catalogues of the institutions of the Conference.

Your committee found a few cases of irregularities in administering the provisions of the Agreement. One particular case was the acceptance of college entrance credit and some forty hours of advance standing credit from unaccredited schools by the president of the institution, the transcripts not being submitted to the committee on credentials. On the whole, however, the provisions are being cheerfully met and ably administered, the only difficulty being the lack of agreement in the interpretation of a number of the provisions.

In conclusion the committee desires to express its appreciation for the courtesy and the coöperation of all members of the Conference, and to reaffirm its faith in the value of the Agreement.

Respectfully submitted,

T. Jennie Green ⎫
J. H. Coursault ⎬ Committee.
John B. Boyd ⎭

APPENDIX E

TYPICAL COMMITTEE REPORT TO THE CONFERENCE OF HIGHER EDUCATIONAL INSTITUTIONS

St. Louis, Mo.,
Nov. 3, 1922

Pursuant to a resolution of the Conference of Missouri State Schools the deans of these institutions met in the Statler Hotel, Friday, Nov. 3, at 9 A.M. to consider uniform requirements for degrees and certificates.

The following were present: Dean J. H. Coursault of the University School of Education, Chairman; Dean C. A. Phillips of the Central Mo. State Teachers College; Dean Geo. H. Colbert of the Northwest Mo. State Teachers College; Dean R. S. Douglass of the Southeast Mo. State Teachers College; M. A. O'Rear, Chairman, Course of Study Committee, Southwest Mo. State Teachers College; and H. G. Swanson representing Dean W. H. Ziegel of the Northeast Mo. State Teachers College.

The meeting was called to order by Chairman Coursault, and R. S. Douglass was elected secretary.

On motion it was decided to take up first the matter of requirements for the degree of B. S. in Education.

It was voted that courses in General Psychology be not credited as Education. Voted to recommend to the Conference that for B. S. in Education degree, one course of at least 2½ hours in Educational Psychology be required. Voted that it is desirable that the course in Educational Psychology be preceded by a course in General Psychology or a course in Biological Science. On motion it was voted to recommend that one course of at least 2½ hours in Principles of Teaching be required for the degree, this course to be preceded by Educational Psychology. It was voted that a course of at least 2½ hours in History and Principles of Education be required for the degree, to be given as late as possible in the student's course.

Voted that a course of at least 2 hours in School Administration, to be called School Economy, be required for the degree. This course should include such topics as: Buildings and Grounds; School Law; Classroom Management; Professional Ethics; Relation of the School to the Community; and Extra-curriculum Activities.

On motion the committee adjourned to meet at 1:30 P.M.

Afternoon Session

The Committee of Deans met at 1:30 and was called to order by Chairman Coursault.

On further consideration of the requirements for the B. S. degree it was voted to recommend that there should be required of the candidate a sufficient amount of practice teaching to demonstrate his ability to teach. This should be not less than one term. This recommendation is not meant to prevent exemption from teaching as provided for in the Conference Agreement, nor does the requirement apply to cases when the diploma is not a certificate to teach.

It is recommended that a course in hygiene with special reference to the health problems of the school be given. The course should carry at least 2 hours' credit. It was voted to recommend that there should be required for the degree a major of at least 15 hours and a minor of at least 10 hours in academic or technical subjects, exception to be made in case of students pursuing fixed curricula in vocational subjects.

It was voted to recommend that for the degree a minimum of 5 hours in English, preferably in English Composition, be required. It was moved, seconded, and carried that the maximum credit in Education should be 30 hours.

The Committee adjourned until 7:30 P.M.

Evening Session

The Committee met at 7:30 P.M. with all members present.

It was voted that the 120 hours required for the degree shall not include credit for physical exercises.

It was agreed that if a Life Certificate is issued upon the completion of 120 hours of work, separate from the degree, requirements specified for the degree should be met.

It was moved, seconded, and carried that at least 5 hours in English, preferably English Composition, be required for the 60-hour certificate. Voted that in addition to the requirement in English and Education candidates for the 60-hour certificate be required to make at least 5 hours in at least three other subjects.

Voted to recommend to the Conference that it reconsider the amount of work permitted to be done by correspondence or extension for degrees and certificates.

The committee adjourned to meet at 8:30 Saturday morning.

Saturday morning, Nov. 4, 1922.

The Committee of Deans met at 8:30, all members present.

It was voted that major and minor subjects be selected and directed on the advice of advisers, preferably in the department in which the major is chosen.

Voted that the minimum requirement in Education for the B. S. in Education degree be 24 hours.

It was voted that it is desirable to restrict, as far as possible, freshman and sophomore students to classes of junior college rank; and to restrict junior and senior students to classes of senior college rank.

It was voted that for the Regent Certificate a course of at least 5 hours in Elementary Education be required. Elementary Education should include such topics as the selection, organization, and presentation of subject matter in the elementary school subjects, and also classroom management.

Voted that for the Regents' Certificate at least 2½ hours in observation and teaching be required.

Voted that one course of at least 5 hours in English, preferably English Composition, be required for the Regents' Certificate.

Voted that Article XII, Section B, Subdivision III under "College Courses in Education," item 6 of the Conference Agreement on uniform terminology should read "Elementary Education" instead of "Elementary Course of Study."

Voted that there should be added to the college courses listed under Psychology in the section on uniform terminology in the Conference Agreement courses in:

Mental Tests

Educational Tests and Measurements

Voted that Section IV, item 1, on uniform terminology in Conference Agreement, under History of Education, should read:

"History and Principles of Education."

Voted that courses in the several departments be not unnecessarily multiplied.

Voted that departments in the various colleges be asked to prepare and exchange syllabi on the required courses for certificates and degrees.

On motion the committee adjourned at 11:30.

APPENDIX F

MINUTES OF A TYPICAL MEETING OF THE CONFERENCE

MINUTES OF THE CONFERENCE OF COLLEGE PRESIDENTS AND STATE
SUPERINTENDENT OF SCHOOLS, HOTEL BALTIMORE,
KANSAS CITY, MO., NOVEMBER 15, 1922

In the absence of State Superintendent of Schools, Sam A. Baker, who
by virtue of his position is chairman of the Conference, President Hendricks presided.

The motions made and adopted by the Conference were as follows:

1. That the minutes of the last meeting receive formal approval at the
next meeting of the Conference.

2. That Presidents Hendricks and Kirk be asked to secure a ruling from
the Attorney-General in regard to the legality of granting a diploma upon
the completion of four years of college work and report same to the other
presidents.

3. That fifty per cent of the required college work for any degree, certificate, or diploma may be completed by extension work, provided that the
existing requirements as to hours in residence remain unchanged.

4. That Dr. J. H. Coursault and President E. L. Hendricks constitute a
committee to compile from our existing rules and regulations a brief of the
essential regulations for the various courses.

5. That the Report of the Committee of the Deans, made at the St.
Louis meeting November 3 and 4, 1922, to the Conference of the College
Presidents, be adopted as a whole. A copy of the report follows:

Report of the Committee of Deans to the Missouri Conference
of State Schools

At a meeting of Deans held in St. Louis, November 3 and 4, 1922, the
following recommendations were agreed upon to be presented to the Conference.

I. Concerning the degree of B. S. in Education and the 120-hour Life
Certificate.

    A. Uniform minimum requirements.
        1. Educational Psychology—2½ hours to be preceded, when pos-
           sible, by a course in General Psychology or Biological Sci-
           ence. (It is recommended that courses in General Psychology
           be not counted as Education.)
        2. Principles of Teaching—2½ hours to be preceded by Educa-
           tional Psychology.
        3. School Economy—2 hours to include a study of buildings and
           grounds, school law, classroom management, professional

ethics, relation of the school to the community, and extra-curriculum activities.

4. Practice Teaching—enough to demonstrate the candidate's ability to teach (at least one term). Exemption may be granted as set out in the Conference Agreement. This requirement is not to apply when the diploma is not a license to teach.

5. History and Principles of Education—2½ hours to be given as late as possible in the student's course.

6. English, preferably English Composition—5 hours.

7. A major of at least 15 hours and a minor of at least 10 hours in academic or technical subjects, to be selected in consultation with an adviser, preferably in the department in which the major is chosen. Exception to be made in case of students pursuing fixed curricula in vocation subjects.

B. Other recommendations concerning the degree and the 120-hour Life Certificate.

1. That a course of at least 2 hours in Hygiene with special reference to the health problems of the school is desirable.

2. That the 120 hours required for the degree shall not include any credit for physical exercises.

3. That the minimum requirement in Education be 24 hours.

4. That the maximum credit to be given in Education should be 30 hours.

II. Recommendations regarding the 60-hour Life Certificate.

A. Uniform minimum requirements.

1. Education—all the courses required for the degree, except History and Principles of Education; namely: Educational Psychology, School Economy, Principles of Teaching, and Practice Teaching.

2. English, preferably English Composition—5 hours.

3. Other academic or technical subjects; at least five hours in each of 3 subjects in addition to Education and English.

B. It is recommended to the Conference that it consider whether a Life Certificate should be granted for less than 120 hours of work.

III. Recommendations regarding the Regents' Certificate.

A. Uniform minimum requirements.

1. Elementary Education—5 hours. This course to include such topics as the selection, organization, and presentation of the subject matter in the elementary school subjects, and also classroom management.

2. Observation and Teaching—2½ hours.

3. English, preferably English Composition—5 hours.

IV. Recommendations regarding Uniform Terminology in the Conference Agreement.

A. That item 6, of Section III, should read "Elementary Education" rather than "Elementary Course of Study."

B. That item 1, of Section IV, should read "History and Principles of Education" instead of "History of Education."

C. That two new courses be added to the courses listed; namely:
    Mental Tests
    Educational Tests and Measurements

V. General Recommendations:
   A. That the Conference re-open the question as to the amount of work permitted to be done by correspondence and extension.
   B. That, so far as possible, freshman and sophomore students be scheduled only in classes of junior college rank; and that junior and senior students should be scheduled only in classes of senior college rank.
   C. That courses offered in the several departments be not unnecessarily multiplied.
   D. That departments in the several colleges which give courses required for certificates and degrees be asked to prepare and exchange syllabi of these courses.

(Signed) J. H. Coursault,
Chairman.

(Signed) R. S. Douglass,
      Secretary.

6. That President Hendricks be elected as chairman of the conference for the ensuing year.

7. That each of the six institutions and the State Department of Education have two votes in the conference meetings.

Since there was no further business to be considered by the Conference, the meeting adjourned.

Dr. E. L. Hendricks,
President.

R. Shoop,
      Secretary.

APPENDIX G

PROPOSED STANDARDS FOR ACCREDITING TEACHERS COLLEGES

By H. A. Brown
President, State Normal School, Oshkosh, Wisconsin
FOR
AMERICAN ASSOCIATION OF TEACHERS COLLEGES

I. Definition of a Teachers College.

A. A teachers college, within the meaning of these standards, is a state, municipal, or incorporated private institution, or an independent unit of a recognized college or university, which has at least one four-year unified curriculum, which is devoted exclusively to the preparation of teachers, which has legal authority to grant a standard bachelor's degree in education, which has granted and continues to grant such degree, and which requires for admission the completion of a standard four-year secondary school curriculum, or the equivalent.

B. A similar institution devoted exclusively to the preparation of teachers, which requires for admission the completion of a standard four-year secondary school curriculum, or the equivalent, which has a curriculum less than four years in length, and does not have legal authority to grant a standard bachelor's degree, or which has a curriculum four years in length but has not granted and does not grant a bachelor's degree, shall be designated as a normal school.

C. Normal schools shall conform to the same standards as teachers colleges except as hereinafter specifically indicated.

II. Requirements for Admission.

A. The quantitative requirement for admission to a teachers college accredited by this association shall be at least fifteen units of secondary school work, or the equivalent. These units must represent work done in a secondary school approved by the state department of public instruction of the state in which the college is located and must conform to the definitions of the various units as recommended by the state department of public instruction, or must be evidenced by the result of examinations.

If the state department of public instruction maintains no accredited list of secondary schools or publishes no definitions of secondary school units, those of a regularly recognized accrediting agency shall be used.

B. Equivalence for entrance units of secondary school work shall be determined only by regularly scheduled written examinations, which shall be of such a character as to satisfy the Committee on Admissions of the college that the applicant is fully prepared to do college work as hereinafter defined.

C. Experience in teaching shall in no case be accepted for entrance or credit toward graduation, except supervised teaching in the training school as a student.

III. Standards for Graduation.

A. The quantitative requirement for graduation shall be the completion of at least one hundred twenty semester hours of credit, or the equivalent in term hours, quarter hours, points, majors, or courses.

B. The requirement for graduation for a normal school with a two-year curriculum shall be at least sixty semester hours, or the equivalent, and for a normal school with a three-year curriculum, at least ninety semester hours or the equivalent.

IV. Size of Faculty.

A. The ratio of students to faculty in the college department shall not exceed twenty students to one member of the faculty, on the basis of current net registration of students carrying a full program in the college department.

B. In the training school there shall be at least one critic teacher for every twelve college students, each of whom does one hundred twenty clock hours of student teaching.

V. Preparation of Faculty.

A. The minimum scholastic requirement for teachers in the training school shall be graduation from a college of recognized standing, presumably evidenced by possession of a bachelor's degree, or equivalent training.

Teachers who have been members of the faculty of the training school for not less than five years and whose training is not equivalent to this requirement, may be considered to have equivalent training for six years after the date on which these standards take effect, provided that the president of the college submits a statement of their training and experience, and files with the Committee on Accrediting and Classification a declaration that such members of the faculty are rendering service in their own teaching and in the supervision of student teaching which is of a superior quality as judged by the standards of the best public school systems in the state in which the college is located.

This declaration must be made annually until each such teacher has secured the required training and shall be based upon actual inspection of the teacher's work.

B. The minimum scholastic requirement for members of the faculty who give instruction in the college department shall be graduation from a college of recognized standing and additional training which shall include at least one year of study in their respective fields of teaching in a recognized graduate school, or equivalent, and presumably possession of the master's degree.

Members of the faculty who have served in their respective positions for not less than five years and who do not meet this requirement, may be regarded as having done so for six years after the date on which these standards take effect, provided that the president of the college submits a statement of their training and experience and files a declaration that such members of the faculty are giving satisfactory instruction of college grade.

This declaration must be made annually until each such member of the faculty has secured the required training, and shall be based upon actual inspection of the work of such members of the faculty.

C. It is desirable that members of the faculty of the college should possess training of a distinctly professional quality, which represents at least three years of study beyond the bachelor's degree, in a recognized graduate school, or corresponding professional or technological training. The effort of a college to maintain a faculty of higher scholarly equipment than is required by the minimum standard shall be held to constitute a strong presumption that superior work is being done.

VI. Teaching Load of Faculty.

A. The following teaching loads, or the equivalent, shall be considered as maximums for the faculty of a teachers college: (a) in English composition, twelve class periods per week, with classes of not more than thirty students; (b) in general classroom subjects other than English composition, sixteen class periods per week; (c) in shop and laboratory work, a weekly program of twenty-four class periods; (d) in physical education, twenty-five class periods per week.

V.II. Training School and Student Teaching.

A. Each teachers college shall maintain a training school under its own control as a part of its organization as a laboratory school for purposes of observation, demonstration, and supervised teaching on the part of students. The use of an urban or rural school system, under sufficient control and supervision of the college to permit carrying out the educational policy of the college to a sufficient degree for the conduct of effective student teaching, will satisfy this requirement.

B. Student teaching shall be so organized as to lead to a proper initial mastery of the technique of teaching and, at the same time, protect the interests of the children in the training school.

C. Each teacher in the training school who is also responsible for a regular amount of supervision of student teaching, shall be required to have charge of not more than forty children at any one time.

D. The standard amount of student teaching required of every graduate of a teachers college shall be one hundred eighty hours of supervised teaching; and of every graduate of a normal school one hundred twenty hours; provided that this requirement shall not be interpreted as preventing a teachers college from exempting a student teacher from further teaching whenever such a student has attained the degree of skill contemplated at the end of the normal period of teaching.

E. For every twelve college students to be given one hundred eighty hours of student teaching, there shall be a minimum group of thirty children, either in the campus training school or in affiliated urban or rural schools under the supervision of the college.

F. No training school teacher shall supervise, in a year, the entire student teaching of more than twelve college students, each of whom does one hundred eighty hours of student teaching, or an equivalent number of student teachers.

G. In the case of use of affiliated urban or rural schools for student-teaching purposes, when the degree of affiliation and control is restricted to such an extent that a teaching force of more limited training than is contemplated by these standards must be used, and which is not capable of effective supervision of student teaching, or which by the terms of the affiliation is not expected to do supervision of student teaching, there shall be one full-time supervisor of student teaching for every twenty-five student teachers, each of whom does one hundred eighty hours of student teaching. Such supervisors must possess the scholastic qualifications required of members of the faculty of the college department.

H. It is recommended that at least two-fifths of the teaching in the training school should be done by regular teachers of the training school or by other members of the faculty.

VIII. Organization of the Curriculum.

A. The curriculum of the college must recognize definite requirements as regards sequence of courses. Senior college courses must not be open to freshmen who have not taken the prerequisites for these courses. Programs consisting mainly of freshman and sophomore courses, carrying full credit, shall not be available for students in the junior and senior years. Coherent and progressive lines of study, leading to specific achievement within definite fields, must be a characteristic of the college curriculum.

Each teachers college must, therefore, adopt an organization of its curricula which will provide in the junior and senior years a sufficient number of advanced courses which require elementary courses as prerequisites, so that at least one-half of the work of a student in the junior and senior years shall consist of advanced courses open only to juniors and seniors.

B. In a normal school with a three-year curriculum, one-half of the work of students in the last year shall consist of advanced courses to which freshmen are not admitted.

IX. Library, Laboratory, and Shop Equipment.

A. Each teachers college shall have a live, well-distributed and professionally administered library bearing specifically upon the subjects taught. At least fifteen thousand volumes, exclusive of public documents, are recommended as a minimum.

B. Each college with less than five hundred students should have a definite annual appropriation for the purchase of new reference books and current periodicals amounting to at least two thousand five hundred dollars. Colleges with five hundred to one thousand students should have a definite annual appropriation amounting to at least five dollars per student registered. Colleges with larger enrollments, should have an amount equal to at least four dollars per student. The foregoing is to be regarded as a recommendation rather than a requirement.

C. Each college shall be provided with laboratory equipment sufficient for instructional purposes for each course offered.

D. Each college must be provided with suitable shops and shop equipment for instructional purposes for each course offered, including gymnasiums for physical education; commercial equipment for courses in commerce; suitable kitchens, dining rooms and laboratories for household arts; and adequate farm buildings and demonstration farms for work in agriculture.

X. Location, Construction, and Sanitary Condition of Buildings.

The location and construction of buildings, the lighting, heating, and ventilation of the rooms, the nature of the lavatories, corridors, closets, water supply, school furniture, apparatus, and method of cleaning, shall be such as to insure hygienic conditions for students and teachers.

XI. Limits of Registration of Students.

A. No teachers college shall be placed on the accredited list, or continued on such list for more than one year, unless it has a regular registration of at least two hundred students of college grade.

B. A notably small proportion of students of college grade registered in the third and fourth years, continued over a period of several years, shall constitute grounds for dropping a teachers college from the accredited list. Fifteen per cent of the enrollment of a teachers college should be in the junior and senior years.

C. A normal school with a two-year curriculum must have an enrollment of at least sixty students of college grade, one-third of whom must be in the second year.

XII. Financial Support.

A. Each state or municipal teachers college must have an annual appropriation sufficient to provide: a faculty of the size, quality, and attainments hereinbefore prescribed; the required library, laboratory, and shop equipment with proper repairs and replacements; sufficient supplies and material in all departments for educational and instructional purposes; repairs and replacements in the physical plant adequate to maintain the plant in good working condition; and suitable staffs, supplies, and material for the effective operation of the physical plant. A marked inferiority or insufficiency in material resources shall be accepted as strong presumption of unsatisfactory educational conditions.

B. If the college is a private incorporated institution, it must have a minimum annual income of $50,000 for its teachers college program, one-half of which shall be from sources other than payments by students; and an additional annual income of $10,000 for each one hundred students above two hundred, one-half of which shall be from sources other than payments by students. If such college is not tax-supported, it shall possess a productive endowment of $500,000 and an additional endowment of $50,000 for each additional one hundred students above two hundred.

XIII. General Requirements.

A. The character of the curriculum, the efficiency of the instruction, the scholarly spirit and the professional atmosphere of the institution, the standard for granting degrees, and the general tone of the college, shall be factors in determining eligibility for accrediting.

B. No teachers college shall maintain a secondary school, or a department in which strictly secondary school academic work is offered as a part of its college organization, except for training school purposes.

XIV. Classification of Colleges.

A. Any teachers college which completely meets these requirements shall be designated as a Class A college; provided that during the first five years of the operation of these standards a college may fail to meet the requirements of three of these standards and nevertheless be given the rating of a Class A college. (Any subdivision of a numbered section indicated by a letter shall be regarded as a standard, except where it is a recommendation only.)

B. Any teachers college which fails to conform to one or more of these standards shall be designated as a Class B college; provided that during the first five years of the operation of these standards a college may fail to meet the requirements of five of these standards and nevertheless be given the rating of a Class B college.

C. Any teachers college which fails to conform to Standards V A, V B, VI A, VII A, VII C, VII D, VII E, VII F, VII G, and VIII A shall be designated as a Class C college.

XV. Accrediting and Classification of Teachers Colleges.

A. For the purpose of administering these standards, a committee of five members, known as the Committee on Accrediting and Classification, is hereby created, one member of which shall be elected annually by the Association for a term of five years. (In 1925 five members shall be elected for terms of one, two, three, four, and five years, respectively.)

B. The secretary of the Association, or the executive secretary, whenever authorized and appointed by the Association, shall be the secretary and the executive officer of the Committee on Accrediting and Classification.

C. Each teachers college accredited under these standards shall file annually with the Committee on Accrediting and Classification a report on a blank provided for that purpose by the Committee.

D. These standards shall go into effect on September 1, 1927. Not later than the date of the annual meeting of the Association in 1928, the Committee on Accrediting and Classification shall prepare an accredited and classified list of teachers colleges on the basis of information contained in the reports submitted to the committee by the colleges.

E. The Committee on Accrediting and Classification may inspect or cause to be inspected any teachers college when it deems such inspection necessary.

APPENDIX H

REGULATIONS GOVERNING LEAVES OF ABSENCE IN MISSOURI TEACHERS COLLEGES

The following statements from Presidents of Missouri Teachers Colleges give the regulations governing leaves of absence at the five schools.

Kirksville:

A sum equivalent to five per cent of a teacher's salary is set aside each month as a fund for foreign travel or graduate study. This fund cannot cover a period of more than seven years. The money is paid in equal payments whenever the teacher is absent for graduate study or foreign travel; provided the program of studies or the planned trip is approved by the President of the School. In order to secure the money set aside the teacher must devote full time to the problem. He or she cannot accept scholarships or pay for part-time teaching. There are two limits; namely, the holder of a B. S. degree or its equivalent cannot receive in any one month more than 60% of one month's salary, and the holder of a higher degree cannot receive in any one month more than 80% of one month's salary.

This plan of leave of absence is operative whenever the teacher has been in the school one year or more. Leave of absence must be taken within the seven-year period or the teacher loses a proportionate part of his accrument.

Warrensburg:

Our plan for leave of absence on the part of faculty members provides that whenever seven years of service have been rendered the institution, the faculty member may be released for one year on half salary. This half pay goes to the faculty member each calendar month. There is no requirement that the faculty member return to us nor that the faculty member spend the year in study.

Cape Girardeau:

We give a leave of absence to two members of our faculty every year, based entirely upon their seniority in service. The leave includes full pay for one semester, and the faculty member may either spend one semester on full salary or an entire year on half pay. Their places are taken care of by substitutes. They may spend their time in any institution acceptable to the President of the Faculty. No member can be away more frequently than once in seven years on salary.

Springfield:

A leave of absence for three months is allowed every three years. Full salary is paid for the three months. Teachers may extend the leave without pay to a full year if they so desire.

Maryville:

"The Board of Regents, recognizing the value of additional preparation of the members of the faculty, states the following to be its policy:

1. To grant such leaves of absence to members of the faculty as from time to time may seem wise to the Board, acting on the recommendation of the President of the college.

216

2. The place and the manner of spending the time covered by leaves, granted under this' section, shall be approved by the Board of Regents on recommendation of the President of the college.

3. No leave under this statement of policy shall be for less than six weeks nor more than one year nor shall any time when the college is not in session be covered by this statement of policy.

4. Faculty members taking advantage of leaves of absence granted may be paid not less than $50.00 nor more than $75.00 per month, in addition to base salary, for as many months after their return to active duty as they have spent in work approved under this statement of policy. The exact amount per month to be determined at the time the leave is granted by the Board.

5. It is to be mutually understood that faculty members taking advantage of this provision regarding leave are to remain with the college at least two years after their return from such leave, provided their services are satisfactory to the college.

6. No faculty member shall be granted a leave under the provision of this section who has not been in the service of the institution for two years or more, nor shall it be granted to any one member of the faculty oftener than one term in seven or one year in seven.

7. The Board reserves the right to limit the number of faculty members on leave to such as in the judgment of the Board can be spared from the college in any one time.

BIBLIOGRAPHY

Agnew W, D.: Administration of Professional Schools for Teachers, 1924.

American Association of Teachers Colleges: Yearbook, 1924.

Babcock, K. C.: Classification of Universities and Colleges with Reference to Bachelor's Degrees. U. S. Bureau of Education, Annual Report, 1911, Vol. I.

Bagley, W. C.: Status of the Critic Teacher. American School, No. 5, 1919.

Bagley, W. C.: The Distinction between Academic and Professional Subjects, Proceedings, N. E. A., 1914.

Benson, C. E.: Output of Professional Schools for Teachers, 1922.

Carnegie Foundation: The Professional Preparation of Teachers for American Public Schools, 1920.

Carnegie Foundation: Curricula Designed for the Preparation of Teachers of American Public Schools, 1917.

Catalogues of Missouri Normal Schools from 1915 to 1926.

Coffman, L. D.: The Social Composition of the Teaching Population, 1911.

Evenden, E. S.: Teachers' Salaries and Salary Schedules. N. E. A. Research Bulletin, Vol. I, No. 3, 1923.

Felmley, David: The Reorganization of the Normal School Curriculum. Proceedings, N. E. A., 1914.

Hamilton, F. R.: Fiscal Support of State Teachers Colleges, 1923.

Herzog, W. S.: State Maintenance of Teachers in Training, 1922.

Humphreys, H. C.: Factors Operating in the Location of State Normal Schools, 1922.

Irion, T. W. H.: Legal Aspects of Normal School Administration. School Administration and Supervision, Vol. 20, p. 319.

Judd, C. H. and Parker, S. A.: Problems Involved in Standardizing Normal Schools, U. S. Bureau of Education, Bulletin, 1916, No. 12.

Kelley, F. J.: The American Arts College, 1925.

Koos, L. V.: The Junior College, 1924.

Leonard, R. J.: The Coördination of State Institutions for Higher Education Through Supplementary Curricular Boards.

Louisiana Survey: Report of the Survey Commission, 1924.

Massachusetts Survey: Report of a Fact-Finding Survey of Technical and Higher Education in Massachusetts, 1923.

Maxwell, R. W.: Report of Committee on Standards of Teachers Colleges. Proceedings, N. E. A., 1923 and 1924.

Moehlman, A. B.: A Survey of the Needs of Michigan State Normal Schools, 1922.

Official Manual, State of Missouri, 1915 to 1926.

Phillips, F. M.: Statistics of Teachers Colleges and Normal Schools. U. S. Bureau of Education, Bulletin, 1924, No. 10.

Randolph, Edgar D.: The Professional Treatment of Subject Matter. 1924.

Revised Statutes of Missouri, 1909 and 1919.

U. S. Bureau of Education, Statistics, State Universities and Colleges, December 21, 1925. A mimeographed letter to college executives.

U. S. Bureau of Vocational Information: Training for the Professions and Allied Occupations, 1924.

Wager, R. E.: Trends and Problems in State-Supported Teacher-Training Institutions. Peabody Journal of Education, 3: 9-25, July, 1925.